Cooperating
for
Peace

STAFF COLLEGE LIBRARY AND INFORMATION SERVICES

ACCESSION NO: _____90670_____

This book should be returned to the Library on or before the last date stamped below.

Cooperating for Peace

The Global Agenda for
the 1990s and Beyond

Gareth Evans

ALLEN & UNWIN

First published in 1993 by
Allen & Unwin Pty Ltd
9 Atchison Street, St Leonards, NSW 2065 Australia

National Library of Australia
Cataloguing-in-Publication entry:

Evans, Gareth, 1944–
 Cooperating for peace.

 Bibliography.
 Includes index.
 ISBN 1 86373 623 9.

 1. United Nations. Armed Forces. 2. Peace. 3. Security,
 International. I. Title.

327.172

Printed by Australian Print Group, Maryborough, Victoria

10 9 8 7 6 5 4 3 2

To the memory of Dr Herbert Vere Evatt, Leader of the Australian Delegation to the 1945 San Francisco Conference and President of the Third United Nations General Assembly, and to all those men and women throughout the United Nations system today who share his vision and commitment.

Contents

Contents

III MAINTAINING PEACE

IV RESTORING PEACE

V ENFORCING PEACE

VI COOPERATING FOR PEACE

Contents

Preface

In June 1992, United Nations Secretary-General Boutros Boutros-Ghali published *An Agenda for Peace*, a 50-page report which stimulated a major international debate about the role of the UN, and the international community generally, in securing peace in the world of the 1990s and beyond. This study is an Australian contribution to that ongoing debate.

The Secretary-General's report—which focused on preventive diplomacy, peace making and peace keeping—was an up-beat and forward-looking response to the world-wide renewal of confidence accompanying the end of the Cold War, and the new era of security cooperation that seemed to be heralded by it. There were high expectations of the UN, particularly in the aftermath of the effective collective response to the Gulf crisis and the inauguration in Cambodia of the UN's biggest ever peace keeping operation.

Since then, events in the former Yugoslavia and Somalia have been sobering reminders of the limits of the UN's authority. Resource limitations, organisational limitations, the number of problems crying out for attention and the intractability of so many of them, have made some of the more exuberant characterisations of the UN's role—as a kind of combination global saviour and police force—now seem rather extravagant.

The present need, as we see it, is to take stock in a systematic, balanced and above all realistic way of the nature of the security problems confronting the international community and appropriate responses to them. In our own contribution to this effort, we have sought to do three things in particular: bring some conceptual clarity, to the extent this is presently lacking, into the definition of problems, responses and the relationship between them; spell out some of the criteria which might guide decision makers in responding to problems; and make some specific proposals for improving structures and processes, particularly in the UN system.

While no study of this size could purport to be exhaustive or definitive, it does try to address the issues comprehensively rather than selectively, and to take full account of the current state of international debate upon them, including ideas and terminology about which there is already significant consensus. We have tried to build on existing thinking, particularly the Secretary-General's, rather than try to reconstruct some new edifice from the ground up.

There are three particular emphases that run through the study. The first is our strong focus on *preventive* strategies rather than post-conflict or post-crisis responses. The second is our emphasis on *peace building* as a particular prevention-oriented concept which, linking as it does to the international community's social and economic agenda, deserves to have a much higher priority in peace and security policy. The third is our utilisation of the concept of *cooperative security* as the appropriate central sustaining idea now for international efforts to secure peace.

The study reflects material available to me and my colleagues as at 15 August 1993. A large number of people have helped me in its preparation, and their contributions are recorded in the Acknowledgements. I am grateful to them all, and hope that between us we have contributed something worth saying on what are unquestionably some of the most important issues now confronting the international community.

Gareth Evans   September 1993

Acknowledgements

This study was conceived and planned by Gareth Evans, who wrote outline drafts for all of it, the first drafts of some chapters, and the final drafts of all chapters. But no serving Minister could possibly produce, in a few short months, a work of this length and complexity without highly dedicated and professional support, and this was very much the case here. The study was a team effort, with input from many serving officers of the Australian Department of Foreign Affairs and Trade and a number of other contributors.

Many ideas for the study came from Peter Wilenski AO, former Australian Ambassador and Permanent Representative to the United Nations, and former Secretary of the Department, whose ground-breaking work on UN reform in New York will hopefully soon bear fruit; from Richard Butler AM, Australia's present Ambassador and Permanent Representative who is, among other things, chairing the UN's 1995 Fiftieth Anniversary Committee; and from a number of past and present members of Australia's Mission to the UN, including Geoff Forrester, Gillian Bird, David Stuart, Kevin Boreham (who, along with Louise Hand and Anita Klima, were the Departmental officers working most closely with the Minister on the overall management of the project), Howard Bamsey, Bruce Osborn, Neil Francis and Richard Rowe.

The Minister's personal staff gave him, as always, great personal and professional support. In particular, Ken Berry, full-time policy adviser and part-time computer buff, performed, with his usual immense good humour, prodigious feats against impossible deadlines in formatting the whole manuscript for publication and preparing the

Acknowledgements

index; Martine Letts played a central role throughout, equally cheerfully, both in coordinating research and contributing ideas and comments; and Christine Evans, who led the secretarial team on this occasion, put in many long hours turning impenetrable notes into readable typescript.

Of the 'outsiders', none played a more important role during the entire project than Dr Connie Peck, formerly a consultant to the Minister, and now conducting preventive diplomacy and peace making training for the United Nations Institute of Training and Research (UNITAR) in Geneva: she was a constant source of inspiration, ideas and detailed information, and contributed especially to the drafting of chapters 5 and 7. Dr Kevin Clements of the Peace Research Centre, Australian National University (ANU), was indefatigable in providing detailed material and sound advice on all facets of the text, and with his colleagues Wendy Lambourne, Betts Featherstone, and Charles Van Der Donckt, produced the Bibliography. Valuable academic input also came from Professors James Richardson and Andrew Mack of the ANU's Department of International Relations, particularly on the definitional issues in Chapter 1. Another especially helpful consultancy contribution came from James Ingram AO, former Executive Director of the World Food Program, who drew on his vast experience in preparing a case study on response to humanitarian emergencies. Former officers of the Department, Tom Critchley and Michael Wilson, also drew on their great experience to produce helpful case studies on Indonesia and the Balkans. Dr William Maley of the Australian Defence Force Academy contributed material on Afghanistan, while Rear Admiral Ken Doolan and other senior officers of the Australian Department of Defence contributed helpfully to round table discussions and the checking of the manuscript.

A good deal of case study source material was developed by Departmental officers in the course of the project. Major case studies were written by Shirley Lithgow (Cambodia), Bruce Lendon (Somalia), Claude Rakasits (the Gulf crisis), and shorter case studies were prepared by Jane Madden (Namibia) Dorothy Holt (Angola), Ian Kemish (South China Sea), Roger Uren (regional organisations), Peter Furlonger (UNSCOM in Iraq), Felicity Volk (Kashmir), David Morris (Cyprus), David Stuart (El Salvador), Robert Newton and Richard Lennane (the Middle East), Peter Lloyd (Iraq), Steven MacIntosh (sanctions, ICJ), Jill Courtney (arms control and disarmament), and Hugh Wyndham (the Falklands). These contributions have added considerably to the body of serious analytical material on international security issues, and it is hoped in due course to publish them in a separate volume.

The Secretary of the Department, Michael Costello, participated actively in a series of round table seminars at which ideas for the study were developed. Other Departmental officers to play particularly helpful roles in drafting, checking or preparing material were David Morris (especially on peace keeping issues), Bryce Hutchesson and Chris Moraitis (on peace building), Karen MacArthur (on case study preparation) and Judy Herron's desktop publishing team (responsible for a number of the charts). Australian Embassies and High Commissions around the world were assiduous in keeping the Minister abreast of developments in what has been throughout the past year a rapidly evolving debate.

Appreciation is also owed to Ministers, officials and others from a number of countries - and in particular those working with the Carlsson-Ramphal Commission on Global Governance - for helpful comments to Gareth Evans on his preliminary paper, *Securing Peace in the Post-Cold War Era: Issues Confronting the International Community*, which was widely circulated in February 1993 as a prelude to this project.

Abbreviations

ANC	African National Congress
APEC	Asia Pacific Economic Cooperation
ASEAN	Association of South-East Asian Nations
BWC	Biological Weapons Convention
CARICOM	Caribbean Community
CD	Conference on Disarmament (UN)
CSCE	Conference on Security and Co-operation in Europe
CSD	Commission on Sustainable Development
CTBT	Comprehensive Test Ban Treaty
CWC	Chemical Weapons Convention
DHA	Department of Humanitarian Affairs
DOMREP	Representative of the Secretary-General in the Dominican Republic
DPRK	Democratic People's Republic of Korea
EC	European Community
ECOMOG	ECOWAS Monitoring Group
ECOSOC	Economic and Social Council
ECOWAS	Economic Community of West African States
ENMOD	Environmental Modification Treaty
FYRM	Former Yugoslav Republic of Macedonia
G7	Group of Seven
G15	Group of Fifteen
GATT	General Agreement on Tariffs and Trade
GCC	Gulf Co-operation Council
IAEA	International Atomic Energy Agency
ICAO	International Civil Aviation Organization
IATA	International Air Transport Association
ICJ	International Court of Justice
ICRC	International Committee of the Red Cross
MFO	Multinational Force and Observers
MINURSO	Mission for the Referendum in Western Sahara
MNF	Multi-National Force
MTCR	Missile Technology Control Regime
NAM	Non-Aligned Movement
NATO	North Atlantic Treaty Organization

NGO	Non-Government Organisation
NPT	Nuclear Non-Proliferation Treaty
OAS	Organization of American States
OAU	Organization of African Unity
OECD	Organisation for Economic Cooperation and Development
OIC	Organisation of the Islamic Conference
ONUC	United Nations Operation in the Congo
ONUCA	United Nations Observer Mission in Central America
ONUMOZ	United Nations Operation in Mozambique
ONUSAL	United Nations Observer Mission in El Salvador
OPCW	Organisation for the Prohibition of Chemical Weapons
OPEC	Organization of Petroleum Exporting Countries
ORCI	Office of Research and the Collection of Information
PAC	Pan Africanist Congress
PCA	Permanent Court of Arbitration
PLO	Palestine Liberation Organisation
SAARC	South Asia Association for Regional Co-operation
SADC	Southern African Development Community
SCR	Security Council Resolution
SPF	South Pacific Forum
START	Strategic Arms Reduction Treaty
SWAPO	South West African People's Organisation
UN	United Nations
UNAMIC	United Nations Advance Mission in Cambodia
UNAVEM	United Nations Angola Verification Mission
UNCED	United Nations Conference on Environment and Development
UNDOF	United Nations Disengagement Observer Force
UNDP	United Nations Development Programme
UNEF	United Nations Emergency Force
UNGA	United Nations General Assembly
UNFICYP	United Nations Peace-keeping Force in Cyprus
UNGOMAP	United Nations Good Offices Mission - Afghanistan and Pakistan
UNHCR	United Nations High Commissioner for Refugees
UNICEF	United Nations Children's Fund
UNIFIL	United Nations Interim Force in Lebanon

Abbreviations

UNIKOM	United Nations Iraq-Kuwait Observer Mission
UNIIMOG	United Nations Iran-Iraq Military Observer Group
UNIPOM	United Nations India-Pakistan Observation Mission
UNITA	National Union for the Total Independence of Angola
UNMOGIP	United Nations Military Observer Group in India and Pakistan
UNOGIL	United Nations Observation Group in Lebanon
UNOMUR	United Nations Observer Mission Uganda-Rwanda
UNOSOM	United Nations Operation in Somalia
UNPROFOR	United Nations Protection Force
UNSCOM	United Nations Special Commission
UNSF	United Nations Security Force
UNTAC	United Nations Transitional Authority in Cambodia
UNTAG	United Nations Transition Assistance Group for Namibia
UNTEA	United Nations Temporary Executive Authority
UNTSO	United Nations Truce Supervision Organization
UNYOM	United Nations Yemen Observation Mission
US	United States
WEU	Western European Union
WFP	World Food Programme
WHO	World Health Organization
$	$US

I

Defining the Issues

1

Peace and Security in the 1990s and Beyond: Problems and Responses

After the Cold War

With the end of the Cold War, there is now far more scope than before for cooperation in the prevention and resolution of conflict. But the irony is that there are now many more disputes, conflicts and crises calling out for such attention. The threat of world devastation posed by the nuclear arms race between the superpowers has been dramatically reduced, raising hopes for the emergence of a new, peaceful international order. But it seems the disappearance of the bipolar strategic balance was only a prelude to new kinds of turbulence and disorder.

So far as the world's major powers are concerned, it is true we can be reasonably confident that conflict is unlikely in the foreseeable future. Serious differences persist, but they are taking the form of economic competition rather than military rivalry. There are a number of reasons for this. One is the degree of interdependence already achieved: not just in ever-increasing trade and investment, but in the emergence of the global communications and media 'village', the global organisation of production, the interlocking of financial markets, and the shared elite culture which accompanies and consolidates all these trends. A second factor is the way in which 'economic well-being' has displaced 'security against threatening great powers' as the dominant theme in the politics of all the major nations:

linked to this, and no doubt reinforced by the continuing realities of the nuclear age, is the more or less universal acceptance, now evident at all levels in these countries, that war is simply not a rational way of advancing national objectives.

But not all these developments have been unequivocally positive. Rates of economic growth have been extraordinarily uneven, with some regions experiencing spectacular advance, but in others deprivation becoming even more endemic—and even more deeply felt in light of the comparison. Some states have simply been unable to cope with exploding internal economic, political and social problems, and for all practical purposes have collapsed, leaving the international community to respond somehow to humanitarian crises often thus created or made worse. Again, communications technology, which has done so much to bring the world together, has also been very selective in its impact: issues tend to be placed on the international agenda less for their intrinsic importance than for their accessibility to television coverage, and this in turn breeds an unhappy tendency for governments to neglect major issues which lack immediate impact but which do have longer term security significance—for example, population pressures and environmental degradation.

The end of strategic competition between the United States and the Soviet Union has created a much more fluid environment for many small and middle size states. While that competition did, during the Cold War years, generate a number of wars and insurrections of its own, it has to be acknowledged that it more often contributed to regional stability, as each superpower ensured the survival of its respective allies but at the same time prevented them from embarking on military adventures that prejudiced the security of their sponsors. There is now more room for states to manoeuvre, and some are bound to seek to do so. Some of the emerging economic powers have yet to acquire political or military profiles commensurate with their wealth, and the process of adjustment certainly has ample potential to generate regional tensions. And should those tensions escalate into conflict, the unhappy reality is that proliferation of more sophisticated conventional weapons, and of the capacity to develop weapons of mass destruction, makes any prospect of major regional conflict an alarming one for the world as a whole.

The release of Cold War pressures has been associated with another major new development of security concern—the resurgence of ethno-nationalism, often taking a violent form. Some ethnic groups have been prepared to pursue their claims for self-determination within the framework of existing states—treating them essentially as claims for minority human rights protection—but many others have made clear that they will be satisfied by nothing less than their nations becoming states, causing the fragmentation of existing states in the process. The proliferating availability of weaponry of every degree of sophistication has given a sharp new edge to these concerns: the devastating impact of hand-held Stinger missiles on the Soviet military in Afghanistan, for example, showed the problems that are faced by even very large states in defeating small non-state forces operating in difficult and remote terrain.

Overall, while there may now be no threat to global security that is comparable to the danger previously associated with the prospect of a nuclear war between the superpowers, a wide array of security problems has become all too apparent in the course of the post-Cold War transition. Diverse in nature, geographically dispersed and often driven by entirely local hatreds, many of these problems have little significance beyond their own immediate areas. But many of them—particularly when they generate, or occur in association with, other problems like famine, massive human rights abuse and large scale refugee flows—are simply too serious for the world community to ignore.

No single government—not even the United States, with all its current pre-eminence—can be expected to contain, let alone resolve, the enormous range of security problems that now confront the world community. If there is to be any meaningful response, it can only be one based on a cooperative approach, with governments tackling these problems—or at least those of them that are capable of being tackled—on a cooperative, multilateral basis.

Defining international security problems

The first stated purpose of the United Nations under its Charter is to 'maintain international peace and security', but these terms are nowhere specifically defined. The traditional approach of the UN security system has been to conceive of threats to international security in terms of threats, by way of actual or potential military incursion, to the territorial and political sovereignty of states. Thus viewed, the system is predicated upon identifying an actual or potential aggressor and responding to immediate causes of conflict. So far as it goes (and there is an argument that it has not gone far enough, particularly in relation to early prevention and attention to the underlying causes of conflicts) this approach is appropriate enough for dealing with problems of a specifically military nature, and will clearly remain essential for reacting to the aggressive behaviour of individual states.

But many more problems than these are now seen, both within the UN system and the wider international community, as being properly described as 'security problems'. It is now generally accepted that security is multi-dimensional in character: that in addition to

5

military threats, the state's security can be menaced, for example, by threats to its economic well-being, political stability and social harmony; to the health of its citizens; or to its environment. At the national level all governments, implicitly, if not explicitly, do give expression to this view to varying degrees in their domestic and foreign policies, although emphases will vary with circumstances: one government may give priority to energy security or food security, another to protecting its border against unregulated population flows, another to domestic cohesion and national resilience, and so on.

The impact of policy choices made by a state in this respect will often reverberate beyond its borders. States acting to protect their security as they see it, in these various non-military contexts, may in the process cause or accentuate similar security problems elsewhere. Many governments seek, for example, to advance their economic security through trade and industry policies of a kind which can cause real pressures and tensions elsewhere in the global economy. Again, current international environment negotiations certainly are seen largely through the lens of national economic security which, while understandable enough, does not make progress in those negotiations any easier.

If security is so broadly defined, then 'international security problems' can be almost anything the international community is prepared to regard as such. To acknowledge this reality, however, is not to make progress with wrestling with the basic question addressed by this study, viz what should be the *response* of the international community to the international security problems of the world as we now find it in the 1990s.

Without making too many assumptions at this stage about matters that will need to be later discussed and tested in detail, it is possible to put at least some order into the analysis by grouping relevant problems into four distinct categories: 'emerging threats', 'disputes', 'armed conflicts' and 'other major security crises'. In the next section an attempt will be made to define, again in a preliminary way, the kinds of responses by the international community which appear possible and appropriate in relation to each of these various categories of problem.

Emerging threats

'Emerging threats' may be defined as developments, either within countries or between countries, which do not in themselves yet involve a dispute, armed conflict, or other major security crisis (as these terms are here defined) but may be seen as having the potential to become so. Such developments might include, for example, the accumulation of large arsenals of sophisticated conventional weapons; the acquisition of capacity to build weapons of mass destruction;

unrestrained population ' growth combined with environmental degradation and emerging food shortages; emerging difference of opinion about responsibility for and methods of dealing with unregulated population flows; an increasing pattern of human rights abuses foreshadowing major internal instability and a possible complete breakdown of governmental structures; or the increasingly strident voicing of competitive ethno-nationalist grievances and aspirations.

Disputes

'Disputes' may be defined as disagreements between states (or in some cases within states) which are serious enough to amount to a potential threat to international peace and security, but which have not yet reached the stage of armed hostilities. Issues here might typically be territorial claims, access to natural resources, access to transport routes and outlets to the sea, other perceived threats to national economic interests, major ideological disagreements or questions about the treatment of ethnic minorities.

Armed conflicts

'Armed conflicts' are hostilities of a kind which breach, or threaten to breach, international peace and security—such as invasions, armed interventions, border clashes and incursions; and also civil strife with some external dimension (most commonly, this dimension would involve either support from external patrons, or the threat of spillover effects in neighbouring countries from refugee flows and the like).

Other major security crises

These represent a not easily defined residual category of situations (involving something more than 'emerging threats' but not easily definable as 'disputes' or 'conflicts') where there is some prima facie expectation—at least following the UN's involvements on behalf of Iraqi Kurds, and in Somalia—that the international community will want to intervene. The terms 'major' and 'crisis' are meant to imply both immediacy and seriousness, usually with large scale loss of life being threatened and the problem being beyond the capacity, or perhaps the will, of an individual government to resolve. The term 'security' crisis is meant to convey that the problem directly or potentially threatens international peace and security (for example, through its spillover effects on neighbours), or that it is seen as justifying in some other way a security related response (as distinct from, say, a disaster relief response) by the international community. The absence of clear, non-circular and generally agreed definitions in this area is a reflection of the reality that there is really much continuing disagreement as to whether there are any 'internal' situations—involving massive human rights abuses, or civil break-down, induced famine or the like—which are such as to compel recognition of a 'right of humanitarian intervention'. This issue will be addressed in some detail later in this study.

Defining possible responses

A fundamental dilemma confronting the international community is that it faces many more international security problems than there are apparent resources available to respond to them. Certainly expectations of the ability of the United Nations to respond effectively to the disputes, conflicts and crises of the post-Cold War years have already far outstripped its present capacity to deliver. And expectations of regional organisations and other actors in the international system in this respect have never been very high to begin with.

One possible—and familiar—response to this dilemma is to conclude that any attempt to resolve it in a systematic, conceptually consistent and comprehensive way is bound to end in failure. There is always bound to be, the argument goes, a shortfall of available resources and institutional capacity to deploy them; involvement by the UN and other international actors is always likely to be not only selective but somewhat arbitrary; each individual problem that forces itself upon the international community's attention has its own distinctive characteristics and, in the nature of things, is bound to be dealt with in an ad hoc way; political and emotional arguments are often likely to be more persuasive at the margin than coolly rational ones; and the best that can be hoped for are marginal improvements here and there.

Needless to say, that is not the approach we have adopted in this study. Of course it is the case that any major adjustment to institutional structures and processes is extremely difficult to accomplish, and very much more so in international relations than in domestic policy. And of course it is true that when the issues addressed by those institutions and processes are themselves bewilderingly complex, and major financial resources are involved as well, then adjustment is even more difficult. But the political process of implementing adjustment cannot even get started unless two preconditions are satisfied: first, a strong measure of intellectual consensus about the nature of the problems which it is appropriate for the international community to tackle, and about the broad scope of appropriate responses; and secondly, a reasonably clearly defined, and widely supported, set of practical proposals for change. It cannot be assumed that if these two preconditions are met, change will follow: that will depend on the commitment and stamina of a great many governments and individuals. But it is certainly worth expending some effort to try to achieve consensus about underlying concepts and desirable practical objectives, and this study is a contribution to that end.

In examining the range of possible responses to international security problems it is helpful, for both conceptual and practical purposes, to group them in four distinct categories: 'peace building', 'peace maintenance', 'peace restoration' and 'peace enforcement'. There follows an outline of what we mean by each of these headings, and by the particular strategic responses—'peace making', 'peace keeping' and so on—grouped under each heading. We have tried here to embrace so far as possible, with only minor qualifications and variations, not only the definitions given in the UN Secretary-General's *An Agenda for Peace*, but also those around which some measure of consensus seems to be emerging in the literature and international practice. Our objective, after all, is to try to reduce such remaining confusion as there is about terminology—not add to it with idiosyncratic prescriptions of our own.

Peace building strategies

'Peace building' is used here to describe a set of strategies which aim to ensure that disputes, armed conflicts and other major crises do not arise in the first place—or if they do arise that they do not subsequently recur. These strategies fall into two broad groups, which in turn may be described, respectively, as 'international regimes' and 'in-country peace building' measures.

- **International regimes**   These are international laws, norms, agreements and arrangements—global, regional or bilateral in scope—designed to minimise threats to security, promote confidence and trust, and create frameworks for dialogue and cooperation. Examples are arms control and disarmament treaties; international legal regimes governing issues like maritime passage or the status of refugees; international dispute resolution mechanisms like the International Court of Justice; and multilateral dialogue and cooperation forums like the ASEAN Post-Ministerial Conference.

- **In-country peace building**   This refers to national and international efforts aimed at economic development, institution building and, more generally, the creation or restoration within countries of the conditions necessary to make them stable and viable states. Peace building has two dimensions. 'Pre-conflict peace building' refers to longer term non-military, economic, social and political measures which can help states deal with emerging threats and disputes (for example, measures to tackle problems associated with population pressures, or with scarce water resources shared with a neighbour or with the absence of telecommunications hot-lines to deal with border incidents). 'Post-conflict peace building', emphasised in *An Agenda for Peace*, is about action taken after a conflict or crisis in order to help ensure there is no recurrence of the problem: it may involve rehabilitation and reconstruction assistance generally, support for various kinds of institution-building, and specific practical programs like de-mining.

Peace maintenance strategies

'Peace maintenance' strategies are those designed to resolve, or at least contain, particular disputes (and some kinds of emerging threats), and prevent them from escalating into armed conflict. These strategies take many different forms, but for present purposes can be conveniently grouped as 'preventive diplomacy' and 'preventive deployment':

- **Preventive diplomacy**   This refers to the full range of methods described in Article 33 of the United Nations Charter—viz 'negotiation, enquiry, mediation, conciliation, arbitration, judicial settlement, resort to regional agencies or arrangements, or other peaceful means'—when applied *before* a dispute has crossed the threshold into armed conflict. Examples include numerous UN Secretary-General's Special Representative fact finding and good offices missions; or the 'unofficial' workshop on competing South China Sea territorial claims sponsored by Indonesia. 'Early preventive diplomacy' involves the provision of skilled assistance through good offices, mediation and the like in order to resolve disputes well before eruption into armed conflict appears likely; 'late preventive diplomacy'—more familiar in the UN system so far—refers to attempts (often involving the Secretary-General himself, working through the Security Council) to persuade parties to desist when such eruptions seem imminent.

- **Preventive deployment**   This is defined here as the deployment of military or police, and possibly civilian, personnel with the intention of preventing a dispute (or, in some cases, emerging threat) escalating into armed conflict. Such deployment could occur on one side of a border only, at the request of the state feeling threatened (as with the deployment of 1000 troops, military observers and civilian police into the Former Yugoslav Republic of Macedonia in 1993); or on both sides of the border at the request of both parties. (In *An Agenda for Peace* the concept of preventive deployment is taken as extending further—to deployment of military personnel within a country, at the request of the government or parties concerned, in order to assist in the alleviation of suffering or the controlling of violence. For present purposes, however, we believe it may be more helpful to regard those in-country prevention or assistance activities that do not involve the use of force as forms of 'peace building', and any kind of deployment that does involve the use of force, other than in self-defence, as being a form of 'peace enforcement'.)

Peace restoration strategies

'Peace restoration' strategies are those applicable to resolve a conflict *after* it has crossed the threshold of armed hostilities: they are premised on the cooperation, and ultimately agreement, of the governments or parties concerned. Two basic kinds of response are addressed here: 'peace making' and 'peace keeping'.

- **Peace making**   This is best understood as a close relative of preventive diplomacy, involving the same range of methods described in Article 33 of the UN Charter—ie 'negotiation, enquiry, mediation, conciliation, arbitration, judicial settlement, resort to regional agencies or agreements, or other peaceful means'—but applied *after* a dispute has crossed the threshold into armed conflict. As with preventive diplomacy, 'peace making' has at least two distinct chronological dimensions. Initial (or 'Stage I') peace making efforts will usually be aimed at the immediate goals of cessation of hostilities, and stabilisation of the situation on the ground; subsequent (or 'Stage II') efforts—which might continue in parallel with the deployment of a peace keeping mission—might be aimed rather at securing a durable political settlement.

- **Peace keeping**   This involves the deployment of military or police, and frequently civilian, personnel to assist in the implementation of agreements reached between governments or parties who have been engaged in conflict.   Peace keeping presumes cooperation, and its methods are inherently peaceful: the use of military force, other than in self-defence, is incompatible with the concept. Although neither described nor defined in the UN Charter itself, peace keeping operations have been—both in the pre-Cold War years and subsequently—the most numerous and visible manifestations of the UN's cooperative security efforts. 'Traditional' peace keeping operations involve not much more than unarmed or lightly armed military contingents being engaged in the monitoring, supervision and verification of ceasefire, withdrawal, buffer zone and related agreements: examples include UNMOGIP in Kashmir, UNFICYP in Cyprus, and UNTSO and MFO (the latter under Egyptian, Israeli and US, rather than UN, auspices) in the Middle East. 'Expanded' peace keeping, by comparison, involves the supplementation of traditional peace keeping with activities such as election monitoring or organisation, human rights protection, and assisting or exercising civil administration functions during transition to independence or democracy: UNTAG in Namibia, and the much more ambitious UNTAC in Cambodia, are the clearest examples.

Peace enforcement strategies

We are concerned here with responses to conflicts or other major security crises in situations where the agreement of all relevant governments or parties is lacking. The strategies are essentially those described in outline in Chapter VII of the UN Charter, and fall into two broad categories: non-military enforcement measures, or 'sanctions'; and military enforcement measures, for which it is convenient, and now common, to reserve the label 'peace enforcement'.

- **Sanctions**   These are measures, not involving the use or threat of military force, designed to compel or bring to an end a course of action by a state or party: they function primarily by denying access to goods, services or other externally provided requirements necessary or important to maintenance of their economic, social or political infrastructure or well-being. The most sustained, and ultimately successful, modern example of sanctions has been in relation to South Africa, although it has to be acknowledged that the mandatory UN Security Council-imposed arms embargo, and the voluntary General Assembly-recommended oil embargo, only went part of the way: they ended up being much less significant than, in particular, the financial sanctions that were imposed by the Commonwealth, EC and many individual countries, reinforced as these were with informal restrictions imposed by the international financial community.

- **Peace enforcement**   This is the threat or use of military force, in pursuit of peaceful objectives, in response to conflicts or other major security crises. The classic case is a UN-authorised military response to cross-border aggression by one state against another, as with the Gulf War in 1991. Also relatively uncontroversial, at least in principle, are actions taken to effectively enforce international arms control, disarmament and similar regimes. A more delicate and difficult application of peace enforcement activity is in support of peace keeping operations, for example, in situations where one or more parties to an agreement have subsequently withdrawn from it, and action is required to enforce a ceasefire or re-establish a buffer zone.   The most difficult of all peace enforcement applications, both in principle and practice, is where military force is used in internal security breakdown situations in support of specifically humanitarian objectives, as for example in Somalia.

Matching responses to problems

When the various response strategies sketched above are matched against the categories of international security problems defined earlier, the result is as described in the accompanying Chart 1. It will be seen how the responses tend to emerge overall as a series of graduated steps—from the least intrusive (peace building and preventive diplomacy in response to emerging threats and disputes) to the most coercive (peace enforcement in response to conflicts and other major security crises). One of the central themes of this study will be the need for much greater attention to be paid by the international community to anticipating and preventing disputes, conflicts or crises, rather than reacting after the event to situations that have already seriously deteriorated. A feature of the presentation in the chart here is that it makes clear just how much of the available response repertoire *is* in fact about peace building and conflict prevention, which are by their nature non-intrusive and non-coercive in character.

Principles of action

The notion that responses should be graduated—with softer options exhausted before harder ones are applied—is just one of the fundamental principles that should properly govern the international community's responses to security problems. In short, the responses should be so far as possible 'timely', 'graduated', 'effective', 'affordable' and 'consistent':

- *Timely* responsiveness means simply involvement at the time best calculated to secure optimal outcomes. Usually the earlier a problem is identified and an appropriate response applied, the more likely is the problem to be solved effectively—and peacefully.

- *Graduated* responsiveness means seeking to resolve disputes and respond to crises by peaceful measures, beginning with preventive strategies and only moving towards enforcement when lower level, more conciliatory, approaches fail. Sometimes circumstances will demand that steps be jumped, but at least consideration should always be given to less intrusive options first.

- *Effective* responses are simply those most likely to resolve the problem in question. That objective should be self-evident—but all too often political, resource or other such considerations have in fact inhibited the application of the response most likely to be effective.

13

Chart 1 Cooperative security: matching responses to problems

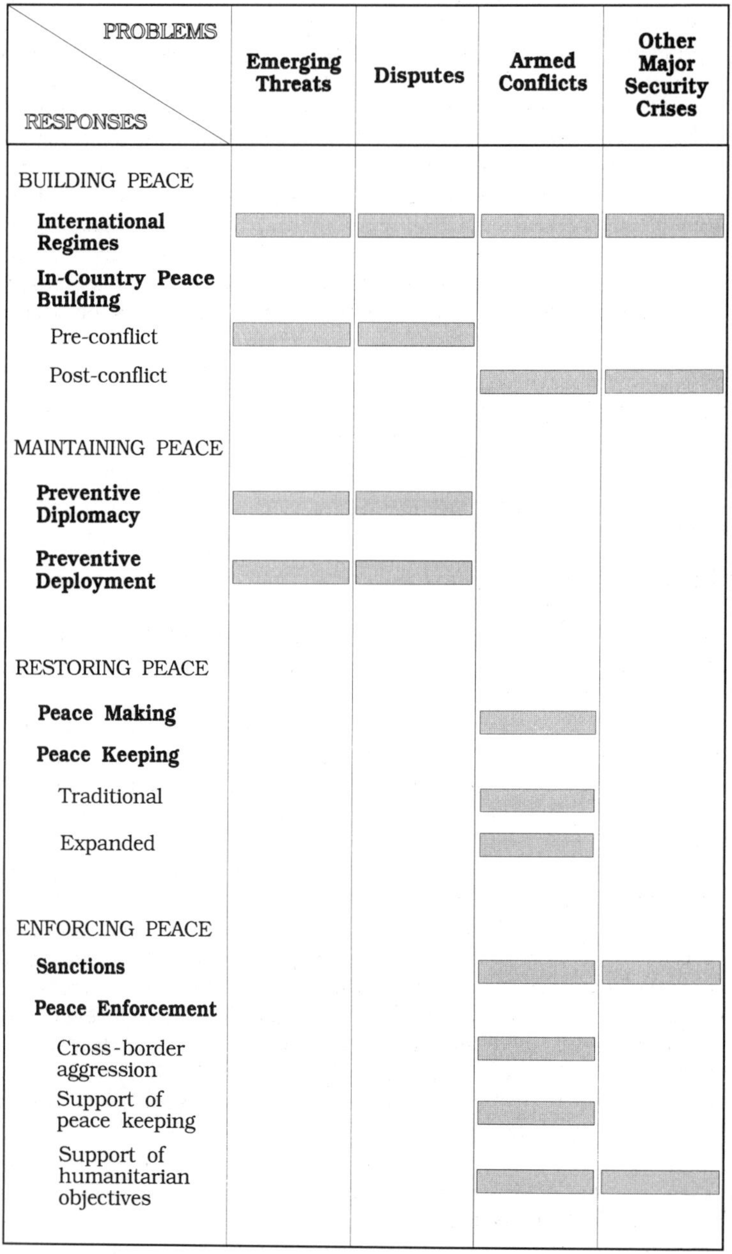

RESPONSES \ PROBLEMS	Emerging Threats	Disputes	Armed Conflicts	Other Major Security Crises
BUILDING PEACE				
International Regimes	■	■	■	■
In-Country Peace Building				
Pre-conflict	■	■		
Post-conflict			■	■
MAINTAINING PEACE				
Preventive Diplomacy	■	■		
Preventive Deployment	■	■		
RESTORING PEACE				
Peace Making			■	
Peace Keeping				
Traditional			■	
Expanded			■	
ENFORCING PEACE				
Sanctions			■	■
Peace Enforcement				
Cross-border aggression			■	
Support of peace keeping			■	
Support of humanitarian objectives			■	■

- *Affordable* responses are crucial: the UN itself is lamentably under-resourced, and there are no other better funded international bodies with anything like the UN's legitimacy to act in response to security problems. Timeliness and graduation principles, if properly applied, should help here: the later the response, and the larger the problem, the greater the likely cost of the necessary response. At the same time the most effective response may on occasion be simply too expensive to be feasible: rather than operations being reduced to affordable ineffectuality, such responses may be better not mounted at all. A more constructive approach—spelt out in more detail later in this study—would be for the UN to develop and streamline its overall response capability, so as to at least ensure the most efficient use of what will almost inevitably be scarce resources.

- *Consistent* responses are also critical in maintaining the international community's credibility. While no two situations will be identical, nor should there be any obvious selectivity or imbalance in responding to security problems which, by their nature, clearly demand some action by the international community.

The idea of cooperative security

A single, coherent, conceptual theme runs through all the response strategies we have been defining: the content, and spirit, of that theme we believe is best captured by the term *cooperative security*.

International relations analysts have been debating for some years how best to describe an approach to the prevention and resolution of conflict which emphasises cooperation more than competition, and does not focus wholly on security as a military issue: 'comprehensive security', 'common security' and 'collective security' all have their advocates. *Comprehensive security* conveys the notion that security is multi-dimensional in character, demanding attention not only to the political and diplomatic disputes that have so often produced conflict in the past, but to such factors as economic underdevelopment, trade disputes, unregulated population flows, environmental degradation, drug trafficking, terrorism and human rights abuses. However, for present purposes, this term does suffer some weaknesses: it is so all-embracing as to lose much of its descriptive force, and it insufficiently emphasises the element of international cooperation which is central to contemporary thinking.

From these perspectives, *common security* is a better expression. The central idea here, as first articulated by the Palme Commission in 1982, is that lasting security does not lie in an upward spiral of arms development, fuelled by mutual suspicion, but in a commitment to joint survival, to taking into account the legitimate security anxieties of others, and to working cooperatively in a number of ways to maximise the degree of interdependence between nations: in short, to achieving security with others, not against them. Although the term is capable of much more far-reaching application, most discussions of common security have had overwhelmingly a military focus, emphasising force structures based on the principle of non-provocative defence, and military confidence-building measures.

The concept of *collective security* is a familiar and useful one, but inherently military focused. It involves the idea of all members of a particular security community—be it the United Nations, or some regional grouping—renouncing the use of force among themselves and agreeing to come to the aid of any member state attacked by a defector from the ranks. Collective security can perhaps best be seen as a corollary to common security: while common security is both an objective, and a way of describing the confidence-building process by which that objective may be peacefully obtained, collective security is the ultimate guarantee that that process will not be blown off course by the aggressive behaviour of any individual state—or that if it is, the reaction will be swift.

The virtue of *cooperative security* as a descriptive theme is that it does embrace and effectively capture the whole content of both 'common security' and 'collective security', neither of which by itself tells the whole story: at the same time, 'cooperative security' picks up some of the multi-dimensional flavour of 'comprehensive security' as well. Cooperative security has been usefully described as a broad approach to security which is multi-dimensional in scope and gradualist in temperament; emphasises reassurance rather than deterrence; is inclusive rather than exclusive; is not restrictive in membership; favours multilateralism over bilateralism; does not privilege military solutions over non-military ones; assumes that states are the principal actors in the security system, but accepts that non-state actors may have an important role to play; does not require the creation of formal security institutions, but does not reject them either; and which, above all, stresses the value of creating 'habits of dialogue' on a multilateral basis. For present purposes, the immediate utility of 'cooperative security' is that it does encompass, in a single, reasonably precise phrase, the whole range of possible responses to security problems through which the international community is now struggling to find its way.

2

The United Nations and the International Community

The United Nations system

This chapter describes the various actors—in particular those in the United Nations system—who make up the 'international community'; it gives an outline sketch of the roles they have played, and are capable of playing, in resolving international peace and security problems. The treatment here is descriptive rather than analytical: those already familiar with the cast, and impatient to get on with the play, should turn immediately to Chapter 3.

The United Nations Charter was signed in San Francisco on 26 June 1945, and entered into force on 24 October 1945. It was, and remains, a bold prescription for maintaining international peace and security and advancing global economic well-being. Under the Charter, the first and primary purpose of the UN is the maintenance of international peace and security (Article 1). The UN's other purposes, also specified in Article 1, are the development of friendly relations among nations, achievement of international cooperation in addressing social and economic matters, and the harmonising of national actions in the attainment of common ends. While related to the maintenance of international peace and security, particularly in the preventive sense, these other purposes stand on their own in affirming the fundamental place of human welfare on the global agenda.

To facilitate the achievement of the UN's declared purposes, the Charter provides for the establishment of six principal organs and such subsidiary organs as may be found necessary (Article 7). These organs are the General Assembly (Chapter IV), the Security Council (Chapter V), the Economic and Social Council (Chapter X), the Trusteeship Council (Chapter XIII), the International Court of Justice (Chapter XIV) and a Secretariat (Chapter XV). With the exception of the largely inactive Trusteeship Council, these organs all have some part to play in addressing matters relating to the maintenance of international peace and security.

In addition to these major organs, the 'UN system' comprises a large number of other related organs, regional and functional commissions, separately constituted peace operations, independent specialised agencies, and other UN-related bodies. The whole structure is extraordinarily sprawling and complex, as is evident from the accompanying Chart 2—which is itself by no means a complete picture of the whole UN organisational landscape.

The UN Charter established a framework for relations between states into the second half of the 20th century, and did so in a way which has proved enduring. Yet during the long years of the Cold War, the Charter's continued relevance to contemporary international relations seemed far from assured. The UN of the Cold War era bore little resemblance to the body envisaged by the founders of the organisation, its basic assumptions diverging fundamentally from the political realities which came with competition between the United States and the Soviet Union. Superpower competition during the Cold War, manifested most evidently through the exercise of the veto power, significantly impaired the effective discharge of responsibilities by the UN's paramount security organ, the Security Council.

The Security Council

The Security Council comprises ten non-permanent members elected for two year terms and five permanent members: China, France, Russia, UK and US (Article 23). The 47th UN General Assembly in 1992 adopted without a vote a resolution (UNGA 47/62) requesting the Secretary-General to invite UN member states to submit comments on a possible review of Security Council membership. Some member states argue that the Security Council does not act consistently and with impartiality, and is inclined to pay less attention to matters in which its members do not have an immediate interest. These states tend to perceive the Security Council as an essentially coercive and manipulative instrument dominated by Western interests. The UN has issued a report on the question of a possible review of Council membership, consisting of comments submitted by member states.

Chart 2   The United Nations system

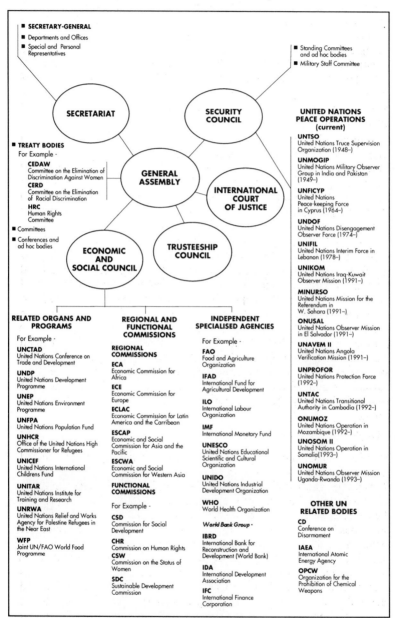

SECRETARY-GENERAL
Departments and Offices
Special and Personal Representatives

Standing Committees and ad hoc bodies
Military Staff Committee

SECRETARIAT

SECURITY COUNCIL

GENERAL ASSEMBLY

INTERNATIONAL COURT OF JUSTICE

TRUSTEESHIP COUNCIL

ECONOMIC AND SOCIAL COUNCIL

TREATY BODIES
For Example -
 CEDAW
 Committee on the Elimination of Discrimination Against Women
 CERD
 Committee on the Elimination of Racial Discrimination
 HRC
 Human Rights Committee
Committees
Conferences and ad hoc bodies

UNITED NATIONS PEACE OPERATIONS (current)

UNTSO
United Nations Truce Supervision Organization (1948–)

UNMOGIP
United Nations Military Observer Group in India and Pakistan (1949–)

UNFICYP
United Nations Peace-keeping Force in Cyprus (1964–)

UNDOF
United Nations Disengagement Observer Force (1974–)

UNIFIL
United Nations Interim Force in Lebanon (1978–)

UNIKOM
United Nations Iraq-Kuwait Observer Mission (1991–)

MINURSO
United Nations Mission for the Referendum in W. Sahara (1991–)

ONUSAL
United Nations Observer Mission in El Salvador (1991–)

UNAVEM II
United Nations Angola Verification Mission (1991–)

UNPROFOR
United Nations Protection Force (1992–)

UNTAC
United Nations Transitional Authority in Cambodia (1992–)

ONUMOZ
United Nations Operation in Mozambique (1992–)

UNOSOM II
United Nations Operation in Somalia(1993–)

UNOMUR
United Nations Observer Mission Uganda-Rwanda (1993–)

RELATED ORGANS AND PROGRAMS

For Example -

UNCTAD
United Nations Conference on Trade and Development

UNDP
United Nations Development Programme

UNEP
United Nations Environment Programme

UNFPA
United Nations Population Fund

UNHCR
Office of the United Nations High Commissioner for Refugees

UNICEF
United Nations International Childrens Fund

UNITAR
United Nations Institute for Training and Research

UNRWA
United Nations Relief and Works Agency for Palestine Refugees in the Near East

WFP
Joint UN/FAO World Food Programme

REGIONAL AND FUNCTIONAL COMMISSIONS

REGIONAL COMMISSIONS

ECA
Economic Commission for Africa

ECE
Economic Commission for Europe

ECLAC
Economic Commission for Latin America and the Carribean

ESCAP
Economic and Social Commission for Asia and the Pacific

ESCWA
Economic and Social Commission for Western Asia

FUNCTIONAL COMMISSIONS

For Example -

CSD
Commission for Social Development

CHR
Commission on Human Rights

CSW
Commission on the Status of Women

SDC
Sustainable Development Commission

INDEPENDENT SPECIALISED AGENCIES

For Example -

FAO
Food and Agriculture Organization

IFAD
International Fund for Agricultural Development

ILO
International Labour Organization

IMF
International Monetary Fund

UNESCO
United Nations Educational Scientific and Cultural Organization

UNIDO
United Nations Industrial Development Organization

WHO
World Health Organization

World Bank Group -

IBRD
International Bank for Reconstruction and Development (World Bank)

IDA
International Development Association

IFC
International Finance Corporation

OTHER UN RELATED BODIES

CD
Conference on Disarmament

IAEA
International Atomic Energy Agency

OPCW
Organization for the Prohibition of Chemical Weapons

Source: Adapted from the *United Nations Handbook*, New Zealand Government, 1992

Article 24 of the Charter confers on the Security Council primary responsibility for the maintenance of international peace and security. Members 'agree that in carrying out its duties under this responsibility the Security Council acts on their behalf'. Under the Charter, the Security Council is granted specific powers to facilitate the pacific settlement of disputes (Chapter VI, Articles 33–38) and to take action with respect to threats to the peace, breaches of the peace, and acts of aggression (Chapter VII, Articles 39–51). These two principal functions are described more fully below.

So long as the Security Council is exercising in respect of any security matter the functions vested in it for such purposes, the General Assembly is precluded from making any recommendation on that security matter, unless requested to do so by the Security Council (Article 12). At San Francisco, delegates agreed that the General Assembly, as the supreme representative body of the world, should work to establish the principles on which world peace and the ideal of solidarity must rest. They envisaged that the Security Council should act in accordance with those principles, and with the speed necessary to prevent any attempted breach of international peace and security. In practice, however, the General Assembly has on several recent occasions adopted resolutions dealing with issues concurrently on the Security Council agenda, notably concerning the conflict in Bosnia–Herzegovina. While such resolutions carry moral and political weight, the Security Council is in no way bound to take them into account.

The veto power The Charter provides that decisions by the Security Council on non-procedural matters shall be made by an affirmative vote of nine members including the concurring vote of the five permanent members (Article 27). The veto power comes from this prescription that the five permanent members must concur with (or at least not reject) a proposed resolution for it to pass. The granting of the veto power was justified largely on the grounds that it saved the Security Council from voting for commitments it was incapable of fulfilling, namely enforcement action against one of the five permanent members or the imposition of sanctions against the will of one of those states. In other words, to convince the permanent members that they should adhere to the Charter and the collective security framework embodied therein, a deliberate decision was taken to establish a collective security system which could not be applied to the permanent members themselves.

Between 1946 and 1990 inclusive, 646 Security Council resolutions were passed—and vetoes cast on 201 occasions (involving 241 actual negative votes). The lack of unanimity and political will

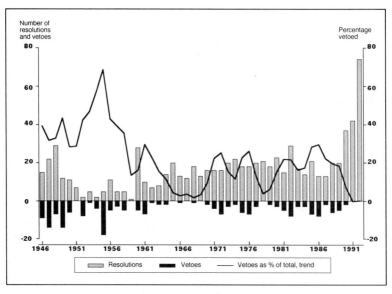

Chart 3   Security Council resolutions passed and vetoed 1946–1992

among the permanent members during the Cold War era, and their unwillingness to allow the Security Council to deal with matters which fell within their respective spheres of influence, effectively prevented the utilisation of the collective security system envisaged in the Charter, particularly Chapter VII, and damaged the UN's international standing.

As demonstrated in the accompanying Chart 3, the Security Council in the 1940s and early 1950s was not incapable of making decisions. There were numerous vetoes, but some decisions as well. The first observer missions and peace keeping operations were established in this period. The veto was often used, principally by the Soviet Union, to block UN membership applications (about half of all vetoes in the 1940s and 1950s, and all eighteen vetoes of 1955) or declaratory or condemnatory draft resolutions. The Security Council was able to authorise the Unified Command in Korea in 1950 only in the absence from the Council of the Soviet Permanent Representative; the action otherwise would almost certainly have been vetoed. The veto prevented the Security Council from discussing the Soviet Union's invasion of Hungary in 1956.

A relatively more constructive environment prevailed in the 1960s. The Security Council was able to authorise a comprehensive

UN peace keeping operation in the Congo (ONUC 1960–64), and considered a number of security matters not directly in the superpowers' spheres of influence, such as the Cyprus question. The crucial issue of Vietnam, however, was never substantively considered by the Council. Few UN membership applications were stymied (44 were accepted and only two vetoed in the 1960s). Yet the veto continued in use, increasing in number again in the 1970s and 1980s, and the Security Council's capacity remained constricted. By this time the composition of the General Assembly had changed, with the addition of many newly independent nations, and Western powers began to use the veto more often on questions related to the Middle East and Southern Africa. The United States repeatedly vetoed applications for UN membership by the Democratic Republic of Vietnam and the Republic of South Vietnam in 1975, and by the united Socialist Republic of Vietnam in 1976. By the 1980s the utility of the UN was being called into question in the United States.

By 1990, however, the Cold War had ended and the five permanent members began to explore anew the potential of the Security Council to take decisions on matters relating to international peace and security. Since 1991 the number of decisions taken by the Council has risen dramatically to a consistently higher level and in 1991 and 1992 there were no vetoes at all. One veto in 1993, by the Russian Federation, was later effectively reversed. Cooperation, rather than confrontation and division, increasingly marks relations between the permanent members of the Security Council. Expectations of the UN are now greater than at any time since the hopes and ideals captured at San Francisco first began to sour. There are now many more, and more complex, international peace keeping operations. The UN's collective security role has evolved from limited monitoring operations ('traditional' peace keeping) to much more multi-faceted peace keeping operations and a range of other quite new roles including peace enforcement in support of humanitarian objectives. For the first time since 1945, there is genuine opportunity for the UN to work as it was intended, for the benefit of all member states. The structure is there already. What is needed now is to adapt it to the challenges of the post-Cold War era.

'Peaceful measures'   The Charter stipulates that the parties to a dispute, the continuance of which is likely to endanger the maintenance of international peace and security, must settle their differences by peaceful means. Article 33 sets out the means by which the pacific settlement of disputes might be pursued: 'negotiation, enquiry, mediation, conciliation, arbitration, judicial settlement, resort to regional agencies or arrangements, or other peaceful means of their own choice'. This same article authorises the Security Council, when necessary, to call upon the parties to settle their disputes by such means. The Security Council is empowered under Articles 36–38 to recommend means of settling disputes peacefully. Under Article 34, the Security Council may investigate any dispute or situation to determine whether its continuance is likely to endanger peace and security.

Article 33 has been the basis for condemnation by the Security Council of acts of violence and outbreaks of armed conflict, and has triggered responses including appeals for the cessation of hostilities and the withdrawal of intervening forces; measures to reduce tension between warring parties; appeals to commence or continue negotiations; requests to the Secretary-General to undertake missions or make available good offices; and requests for the Secretary-General to name a Special Representative as part of efforts to promote resolution of disputes or conflicts. Article 34 has mandated fact finding and inquiry missions and other investigative bodies. Under Chapter VI, the Security Council has also dealt with questions of hostage-taking and abduction (eg Israel's abduction of Adolf Eichmann) and terrorism, condemning all acts of unlawful interference against civil aviation.

Other than the moral suasion derived from Article 33, the Security Council's principal activity under Chapter VI has been to establish, through recommendations under Articles 36–38, military observer missions and peace keeping forces mandated to determine whether agreed ceasefires are being maintained, and to act as a disincentive or provide a buffer to reduce the possibility of renewed conflict. These have included unarmed observer missions to observe ceasefires (eg UNTSO, UNMOGIP), missions to verify redeployment or force withdrawal (eg UNAVEM), and lightly armed forces dispatched to maintain peaceful conditions along armistice lines or international frontiers (eg UNFICYP, UNIFIL).

The Congo (ONUC 1960–64) saw the first example of a UN peace keeping mission expanded to include a civilian component mandated to create or strengthen local institutions designed to foster conditions conducive to economic rehabilitation and reconstruction, and to avoid a recurrence of conflict. In the post-Cold War period such expanded mandates have become almost commonplace. The UN Transition Assistance Group (UNTAG 1989–90), established to facilitate the Namibian independence process, was involved particularly in electoral assistance and monitoring, while the UN Transitional Authority in Cambodia (UNTAC) and the UN Operation in Somalia (UNOSOM), discussed in detail in subsequent chapters, were both multi-dimensional operations extending well beyond the scope of traditional peace keeping.

23

Enforcement measures   The Security Council is empowered under Chapter VII to take action with respect to threats to the peace, breaches of the peace, and acts of aggression. This Chapter sets out the Council's principal enforcement powers. Under Article 41, the Security Council may decide what measures (not involving the use of armed force) are to be employed to give effect to its decisions, including economic and communications sanctions. Article 42 authorises the Security Council to 'take such action by air, sea or land forces as may be necessary' to maintain or restore international peace and security. Such action may include demonstrations, blockades and other operations by air, sea or land forces of UN member states.

The Unified Command in Korea in 1950 was the only example during the Cold War of a Chapter VII enforcement action employing armed force. The operation proceeded under a unified command led by the US, but flying the UN flag. While not explicitly invoking Chapter VII, the Security Council also authorised ONUC to use force, as a last resort, to prevent civil war in the Congo, and later authorised the Secretary-General to use force to complete the removal of mercenaries. Since the end of the Cold War, there have already been operations mandated to use military force: in the Gulf (1991), Somalia (1993) and on a more limited basis in Bosnia–Herzegovina (1993). Enforcement actions instituted under Article 41 during the Cold War era include the imposition of sanctions against Southern Rhodesia (1966 and 1968) and South Africa (1977); in more recent times, sanctions have been imposed against Iraq (1990), former Yugoslavia (1991–93), Somalia (1992), Libya (1992) and Haiti (1993).

The Military Staff Committee was intended under Article 47 to advise the Security Council on all questions relating to military matters and to take responsibility for the strategic direction of any armed forces at the Security Council's disposal, including any national forces made available to the Security Council by special agreement under Article 43. It was rendered inoperable by the Cold War. The only task undertaken by the Military Staff Committee during this period was the preparation for the Security Council of a report on the general principles governing the organisation of forces made available to the Council under Article 43. The Committee ceased to function for all practical purposes following the failure by members to agree on fundamental aspects of the report.

The Secretary-General

The Secretary-General is empowered under Article 99 of the Charter to 'bring to the attention of the Security Council any matter which in his opinion may threaten the maintenance of international peace and security': his responsibility on security matters is to the Security Council rather than the General Assembly. As well as being the UN's chief administrative officer (Article 97), the Secretary-General has wide-ranging (albeit unclearly defined) political responsibilities and powers. The Secretary-General is the symbol of international organisation, and has the capacity to act as independent spokesman for the global interest. He or she has the power to influence the international agenda and its substance, and to intervene freely in debates, subject to the injunction in Article 100 demanding of the Secretary-General and Secretariat staff neutrality and independence from the UN's member states. In short, the Secretary-General is in a position to make what he or she will of the office, taking due account of precedents well established in practice.

There are numerous ad hoc examples of involvement by the Secretary-General and Secretariat staff in the pacific settlement of disputes without a mandate from the Security Council. These responsibilities have sometimes been taken on by the Secretary-General himself (eg U Thant's quiet, pro-active good offices initiative during the Cuban Missile Crisis in 1962 or Javier Perez de Cuellar's efforts in 1988 in the negotiation of the Iran–Iraq ceasefire and the conclusion of the Geneva Accords on Soviet withdrawal from Afghanistan) or, more frequently, by senior staff or diplomats acting as the Secretary-General's Special Representatives, Personal Representatives, envoys or emissaries to assist in tracking particular situations and in providing good offices and mediation. Brian Urquhart, for one, spent many years of his UN life engaged in such missions in the Congo, Middle East, Cyprus and Namibia.

The General Assembly

The General Assembly, comprising all member states—now 184 of them—embodies the universality of the UN as the world organisation. It is empowered under Article 10 to discuss any matters within the scope of the Charter, including those relating to the Security Council's powers and functions and, except as provided in Article 12, may make recommendations to member states or to the Security Council on such matters. Article 11 authorises the General Assembly to consider any questions, and general principles of cooperation, relating to the maintenance of international peace and security, and to make recommendations with regard to such questions and principles. Under Article 14, and again subject to Article 12, the General Assembly may recommend measures for the peaceful adjustment of any situation which it deems likely to impair the general welfare or friendly relations among nations.

In exercising its authority under Article 11, the General Assembly approved the 1982 Manila Declaration on the Peaceful Settlement of International Disputes (UNGA 37/10) and the 1988 Declaration on the Prevention and Removal of Disputes and Situations

Which May Threaten International Peace and Security and on the Role of the United Nations in this Field (UNGA 43/51). It also adopted the 1991 Declaration on Fact-Finding by the United Nations in the Field of the Maintenance of International Peace and Security (UNGA 46/59).

A number of the main Committees of the General Assembly, in particular the First (Political and Security) Committee and the Special Political Committee, as well as the Plenary of the Assembly itself, provide major forums for addressing international security issues. The Fourth (Decolonisation Issues) and Special Political Committees have been amalgamated and other proposals to reform the General Assembly's committee structure, including rationalising diffuse agendas by re-allocating certain items to the First Committee, are currently under consideration.

One product of the Cold War 'gridlock' in the Security Council was a limited intrusion by the General Assembly into the Council's sphere of responsibility. This was signalled in the first instance by the 1950 Uniting for Peace resolution, which empowered the General Assembly to call for (but not impose) action to maintain or restore international peace and security in situations where such action had been vetoed by the Security Council. The Assembly's membership and potential influence grew significantly during this period, particularly in the 1960s, as former colonies became independent sovereign states and the Non-Aligned Movement (NAM) consolidated its position. Yet developing member states, attracted to the idea of holding sway in the General Assembly in a manner they could not in the Security Council, found their influence was still overshadowed by the Cold War power blocs.

Since the Cold War, the General Assembly has been used as a forum for expressing dissatisfaction with the Security Council's handling of the conflict in Bosnia–Herzegovina and to urge the Council to consider further measures, such as lifting the arms embargo. The General Assembly has also played an important role in broader peace building efforts. It has, for example, sent a civilian mission to monitor the human rights situation in Haiti in support of joint UN/Organization of American States (OAS) peace making efforts there. The General Assembly has also initiated electoral monitoring missions (eg the elections in Haiti and the referendum in Eritrea), in addition to the Security Council's involvement in electoral issues through expanded peace keeping operations.

The International Court of Justice

The UN Charter establishes the International Court of Justice (ICJ) as the UN system's principal judicial organ (Article 92). All members of the UN are deemed, by the very fact of their membership, to be parties to the ICJ Statute (Article 93), and undertake to comply with the ICJ's decision in any case in which they voluntarily submit to the Court's jurisdiction (Article 94). Under Article 93, non-member states can also be party to the ICJ Statute. States may bring their disputes before tribunals other than the ICJ (Article 95). The General Assembly and the Security Council may request the ICJ's advisory opinion on any legal question, and the former may authorise other organs of the UN and its specialised agencies to likewise request an opinion on any legal question arising within the scope of their activities (Article 96). In making recommendations under Article 36 for the pacific settlement of disputes, the Security Council is enjoined to take into consideration that legal disputes should as a general rule be referred by the parties to the ICJ.

In practice, the ICJ has been under-utilised. Only 21 advisory opinions have been sought under Article 96 since 1945. Notwithstanding Article 93, only 57 UN member states have accepted the general jurisdiction of the Court, and others impose conditions in agreeing to submit to its jurisdiction. The ICJ itself, in accordance with its own Statute (Article 36), has conscientiously accepted the principle that it can consider contentious cases only if both parties have clearly signified their assent for it to do so. Under Article 36 of the Statute, states party to the Statute may at any time declare that they recognise as compulsory and without special agreement, in relation to any other state accepting the same obligation, the jurisdiction of the Court in all international legal disputes. This declaration may be made unconditionally or on condition of reciprocity on the part of several or certain states, or for a certain time. The Court has been wary of efforts by the UN's political organs to tempt it to render advisory opinions on contentious cases without the consent of the parties. That said, the ICJ has been influential both in dispute and conflict resolution and in assisting the activities of other actors in the international security community, and could become a more valuable adjunct for the Secretary-General in extending the range of responses available in problem situations.

ECOSOC and the specialised agencies

The Economic and Social Council (ECOSOC) and the specialised agencies have potentially important roles in contributing to peace building efforts, including in addressing emerging non-military threats to security. Under Article 62, ECOSOC is empowered to make recommendations to the General Assembly, to member states and to the UN specialised agencies, concerning international economic, social, cultural, educational, health and related matters, and for the purpose of promoting respect for and observance of human rights and fundamental freedoms. Under Article 65 of the Charter ECOSOC may furnish information to the Security Council, and shall assist the Council upon its request.

ECOSOC, as the economic and social arm of the UN system, is mandated to coordinate the activities of the UN's specialised agencies through consultation with and recommendations to these agencies, and through recommendations to the General Assembly and member states (Article 63). Responsibility for the discharge of the functions of these agencies is vested in ECOSOC under the authority of the General Assembly (Article 60). In practice, however, the majority of UN member states to date have preferred to deal with the specialised agencies directly, rather than through ECOSOC. Proposals to reform ECOSOC, and to enhance its ability to play its coordination role effectively, are currently under consideration.

The UN's specialised agencies deal with a range of global issues like health and food security which can become critical features of conflicts and crises threatening international peace and security. Other UN bodies with similar functions include the UN Children's Fund (UNICEF) and the Office of the UN High Commissioner for Refugees (UNHCR), which play an acknowledged humanitarian role, those providing emergency relief such as the World Food Program (WFP), and developmental programs like the UN Development Program (UNDP). By themselves or in conjunction with others, the specialised agencies and these other bodies play a major role in alleviating international crises, including those arising as extensions of conflicts. To the extent that they encourage processes of development and cooperation, these agencies and programs actively foster international peace and security by tackling some of the structural roots of conflict. For example, UNHCR in working to facilitate the voluntary return or resettlement of refugees is providing both humanitarian assistance and promoting regional stability (eg Rohingya refugees returning from Bangladesh to Burma).

The UN Secretariat's recently established Department of Humanitarian Affairs (DHA), which reports to ECOSOC, is charged with better co-ordinating the involvement of these and other agencies in crises and other humanitarian situations, including in expanded UN peace keeping operations. Although DHA's coordinating mechanisms are not yet fully developed, and certain states continue to resist (on sovereignty grounds) a greater role for the UN's specialised agencies, the international community can be expected to continue efforts to develop integrated responses to the multi-dimensional and non-static security problems of the post-Cold War era. This will require closer links in practice between the military, political, developmental and humanitarian facets of international cooperative security operations.

Other international bodies linked to the UN

Such bodies with a peace and security role include the Conference on Disarmament (CD), the International Atomic Energy Agency (IAEA), and the Organisation for the Prohibition of Chemical Weapons (OPCW). The CD, established by agreement among states and subsequently endorsed by consensus in its current configuration at the General Assembly's 10th Special Session in 1978 (UNGA 33/71F), is an autonomous negotiating forum for multilateral disarmament agreements. The IAEA is an independent inter-governmental organisation under the aegis of the UN which implements, most importantly, safeguards provisions of the Nuclear Non-Proliferation Treaty (NPT) and other equivalent agreements. The OPCW, established under the Chemical Weapons Convention, is intended to implement and supervise global chemical disarmament and non-proliferation.

Regional organisations

The Charter, under Chapter VIII, addresses the place of regional arrangements or agencies—for present purposes described collectively as regional organisations—in the cooperative security system. Regional organisations are empowered to deal with such matters relating to the maintenance of international peace and security as are appropriate for regional action, and are encouraged to make every effort to achieve pacific settlement of local disputes before referring them to the Security Council, whether on their own initiative or by reference from the Security Council (Article 52). Where appropriate, the Security Council is empowered to utilise regional organisations for enforcement action under its authority, with no regional organisation being permitted to take enforcement action unless so authorised by the Security Council (Article 53).

The Secretary-General in *An Agenda for Peace* observes that the Charter deliberately left open, for reasons of flexibility, the interpretation of what constituted regional arrangements or agencies under Chapter VIII (para 61). Such organisations could include treaty-based organisations, organisations for mutual security and defence, those established for regional development or for cooperation on a particular topic or function, or groups created to deal with a specific issue of current concern. The Secretary-General notes that the Cold War not only impaired the use of Chapter VIII, but also resulted on occasion in regional organisations working against, not for, the resolution of disputes (para 63). He adds that regional arrangements or agencies during the Cold War period often owed their existence to the absence of a universal collective security system.

While there is no precise guide to which regional organisations have the standing or mandate to address and respond to security problems, such bodies might broadly be divided between 'existing organisations with a peace and security role', and 'discussion forums and emerging new bodies'.

Existing organisations with a peace and security role

A number of regional bodies already have a standing invitation to participate in the General Assembly's work, and have worked closely with the Security Council on peace and security matters. These include the Organization of American States (OAS), the Organization of African Unity (OAU), the Organisation of the Islamic Conference (OIC), and the Arab League. All but the OAS have entered into framework agreements for cooperation with the UN (the OAU in 1965, updated in 1990, the OIC in 1982, and the Arab League in 1989). These organisations have an express mandate to address and respond to security issues or, in the absence of such a mandate, have developed the necessary functions through practice or need.

The OAS was founded with the aim of fostering peace, security, mutual understanding and cooperation among the nations of the Western Hemisphere. The OAS Charter includes provisions relating to non-aggression against other member states (Article 14), diplomatic measures to resolve bilateral disputes (Articles 6, 9 and 14), and sanctions (Article 18). The OAS has established a Working Group on Hemispheric Security (a forum for debate, assisted by experts, on major regional and international security issues) and is currently considering organising a Hemispheric Security Conference. The OAS has taken a number of specific security measures in recent years. Through the Inter-American Defence Board, it has sent demining teams to Nicaragua. It has provided election monitors (eg in Nicaragua, Dominican Republic, Guatemala, Haiti, Surinam and Paraguay) as part of efforts to promote regional peace and security. The OAS worked closely with the UN to reach an agreement to the dispute in El Salvador (five Central American presidents, known as 'Friends of the Secretary-General', assisted senior UN Secretariat officials to this end), and is also cooperating closely in the case of Haiti (the Special Representative appointed by the UN Secretary-General to deal with the situation in Haiti is deemed to represent both the OAS and the UN).

The OAU Charter identifies as one of the organisation's principal aims the defence of the sovereignty, territorial integrity and independence of African states (Article II). Under Article III, OAU member states are required to settle disputes by peaceful means. Article XIX establishes for these purposes a Commission of Mediation, Conciliation and Arbitration. The Commission itself has been virtually dormant since its establishment. However, through the appointment of ad hoc commissions, the OAU has taken up some of the more difficult regional issues (eg Western Sahara, Chad/Libya, Mauritania/Senegal), but has not found it easy to implement its findings. As part of its continuing efforts to effect conflict resolution, the OAU agreed at its summit meeting in Cairo in June 1993 to establish a mechanism for preventing, managing and resolving conflicts in Africa. The mechanism will be grafted onto pre-existing organisational structures and will have to overcome problems that have dogged similar initiatives in the past—including lack of resources and reluctance of member states to become involved in the intra-state conflicts of others.

The OIC and the Arab League, although encompassing members drawn from several regions (the entire Islamic world in the former case, North Africa, the Arabian peninsula and the Eastern Mediterranean in the latter), clearly fall within the spirit of Chapter VIII. The OIC aims, inter alia, to take necessary measures to support international peace and security, founded on justice (OIC Charter 1972). Although focused to a considerable extent on the Israeli/Arab dispute, the OIC has also responded (albeit with limited effect) to the Soviet invasion of Afghanistan, the Iran/Iraq War, Iraq's invasion of Kuwait, conflicts in Chad and Lebanon, and the civil war in Somalia. In 1992, the General Assembly approved a resolution introduced by the OIC calling on the Security Council to act forcefully to defend Bosnia–Herzegovina's non-Serbian population and its territorial integrity. The Arab League, through its Political Committee, Joint Defence Council and Permanent Military Commission, has been concerned with much the same security issues, but not to date with much evident success.

The Conference on Security and Co-operation in Europe (CSCE) has an explicit security role and, through the Helsinki Document 1992, declared itself a regional arrangement within the meaning of Chapter VIII. It is currently considering the possibility of formally seeking UN observer status. Under the Helsinki Document, the CSCE may request the use of the military resources of NATO, WEU, the EC and other organisations to facilitate planning for peace keeping operations in which it has an interest. The CSCE has recently undertaken several regional missions, including to the Balkans and to the former Soviet Union, to resolve disputes and address conflicts, and in May 1993, the UN Secretary-General and the Chairman of the CSCE Council agreed on a framework for cooperation and coordination between the UN Secretariat and the CSCE.

NATO, although clearly a regional organisation within the meaning of Chapter VIII, does not have any formal UN status. Founded at the end of the Second World War in response to the Soviet military threat, NATO represents a system of collective security serving a limited number of states for the specific purpose of self defence (as envisaged under Article 51). It was established as an alliance dedicated to fill a perceived gap in the collective security system envisaged by the UN Charter (the gap being the collective security system's inability, on account of the Security Council veto power, to deal with aggression launched or supported by a permanent member of the Security Council).

With the end of the Cold War, and the removal of NATO's fundamental raison d'etre, the organisation has been compelled to find a new and relevant role, or else face obsolescence in the manner of the Warsaw Pact. NATO's new role is predicated on provision of a rapid reaction force, and close cooperation with the CSCE, WEU, EC and other such organisations. The NATO/CSCE relationship (like the relationship between the Front-Line States in Southern Africa and the OAU) demonstrates that sub-regional organisations can play a security role without being subordinate to broader regional groupings which embrace all their members.

Discussion forums and emerging new bodies

Included here are regional organisations of one kind or another which have assumed a security role, or which have the potential to do so, even though this may not have been their original rationale or their primary or sole purpose. There are many groups, especially sub-regional, which fall into this category. They have no formal standing with the UN, but in some cases increased interest has been expressed in their potential collective security roles. ASEAN, the South Pacific Forum, the Gulf Co-operation Council, and the Economic Community of West African States provide useful examples. The Commonwealth, although covering a broad spectrum of activities, played a central role in the Rhodesian peace settlement (1979-80) and continues to be closely involved in Southern African affairs, including those of a security nature.

ASEAN (Association of South-East Asian Nations) was established primarily to accelerate economic development in the South East Asian region. The organisation acquired a more overt security dimension in 1976 with the Treaty on Amity and Co-operation in South-East Asia (Bali Treaty), which set out principles of mutual respect for the independence and sovereignty of all nations, non-interference in the internal affairs of one another, and settlement of disputes by peaceful means. With the end of the Cold War, and the diminished US security presence in the region, ASEAN members have concluded that there should be greater cooperation within the organisation on security matters. This process is being pursued through ASEAN Ministerial Meetings, Post-Ministerial Conference

(PMC) discussions with dialogue partners, and several levels of 'second track' diplomacy. An ASEAN-sponsored resolution adopted by the General Assembly (UNGA 47/53B) identified the Bali Treaty as consistent with the Secretary-General's call in *An Agenda for Peace* for a closer relationship between the UN and regional organisations. In July 1993, it was agreed at the ASEAN PMC to inaugurate, as an important new vehicle for dialogue and cooperation on security matters, an 'ASEAN Regional Forum'—including not only the ASEAN six and their existing regional dialogue partners (Australia, New Zealand, Japan, Korea, the United States and Canada), but also Russia, China, Vietnam, Laos and Papua New Guinea.

The South Pacific Forum (SPF) has an economic and social focus, with attention turning on occasion to specific security issues, such as French nuclear weapons testing in the region. There has been recent discussion, as yet unresolved, about the possibility that the SPF might in due course formalise its status with the UN as an observer at the General Assembly.

The Gulf Co-operation Council (GCC) was established to enhance economic, social and cultural cooperation among member states. It was compelled by the Iran/Iraq war to address at least to a degree questions of regional security cooperation. This process was considerably accelerated by Iraq's invasion of Kuwait, and the subsequent Gulf War in 1991. Following this war, the GCC announced in the Damascus Declaration the establishment of a regional peace keeping force. The Declaration is yet to be implemented, and the proposed regional peace keeping force is dormant.

The Economic Community of West African States (ECOWAS) was instituted with a strong trade orientation. This emphasis shifted to an extent when a Mutual Defence Assistance protocol was agreed between member states in 1981. In 1990, a Standing Mediation Committee was formed to mediate in regional disputes. An ECOWAS Monitoring Group (known as ECOMOG) was sent the same year to restore peace and establish an interim government in Liberia.

Regional bodies with a potential security role might include the South Asia Association for Regional Co-operation (SAARC), and the Andean Pact. Both organisations to date have focused exclusively on economic and social matters, but by their regionally inclusive nature might have the potential in due course to develop a complementary security dimension. There have been suggestions of a CSCE equivalent being established for the Middle East as a possible outcome of the present peace process.

Sovereign states

The sovereign state remains the basic unit in international affairs and is so recognised by the UN Charter. Article 2.7 provides that nothing in the Charter authorises the UN to intervene in matters which are essentially within the domestic jurisdiction of any state, nor are states required to submit to the UN such matters for settlement (the application of Chapter VII enforcement measures excepted). States have played a variety of roles in international security matters, acting individually or as members of coalitions. Under Article 51, states have an inherent right of individual or collective self-defence against armed attack, until such time as the Security Council takes such action as it deems necessary to maintain international peace and security. States may also take initiatives to settle disputes and resolve conflicts to which they are third parties: the role played by the United States in initiating in 1991 the Middle East peace process is a clear example. Indonesia's sponsoring of workshops on South China Sea issues is another good example of a preventive initiative. The role played by the United States in 1993 in an ongoing series of bilateral discussions with the DPRK to secure continued DPRK commitment to the NPT and to the obligations it has assumed under its membership of the NPT is another. The Soviet Union's mediation after the 1964 Indo-Pakistan war illustrates third party involvement in peace making diplomacy as a post-conflict assistance measure. Development assistance contributions by national governments have also been important in facilitating political reconciliation and economic reconstruction in post-conflict situations.

Other international peace and security actors

Non-government organisations

Non-government organisations (NGOs) have played important security roles in particular situations or more generally. Pre-eminent among these is the International Committee of the Red Cross (ICRC) which, in recognition of its formal mandate under the Geneva Conventions and its Protocols and its commendable humanitarian record in conflict situations, is the only NGO invited to participate in the work of the General Assembly. International NGOs are motivated by essentially humanitarian or developmental concerns but, in working to foster local economic and social processes, can also have a positive impact on international peace and security, particularly through peace building activities. Groups like OXFAM, Save the Children, Community Aid Abroad and Médecins sans Frontières, for example, have played a useful role not only in supplying humanitarian relief and development assistance, but also in alerting the world community to diverse humanitarian crises (eg in Uganda, Cambodia and the Sudan). They are in this sense not unlike a number of the UN specialised agencies (perhaps with the exception of UNHCR, which has a more overt security role through its interest in mass movements of people). Most NGOs stand outside the system of government action and cooperation, and will often seek to avoid an overtly political role. Indeed, this impartiality is often essential to their effectiveness and access, as well as to the safety of their own personnel.

National liberation movements

National Liberation Movements and similar political groups can be key players in international disputes and conflicts. Concern to ensure the territorial integrity and political independence of UN member states (Article 2.4) has in most instances precluded the UN from formally recognising these organisations in any way. There have been some exceptions to this, including the standing invitation to the Palestine Liberation Organisation (the PLO) to participate (as 'Palestine') as an observer in the General Assembly's work. Prior to Namibia's independence, the South West African Peoples Organisation (SWAPO) was also accorded observer status following its recognition by the General Assembly as the 'sole legitimate representative' of the Namibian people. A lesser category of observer status has been accorded the African National Congress (ANC) and the Pan Africanist Congress (PAC), which are invited to participate in the General Assembly's consideration of questions concerning South Africa.

Lack of formal recognition by the UN has not prevented informal contact (particularly away from New York) between UN officials (including Special Representatives and emissaries) and important liberation groups. There has, for example, been regular contact between UN officials and the various Mujahadeen factions in Afghanistan, and with rebel movements and other groups in Africa's several civil wars. (UN contact with the Afghan rebel groups was an unusual departure at the time, and one which could not have occurred in the pre-Gorbachev era, as the Najibullah regime still occupied Afghanistan's seat in the General Assembly). Several of these factions and groups have participated in UN-sponsored settlement talks and/or been referred to as parties in UN resolutions endorsing agreements reached.

Thinkers and think tanks

Academics and professional institutions, and ad hoc groups of eminent persons, also play a significant role contributing to debate on improving international responses to security situations and, in many specific situations, putting forward ideas and analyses which are eventually reflected in the policies and proposals of governments. Examples of significant bodies in this respect, from a myriad that could be cited, are the 1982 Independent Commission on Disarmament and Security Issues (the Palme Commission) and the current Carlsson–Ramphal Commission on Global Governance; the International Peace Academy, Ford Foundation, Stockholm and Oslo International Peace Research Institutes, Australian National University Peace Research Centre, Frankfurt Peace Research Institute, United States Institute for Peace, Harvard Program on Negotiation and International Peace Research Institute (Meigaku) in Japan; and the proposed Council on Security Cooperation in Asia and the Pacific (linking a number of regional Centres for Strategic and International Studies and other think-tanks).

II
Building Peace

3

International Regimes

The concept of peace building

Peace building strategies are those that seek to address the underlying causes of disputes, conflicts and crises: to ensure either that problems don't arise in the first place, or that if they do arise they won't recur. In *An Agenda for Peace*, the Secretary-General focused his attention on non-recurrence—what he described as 'post-conflict peace building'. But peace building has a strongly *preventive* character as well. If the foundations are properly laid by efforts, among other things, to create fair systems of rules, fair ways of distributing scarce resources, and to meet basic human needs for survival and dignity—then the chances are that many potential problems, whether international or internal, will remain manageable.

At the heart of the notion of peace building is the idea of meeting needs: for security and order, for a reasonable standard of living, and for recognition of identity and worth. Conflict, whether cross-border or in-country, typically begins, and continues, when important interests or needs of one or more parties are frustrated, threatened or remain unfulfilled. Of course many of the strategies discussed in later chapters—especially preventive diplomacy (see Chapter 5) and peace making (see Chapter 7)—are built around this same approach, of identifying needs and interests and seeking so far as possible to accommodate and reconcile them. But whereas there the focus is on resolving a particular dispute or conflict, here it is more general: on creating the conditions that will ensure that problems needing such attention won't occur, or recur, at all.

To a large extent peace building involves doing exactly the sorts of things that a civilised international community, and the states that make it up, should be doing anyway—ie putting in place effective international rules-systems, dispute resolution mechanisms and cooperative arrangements; meeting basic economic, social, cultural and humanitarian needs; and rebuilding societies that have been shattered by war or other major crises. But too often in the past these things, while seen as worthwhile in their own right, have not been identified clearly enough as absolutely integral to the achievement and maintenance of peace and security, and as a result have been given less than the attention they deserve. If we are to achieve just and durable peace in the post-Cold War world, it is crucially important that the international community not continue to make that mistake. The Secretary-General made the necessary connection in *An Agenda for Peace*, but his message should be given even wider application by applying it to pre-conflict as well as post-conflict situations.

Peace building strategies fall into two broad groups which may be described, respectively, as 'international regimes' and 'in-country peace building'. The former refers to strategies which by their nature are general in application, embracing more than one country; the latter refers to efforts—whether internationally assisted or not—to build the conditions for peace within particular countries. Each group of strategies has both preventive and post-conflict dimensions. In the case, for example, of most of the legal regimes described below, the creation of the regime has been designed to prevent disputes arising, but there will also be provisions within the same regime for the resolution of disputes if they do occur.

'International regimes' are defined here as international laws, norms, agreements and arrangements—global, regional and bilateral in scope—designed to minimise threats to security, promote confidence and trust, and create institutional frameworks for dialogue and cooperation. They can conveniently be discussed, in turn, under three headings: 'legal regimes and dispute resolution mechanisms', 'arms control and disarmament regimes' and 'dialogue and cooperation arrangements'.

Legal regimes and dispute resolution mechanisms

There is already in place today a substantial framework of rules and structures permeating every facet of international relations. They operate at the global, regional and bilateral level. They tend to operate habitually and, for the most part, invisibly. They cover virtually every field of interstate activity—including diplomatic relations, maritime affairs, international environmental protection, human rights and international trade and communications. Without them, much of contemporary international intercourse—and its routine and orderly nature—would be inconceivable.

A significant part of the present framework is the legacy of centuries of international state-craft and diplomacy. Building on these foundations through processes of cooperative law making, states have created a substantial body of law matching modern needs. This activity of states—seeking to secure common objectives and meet common needs through treaty-based law making—is a welcome development, with the potential to benefit all members of the international community equally. It is a crucial tool in promoting international peace and stability and is fundamental to good habits of cooperating for peace. A clear recognition of this reality is the declaration of the 1990s as the Decade of International Law. This rapid growth in law-making among states has been made possible in turn by the rapid growth, following the establishment of the United Nations, of cooperative multilateralism as a primary focus of international relations. The development of global standards and global regimes, for example for the protection of the natural environment, would have been impossible if there had not been international forums such as the United Nations and its specialised agencies in which all states—large and small, the weak as well as the powerful—participate as equals.

An important dimension of these international legal regimes is the bringing into existence of formal and informal processes which states and non-state actors can use to protect their interests and to address at their most innocuous stage those situations with the potential to generate friction and conflict if left unattended. In encouraging the necessary further development of legal frameworks in this field, states should keep in mind the need to build mechanisms into legal frameworks which—of themselves—are capable of triggering adequate and credible responses to breaches of such regimes. Mechanisms for verification and reporting of compliance, challenge inspection and dispute settlement procedures are essential for guaranteeing the integrity of a legal regime and for engendering confidence in its effectiveness.

Some specific regimes

International legal regimes can offer security benefits not only to the parties to an agreement but the international community in general. The Antarctic Treaty regime, for example, has ensured that Antarctica has remained a demilitarised zone. The treaty, moreover, provides parties with a framework for consultation and exchange of information. It is one of the earliest examples of 'anywhere, anytime' on-site inspections in response to possible or emerging threats to the Treaty's integrity.

Distributive justice—fair rules about resource allocation—is particularly important to a smoothly functioning international system. Perceived unfairness in rules of distribution or the violation of agreed-upon rules about how resources (including territory) will be divided are potent sources of conflict. Resource shortages (of, for example, territory, water, oil, minerals, or even basic supplies such as fish) can exacerbate such problems and make conflict more likely. The bilateral agreement between Australia and Indonesia in 1989 to establish a 'Zone of Cooperation' in a disputed maritime border area in the Timor Sea, enabling joint exploration for and equal sharing of petroleum resources within the area, was a creative solution to the kind of problem which has often led to conflict elsewhere. More generally, the 1982 Convention on the Law of the Sea has a role in promoting international peace and security by regulating conflicting claims over waters and continental shelves and the passage of vessels and aircrafts. The Convention, even though not yet formally in force, is generally regarded as declaratory of international law on these issues, and so plays an important role in managing relations between states in this area to the point where conflict, so often the case historically on these issues, need no longer arise.

International environmental issues are linked intrinsically to international security issues and require global solutions. Global rules are required to manage responses to issues such as ozone depletion, the civil application of nuclear energy, climate change and the international movement of hazardous wastes. Without such rules, the international community risks both global environmental degradation, with its serious consequences for all people, including problems of food security, refugee flows and civil disorder, and disputes among states in response to specific local problems such as acid rain and access to fresh water. The implementation of such rules can help avert some of the complex humanitarian crises that have placed acute pressures on the UN and its member states, sometimes to the point of requiring military intervention.

The nexus between environment and development is also an important element in achieving and maintaining international security. Environmental degradation hinders development and exacerbates poverty in a vicious cycle; unbalanced consumption patterns and excessive population growth also carry serious consequences for stability. Progress towards the achievement of global sustainable development may lead to greater long term global resources security and hence reduce potential for conflict and human suffering. Monitoring the implementation of the results of the 1992 Rio UN Conference on Environment and Development (UNCED), including its blueprint for the future, *Agenda 21*, through the Commission on Sustainable Development (CSD) will be an important step in encouraging the kind of global partnership necessary to achieve sustainable development. Governments should accord priority to these policies if they want to avert the unhappy consequences for national and international security which are all too likely to flow from continuing neglect. An important adjunct to the UNCED process will be the International Conference on Population and Development to be held in Cairo in September 1994. The Conference should encourage a greater understanding of the relevance and interaction between population issues and economic and social well-being within nations as well as between nations, and as such should be an important step towards enhancing global security.

International humanitarian law

This is a major body of rules and practice governing conduct of international and non-international armed conflict. While the four 1949 Geneva Conventions and the 1977 Additional Protocols have a primary focus in regulating and controlling the conduct of conflict, they also have important preventive and deterrent functions which merit support and wider promotion. There should be universal adherence to both the Conventions and Protocols. In peace-time states must ensure familiarity with this body of law among their military through active programs of legislation, education and training. There should be universal acceptance of the International Fact-Finding Commission to enquire into all allegations of violation of the Geneva Conventions. The international community must be prepared to pursue measures to strengthen the effectiveness and deterrent value of the Conventions.

A feature of the post-Cold War world has been a growing call for a mechanism to try individuals for breaches of international humanitarian law and other international crimes. Security Council Resolution 827 in 1993 has taken the positive step forward of creating under Chapter VII an ad hoc War Crimes Tribunal to investigate cases in the former Yugoslavia, which should at least have a useful deterrent effect in the present situation. The International Law Commission, an advisory body established by the UN General Assembly, has been working for some time drafting a statute for an international criminal court. The creation of such a court would certainly further underline the resolve of the international community to respond to breaches of humanitarian law and gross violations of human rights, and have an even stronger general deterrent effect—provided the commitment of the international community to pursue perpetrators was firm and clear, which may not be easily achievable in the short term.

A myriad of international legal regimes contain their own dispute resolution procedures, accepted by the parties to those regimes when they create or join them: many are described in the 1991 UN *Handbook on the Peaceful Settlement of Disputes Between States* (A/46/33). The perennial problem for the international community, however, has been to win general acceptance for international dispute resolution mechanisms of more general application. When the sovereign state is the basic unit of the system and there is no supranational authority that can routinely enforce compliance, the rule of law does not have quite the same resonance as it does within states.

Dispute resolution institutions

The Permanent Court of Arbitration (PCA) established under the 1899 and 1907 Hague Conventions for the Pacific Settlement of International Disputes—and for which Andrew Carnegie originally built the Peace Palace in The Hague—was the first serious attempt to create a tribunal to which states could routinely resort to resolve their problems. Busy in the years before World War I, the Court became increasingly under-utilised in subsequent decades and, until 1992, its last significant arbitration had been in 1970. But the Court still exists—albeit now occupying only a small corner of the Palace—and is currently showing signs of successful revitalisation as arbitration comes to be seen again by states as an extremely helpful way of addressing commercial and other problems that increasingly arise between them in an ever more interdependent world.

Since its establishment under the UN Charter in 1945, the International Court of Justice—or World Court—has been very much *the* judicial organ of the international community, long ago displacing the PCA as the Palace's major tenant. But it lacks compulsory jurisdiction; less than a third of member states have submitted voluntarily to its jurisdiction; when they have done so, in many instances this has been subject to highly restrictive conditions; and to the extent that the Court does have jurisdiction, it has been conspicuously under-utilised. Secretary-General Boutros Ghali, in *An Agenda for Peace*, made a series of recommendations about taking greater advantage of the Court—including its advisory jurisdiction. They not only are worth reproducing in full, but should be wholeheartedly endorsed by the international community:

> 38.   The docket of the International Court of Justice has grown fuller but it remains an under-used resource for the peaceful adjudication of disputes. Greater reliance on the Court would be an important contribution to United Nations peacemaking. In this connection, I call attention to the power of the Security Council under Articles 36 and 37 of the Charter to recommend to Member States the submission of a dispute to the International Court of Justice,

arbitration or other dispute-settlement mechanisms. I recommend that the Secretary-General be authorized, pursuant to Article 96, paragraph 2, of the Charter, to take advantage of the advisory competence of the Court and that other United Nations organs that already enjoy such authorization turn to the Court more frequently for advisory opinions.

39. I recommend the following steps to reinforce the role of the International Court of Justice:

(a) All Member States should accept the general jurisdiction of the International Court under Article 36 of its Statute, without any reservation, before the end of the United Nations Decade of International Law in the year 2000. In instances where domestic structures prevent this, States should agree bilaterally or multilaterally to a comprehensive list of matters they are willing to submit to the Court and should withdraw their reservations to its jurisdiction in the dispute settlement clauses of multilateral treaties;

(b) When submission of a dispute to the full Court is not practical, the Chambers jurisdiction should be used;

(c) States should support the Trust Fund established to assist countries unable to afford the cost involved in bringing a dispute to the Court, and such countries should take full advantage of the Fund in order to resolve their disputes.

Arms control and disarmament regimes

Arms control and disarmament regimes have a particular and powerful role in peace building. The very process of their negotiation can have a highly beneficial impact on international peace and security as states agree, and are seen to agree, on the elimination of, or lower limits and controls on, armaments—in short, as they cooperate for peace. In their operation over time, these regimes build confidence further as their restraints on arms procurement or military holdings begin to stick, and as on-site verification measures ensure transparency of state behaviour. As a method of security enhancement, arms control and disarmament measures have been this century—and particularly since 1945—a regular feature of the international community's efforts to respond to technological developments with potential or actual military applications.

Nuclear

Nuclear non-proliferation and disarmament measures, even in the less fearful environment of the post-Cold War world, remain a critical element in peace building. The agenda here should include indefinite extension and enhancement of the Nuclear Non-Proliferation Treaty (NPT) when it comes up for review in 1995; adherence to the NPT by the nuclear threshold countries presently not party to it; effective implementation of the Strategic Arms Reduction Treaties of 1991 and 1993 (STARTs I and II); the resolution of outstanding questions about the nuclear status of former republics of the Soviet Union, especially Ukraine; the timely conclusion of a Comprehensive Test Ban Treaty (CTBT) in the Conference on Disarmament (CD) in Geneva; strengthened 'negative security assurances' from the nuclear weapon states (ie that they will never use such weapons against non-nuclear weapon states); and a treaty providing for the cessation or 'cut off' of the production of fissionable material for weapons purposes. The recent extension by a number of nuclear weapon states of their nuclear testing moratoriums—even though conditional and time limited—is a welcome interim step towards further progress on both nuclear non-proliferation and nuclear disarmament.

Chemical and biological

The Chemical Weapons Convention (CWC), opened for signature in 1993, is a model for multilateral efforts in the arms control and disarmament field. It establishes comprehensive and unambiguous legal prohibitions on the possession and use of an entire category of weapons—the feature of the regime most obvious when compared to its predecessor, the 1925 Geneva Protocol. The Convention encompasses both complete disarmament and future non-production of chemical weapons and includes a detailed verification regime with both military and civilian reach. The prohibitions in the CWC regime are reinforced by a detailed and graduated regime for addressing non-compliance through bilateral consultative mechanisms, disputes settlement procedures and, as a matter of last resort, intrusive challenge inspection conducted by a neutral and professional third party. At the same time, the regime accommodates the legitimate requirements of industry, international trade in chemicals and legitimate technological cooperation in the field.

Not all existing regimes are geared to respond comprehensively to proliferation of weapons of mass destruction or destabilising build-ups of sophisticated conventional weaponry. A number of these regimes have procedures for responding to emerging security threats, in particular through giving parties recourse to the Security Council. But it is timely to consider how existing regimes such as the Biological Weapons Convention (BWC) can be further improved, especially by more effective verification procedures, in order to maximise their peace building capacity.

Missiles

It is even more timely to be developing formal treaty regimes in areas where none now exist at all. The area of greatest immediate proliferation concern in this respect is missile technology. In the absence of any multilateral treaty, the Missile Technology Control Regime (MTCR) has been developed by like-minded countries in order to develop strategies and practical responses to what has been perceived to be an immediate threat to international security. (The 'Australia Group' has been a similar 'self help' export control exercise, which evolved in the mid 1980s, in response to the mounting evidence of chemical weapons proliferation, pending the finalisation and entry into force of the CWC.) While there have been an increasing number of adherents to (and countries making less formal commitments to observing) this Regime, this is ultimately no substitute for a properly verifiable and enforceable, internationally agreed control system.

Conventional weapons

Of course it is not only weapons of mass destruction, and their delivery systems, that need to be addressed in developing peace building strategies. Conventional weapons continue, after all, to be responsible for the overwhelming majority of the fatalities and casualties in contemporary armed conflict. One writer (Michael Renner) has put the scale of the problem in these terms:

> The world's nations have acquired a collective arsenal of unprecedented lethality. In 1992, they had either deployed or stockpiled some 45,000 combat aircraft, 172,000 main battle tanks, 155,000 artillery pieces, more than 1,000 major surface warships, and about 700 military submarines. Added to these are tens of thousands of light tanks, armoured vehicles, helicopters, mortars, missiles and smaller naval vessels. Assault rifles, machine guns and other small arms meanwhile are far too abundant to keep track of...since 1960 at least 1 trillion dollars worth of arms crossed international borders, much of it going to the third world.

Every state of course has the right to defend itself against both foreseeable and unforeseeable defence contingencies, and it is much more difficult to get agreement about effective control regimes in this area than it is for weapons of mass destruction. But because demilitarisation—or at least the avoidance of new arms races—is such an important contributor to peace and stability, it ought at least to be possible to put in place arrangements and processes which contribute to that objective of states having defence self-sufficiency, but no more than that. Bilateral and regional discussions about what constitutes self-sufficiency are increasingly being accepted as ways of removing at least the kind of rationally-based motivations countries might have for making arms purchases. There is increasing acceptance, in this context, of the confidence-building virtue of greater transparency—in military holdings, force structures and even in the strategic assessments countries make about their security environment.

It is important that these processes continue to be encouraged through the United Nations itself. The recently introduced UN Arms Transfer Register is a cautious but welcome start in achieving transparency in new arms purchases from external sources: next steps here should extend to the supplementation of that with information about existing holdings and domestic production. In this context, the problems posed by the indiscriminate use of landmines are so serious that the international community should seek ways of strengthening or extending existing treaty proscriptions, in particular through a review of the 1981 Inhumane Weapons Convention, especially Protocol II which covers landmines, booby traps and similar devices: as a minimum, this treaty must be strengthened through increased adherence (it currently only has 38 parties) and more stringent verification and enforcement mechanisms.

Other treaties

Another existing regime which could be upgraded in scope is the 1977 Environment Modification Treaty (ENMOD), designed to prohibit military or other hostile uses of certain environmentally destructive techniques. Again, while the 1967 Outer Space Treaty bans the emplacement of weapons of mass destruction in outer space, there is still no legal regime in place to prevent the emplacement of other weapons systems in space. The gap should be filled. Conclusion of agreements on a range of confidence-building measures governing uses of space, particularly those with military and security applications, would also make an important contribution to peace building.

Role of the Security Council

With the end of the Cold War, there is greater scope than ever for the Security Council to play a more active role in disarmament and arms control, not least by becoming a forum for more systematic discussion and consideration of arms control and disarmament priorities. Other functions which the Security Council could undertake include:

- promoting non-proliferation objectives, particularly in respect of weapons of mass destruction and their delivery systems;
- calling high-level meetings aimed at accelerating the negotiation of disarmament treaties;
- proposing—in accordance with the terms of the Charter—qualitative and quantitative limits on conventional weapons, whether on a global or regional basis;
- using arms embargoes as a preventive measure to limit the level of armaments available in times of conflict; and

- promoting the Security Council as an agent of last resort in the case of treaty violation.

A pioneer regime in the last-mentioned respect has been the International Atomic Energy Agency (IAEA). Article 12(c) of its Statute requires that its Board of Governors report cases of parties' non-compliance with safeguards obligations to the Security Council, the General Assembly and all other IAEA members, following which the Security Council is able to consider whether the action reported warrants action pursuant to Chapter VII. This reporting mechanism was used early in 1993 to trigger Security Council consideration of North Korea's non-compliance with its NPT safeguards agreement and announced intention to withdraw from the NPT. The Security Council initially responded with a statement expressing concern and asking the IAEA to continue consultations with North Korea. When no progress was made in these consultations, it asked North Korea, through a follow up resolution in May 1993, to reverse its decision to withdraw from the NPT and to fulfil its safeguards obligations. It indicated that it was prepared to consider 'further action' if necessary. This response implied that any such action could be taken under Chapter VII in the form of sanctions. North Korea has now suspended its withdrawal and has agreed, following a series of bilateral meetings with the United States, to resume negotiations with the IAEA on the implementation of its safeguards agreement. The Security Council remains seized of the issue.

The action which the Security Council took with respect to Iraq following the Gulf War constitutes a novel form of enforcement of arms control measures. Reacting to evidence of Iraq's development of nuclear, chemical and biological weapons and related delivery systems, the Security Council imposed a new and comprehensive regime on Iraq to eliminate its capacity to manufacture and deliver such weapons which contains far-reaching international inspection and verification procedures to ensure that Iraq's weapons of mass destruction capacity is not rebuilt. The United Nations Special Commission (UNSCOM) was established to carry out inspections and destruction. With the ready backing of the Security Council, UNSCOM has persevered and has been generally successful in meeting its objectives.

Enforcement of arms control regimes by the Security Council will obviously continue to be an avenue of last resort when other efforts to assure compliance with an arms control regime have failed. The destructive potential of weapons of mass destruction and their vigorous pursuit by a small number of countries, along with the inexorable spread of relevant technologies, suggest that the Security Council will need to keep open the enforcement option in the future.

Dialogue and cooperation arrangements

It is not only formal legal regimes, and institutions with a specifically defined dispute resolution function, that have an international peace building role in the sense being discussed in this Chapter. Important foundations for peace are also regularly laid around the world in the innumerable bilateral, regional and global-scale arrangements that bring countries together for dialogue and cooperation purposes. What is important, for present purposes, about these arrangements is not so much the specific outcomes that may be the product of such meetings and exchanges, but the sense of familiarity, comfort and understanding that tends to flow, other things being equal, from the mere fact of their occurrence. It would be naive to overstate this point, but wrong to ignore its significance.

Bilateral exchanges between countries, of varying degrees of frequency and formality, are a long familiar part of this landscape. On a global scale, the United Nations General Assembly itself, the Non-Aligned Movement, the Commonwealth of Nations and the Inter-Parliamentary Union—not to mention economically-focused groupings like the GATT, OECD, G7 and G15—all create endless opportunities for contact between elected and public officials. And at the regional level there are all the organisations described in the last chapter: well established ones with an explicit peace and security role—like the OAU, OAS, OIC and Arab League, together with the European constellation (CSCE, EC, NATO and WEU)—and also discussion forums and emerging new bodies like the South Pacific Forum (SPF), the Gulf Co-operation Council (GCC), the Economic Community of West African States (ECOWAS), the South Asia Association for Regional Co-operation (SAARC), the Andean Pact and the ASEAN Regional Forum.

As well as helping to create the kind of deep and durable relationships which make conflict improbable, these various forums can—and sometimes already do—play more specific peace building roles, for example in supporting, urging respect for, and calling for consistent resort to, international law and the conduct of international relations; identifying areas and issues requiring new rules or arrangements for political, social, economic or security cooperation; and creating new mechanisms for developing more effective and relevant regimes and arrangements as new needs emerge, eg as the UN General Assembly did in respect to the law of the sea.

The organisations that have been most successful in promoting security through social, economic and political growth in their regions have tended to be those offering a series of practical and positive inducements to cooperation. The impetus may be the expectation of economic benefits, as with the European Communities (EC), a desire to be part of a broader political framework for defence and security purposes, or a response to small size or lack of particular resources. The functional relationships that have developed in the EC, ASEAN, the South Pacific Forum, the Southern African Development Community (SADC), the Andean Group, the Caribbean Community (CARICOM), and now the Asia Pacific Economic Cooperation (APEC) organisation are good examples of effective socio-economic and political peace building through regional organisations.

In the military sphere, the new commitment to the pursuit of cooperative security in Europe, and increasingly in recent years in the Latin American and Asia Pacific regions, are good examples of peace building with a clear security focus. The very fact of the substantial recent discussions about the development of a new regional security architecture in the Asia Pacific region, for example, and the practical range of specific confidence-building measures starting to emerge from them, have served to create a greater sense of security and confidence among the countries involved. The pursuit of security in cooperation with rather than against others is the great strength of these processes. These positive developments in the security area have, moreover, been matched by sustained rapid economic growth: both trends reinforce each other.

States and non-state actors in different geographical areas should be encouraged to look beyond purely national concerns and work for the gradual development of broad, regional agendas for economic and social growth, mutually reinforcing confidence-building measures and mechanisms for the non-violent resolution of conflict. Contrast, for example, the inconceivability of armed conflict among the member states of the European Communities with the conflict and instability which has marked the collapse of an arbitrary and oppressive regional arrangement in Eastern Europe. Robust regional economic and political institutions in turn become important building blocks in the evolution of effective global institutions just as robust, peaceable states help to reinforce good global governance.

4

In-Country Peace Building

Pre-conflict peace building

Preventive peace building within states, in which both the international community and individual states themselves have mutually supportive roles to play, should aim to achieve progress in reducing the gap between rich and poor, to extend basic human rights to all people (including minorities), to promote sustainable development and to advance a just and fair society which does not discriminate on grounds of gender and race. Preventive peace building at this level also seeks to promote adherence by states to the established standards of good international citizenship. Good internal government is the necessary foundation of good global governance.

Peace building through national effort

At the national level appropriate preventive peace building techniques include social and economic development, democratisation, observance of fundamental human rights, the elimination of all forms of gender or racial discrimination and respect for minorities. Many states spend disproportionate amounts of their scarce resources for military purposes, thus depriving their populations of vital economic and social infrastructure needs which would be, in general, far more effective in enhancing their national security and well-being. In all regions of the world—and this is just as true of developed as of developing countries—the conversion from defence industry and expenditure to civilian programs and the adoption of disarmament and arms control measures could, if appropriately managed, result in substantial economic benefits.

That said, a great many states simply do not have the physical or financial capacity by themselves to deliver material well-being to their people: to do so involves not just good will and sound priorities but resources, and those are often in desperately short supply. What every state *does* have the capacity to deliver to its people, however, is distributive justice (ensuring, through taxation and related policies, that gross inequalities of wealth and income are minimised), and also political and civil rights—in particular, giving to everyone a direct say in how they are governed, and a capacity to think, talk and act freely subject only to reasonable respect for the rights of others.

Democracy and human rights issues these days are acknowledged much more widely to be everybody's business. Secretary-General Boutros-Ghali put the point with absolute clarity in *An Agenda for Peace:*

> The authority of the United Nations system to act in this field would rest on the consensus that social peace is as important as strategic or political peace. There is an obvious connection between democratic practices—such as the rule of law and transparency in decision making—and the achievement of true peace and security in any new and stable political order.

It is much remarked that, as a matter of evident historical fact, democracies have not gone to war against each other. It would seem, for this reason alone, to be in everyone's interests to safeguard and extend democratic processes, individual and collective rights, and the interests of minorities—and to ensure that authoritarian societies are encouraged to move in a democratic direction. A good recent example of a country dealing constructively with a potentially explosive minority human rights issue was Romania's agreement in July 1993 to a package on language and related measures sought by its Hungarian minority.

It is essential, in all these respects, that states protect and promote the independence of the judiciary, underline the primacy of the rule of law and periodically review their compliance with international humanitarian, human rights, refugee, economic and social agreements. Where national laws or practices contradict or diverge from international agreements, states should seek to, and be urged to, bring domestic practices into line with international standards. States should periodically review the extent to which national policy and practice conform to international standards, and should be encouraged to become parties to the key human rights conventions, in particular the International Covenants on Civil and Political Rights, and Economic, Social and Cultural Rights; the Conventions on the Elimination of All Forms of Discrimination Against Women, and of Racial Discrimination; the Convention Against Torture and Other Cruel, Inhuman or Degrading Treatment or Punishment; and the Convention on the Rights of the Child. Importantly, all these Conventions have mechanisms for the regular examination by expert tribunals of the practice of states parties.

Peace building with international support

The United Nations system has a strong supportive role to play in promoting peace building within states in some of the areas just mentioned. The Secretary-General's conviction that the UN has both the authority and responsibility to act in the fields of democracy and human rights has already been mentioned. One recent manifestation of that commitment, which is much to be applauded, is the establishment of an electoral assistance unit within the Department of Political Affairs. The UN Centre for Human Rights in Geneva can provide expert advice and technical assistance on the establishment of national institutions to promote and protect human rights and thereby to further democracy generally.

International development assistance and the promotion of cooperative development projects, especially in areas of potential dispute, are important to economic peace building within states. Projects aimed at bringing adjoining states together around joint agricultural development projects, transportation, water and electricity utilisation schemes are important confidence-building measures in their own right and should be encouraged. An example is the ability of the Interim Mekong Committee to foster development related cooperation even while post-Vietnam War hostilities continued in the area.

UN economic and technical assistance can relieve many of the social and economic tensions underlying disputes: it is important here to ensure that the UN does not lose sight of the fact that peace and security involves the security of peoples and societies as much as it does that of states, and that the promotion of popular, as well as state, well-being should be a criterion for determining resource allocation. ECOSOC could play a role in accordance with Article 65 of the Charter of the UN in alerting the Security Council to economic and social developments threatening to international peace and security. This role should be aimed in the first instance at better coordination of those UN organisations and agencies devoted to economic and social progress.

There is a particular need to strengthen the coordination of UN humanitarian emergency assistance, to improve its capability in prevention and in preparedness for natural disasters and other emergencies, particularly those involving food. Improving the UN early warning capability for potential humanitarian emergency situations, including the involvement of national institutions, is an important peace building function which can avert destabilising situations. In responding to such emergencies, one option—where the government of the country concerned, or all relevant parties, consent—is for military personnel from other member states to be deployed to give urgent assistance: this is described in *An Agenda for Peace* as a form of 'preventive deployment', but 'peace building' may better capture the flavour of what is involved. (If the use of force is thought likely to be necessary to maintain security in such a situation, then the exercise is perhaps better treated as 'peace enforcement in support of humanitarian objectives': see Chapter 10.)

More generally, there is a need for much more integration of activities within the whole UN system, so that the pursuit of peace and security is seen to include the satisfaction of basic human needs as well as the prevention, containment and settlement of violent conflict. This will inevitably require linkages between visions of a more peaceful world and greater integration within the system, particularly in relation to program planning, the application of resources and the development of smooth functioning coordination mechanisms.

The Secretary-General as Chief Administrative Officer of the UN, and Chairman of the Administrative Committee on Coordination, has the major responsibility in this regard. There is a case for establishing a new section within the Secretariat—possibly in the Department of Political Affairs, or the Department of Humanitarian Affairs—to assist in this regard, stimulating and coordinating peace building processes across the whole UN system.

Post-conflict peace building

All the strategies appropriate to pre-conflict peace building are just as applicable to post-conflict situations, but there are some additional things that will often need to be done—again through a combination of national effort and international support—to meet the special needs of countries and peoples shattered by warfare.

Democratic institutions

The task in these situations will often be no less than the total reconstitution of broken and devastated societies. The lessons to be learned from past experience show how essential it is for the people and their leaders to reach agreements about what sort of society and polity they wish to develop after the conflict. In these situations, the international community—not just the UN itself, but regional organisations and other international actors as well—has a responsibility to promote democracy and human rights as part of the linked processes of peace making and post-conflict peace building.

The 1993 World Conference on Human Rights in Vienna showed that differences of emphasis between North and South on human rights issues can be accommodated. It also underlined the principle that democracy, development and respect for fundamental human rights are interdependent and mutually reinforcing. Where a state has been the object of massive and intrusive UN intervention, the UN may have to contend with an impatience to dispense with its services at the military and political levels so that internal approaches to managing the affairs of state can be pursued unhindered. But the goals of democratisation and human rights cannot be compromised. These goals cannot be reached without a functioning and effective police system, the restoration of an independent judiciary and the creation of security personnel committed to democratisation. In countries that have had no tradition of democratic government and where there is understandable residual suspicion of state authorities after a conflict, there is a need to make a special effort to generate education campaigns about what a democratic, participative and human rights respecting political system could look like, and why parties in the post-conflict situation should suspend judgement and give new approaches a chance. This is an area again where the international community can give crucial support.

The building of a functioning criminal justice system is a particularly crucial priority if the gains of a peace keeping operation are to be consolidated and a relapse into conflict avoided. We support the idea, advanced by lawyers in Cambodia troubled by their inability to effectively implement UNTAC's human rights mandate, that UN 'justice packages' be part of any peace keeping and post-conflict peace building exercises in countries where the rule of law, and the institutions needed to support it, have manifestly broken down. Elements of such a package would include provision, as appropriate, of a body of criminal law and procedures, drawing on universal principles; civil police, with training as well as law enforcement responsibilities; a panel of judges, prosecutors and defenders able to work with available local professionals during the transitional period, again with an obligation to train their local successors; and adequate correctional facilities, and personnel to staff them while developing local replacements. Basic as all these requirements may be, no viable government or social order can be built without them, and there will be situations where only the authority of the UN is capable of delivering them.

Economic reconstruction

The rebuilding of a peaceable post-conflict society and democratic polity must also be accompanied by economic assistance sufficient to satisfy basic needs and able to stimulate new development. This will require, among other things, special UN teams to develop post conflict reconstruction programs, incorporating the existing UN specialised agencies and empowered to stimulate support from governments and international and private financial institutions as well.

The mobilisation of these resources is a difficult task. Donor fatigue is already beginning to show in relation to a number of current UN operations. But donor enthusiasm must be revived and maintained, not least because peace building strategies, while expensive in themselves, are certainly less expensive than peace keeping or peace enforcement activities which the international community must consider once conflict has erupted. Much more national, regional and global attention needs to be directed to post-conflict rebuilding to counter the tendency of the international community to think that a successful conclusion to peace making, peace keeping or peace enforcement ends its responsibilities.

Other problems

There are a number of other problems that will often loom very large in post-conflict peace building. One of them, strongly emphasised by the Secretary-General in *An Agenda for Peace,* is de-mining. It has been estimated that there may be more than 100 million uncleared mines world-wide left over from recent conflicts, and—with some 800 new casualties every month—they continue to take a terrible toll. As Afghanistan and Cambodia have highlighted particularly graphically, de-mining operations are essential not only for the immediate safety of people in the areas in question, but for the resumption of normal agriculture and commerce—and for the return of civilians to areas previously subject to conflict.

Another recurring problem—whose solution will often partly depend on the success of de-mining—is the repatriation of refugees and displaced persons, and the provision of adequate support for them on return. This requires, to be successful, not only skilful diplomacy but proper resources. The Office of the United Nations High Commissioner for Refugees (UNHCR) is currently subject to overwhelming demands in this area—not least in relation to internally displaced persons, for whom neither it, nor any other international agency, has any mandate to act, but whose needs are just as compelling as those forced across borders. There is a need for the UNHCR—and other agencies like UNICEF and WFP who assist it in this area—to be explicitly recognised as having a crucial peace building role; they should be better resourced in their tasks of ensuring that host populations are willing to reabsorb returnees, and that returnees do not generate further conflicts on their return.

A further problem that may cause special difficulties is demilitarisation and disarmament. We have already discussed the application of arms control and disarmament regimes in this area, and the possible need in extreme cases for Security Council intervention;

in later Chapters we consider how to deal with other dimensions of this issue, in the context of peace keeping and peace enforcement operations. Yet another concern that may need to be addressed is the pursuit of serious breaches of international humanitarian law, for example through war crimes tribunals: again, this is an issue already mentioned in the context of our earlier discussion of 'international regimes'.

The list of peace building problems and tasks can be a never ending one. Certainly the UN cannot expect by itself to address them all. But there is perhaps a leadership role for the UN to play in giving a new prominence to peace building—both in pre-conflict and post-conflict situations—in a way that will stimulate regional organisations, states themselves and non-governmental relief and development agencies to assume more responsibility for, and devote more resources to, the necessary tasks. An integrated approach bringing together global and regional organisations and states to respond to the needs of peace building is required in order to eliminate fractured effort, duplication and competition. Finding additional resources, both within and outside the UN system, is always going to be a problem. But the returns from this investment—in the attainment of sustainable, equitable growth; in crises averted; and in a new capacity and willingness to resolve disputes peacefully—can be immeasurable.

Here as elsewhere, what is most fundamentally necessary if we are to achieve these outcomes is the emergence of a new mind-set in the conduct of international relations: one that pays as much attention to the satisfaction of basic human needs as it does to the interests of states; one which evaluates assessments of threats to peace and security in non-military as well as traditional military terms; and one which endeavours to move beyond power politics towards cooperative problem solving.

III

Maintaining Peace

5

Preventive Diplomacy

The concept of preventive diplomacy

'Peace maintenance strategies' are those designed to resolve, or at least contain, particular disputes (and some kinds of emerging threats) and prevent them from escalating into armed conflict. They include 'preventive deployment'—the use of military resources for containment purposes—a subject discussed in the next chapter. They also embrace a variety of strategies, best described collectively as 'preventive diplomacy', which rely on diplomatic and similar methods rather than military ones. Included here are the full range of 'peaceful means' described in Article 33 of the UN Charter, ie 'negotiation, enquiry, mediation, conciliation, arbitration, judicial settlement, resort to regional agencies or arrangements, or other peaceful means of their own choice', all of which are described in detail in the *Handbook on the Peaceful Settlement of Disputes between States*, prepared by the UN Secretariat and welcomed unanimously by the General Assembly in 1991. We believe there is particular scope for the further development of preventive diplomacy—particularly in the UN's mediation role—and it is this subject to which we devote most attention in this chapter.

As signatories to the UN Charter, member states are under an obligation—made express in Chapter VI, Article 33 of the Charter—to resolve their disputes peacefully. The Charter, however, gives members a choice of the dispute resolution method which they will employ. When it deems necessary, the Security Council may also call upon members to resolve their disputes peacefully and even recommend a particular method which they should use. In practice, however, peaceful methods of dispute resolution can only be effective if the parties consent to participate in this process. For this reason, approaches which allow the parties more control over the process, and which seek to address their interests, are more likely to be attractive to disputants and more likely to be used. This explains why methods such as negotiation and mediation have been used with much greater frequency than those such as arbitration and judicial settlement.

The difficulty of resolving disputes peacefully, however, suggests that disputing parties may sometimes need assistance from a third party in order to comply with their obligations under Chapter VI of the Charter. Increasingly, the international community is looking to the UN to assist in this regard and, in the following pages, our primary focus is on outlining ideas for strengthening the preventive diplomacy activities of the UN, both at its headquarters and in the field: a central theme of this study is that preventive action, as early as possible, is the least complex, the most humane and the most cost-effective path for the international community to take in resolving disputes.

It is well recognised that, quite apart from the UN, regional organisations, individual states or groups of states, and various groups of non-government actors all have important roles to play in preventive diplomacy. Indeed, it has to be acknowledged at the outset that it is likely to remain well beyond the capacity of the UN to identify and monitor, let alone manage, all the disputes which might lead to international friction or otherwise endanger international peace and security. The UN's founders certainly did not envisage that the organisation would deal with *all* international disputes: the UN membership is empowered, but not compelled, to respond collectively to problems short of threats to or breaches of the peace or acts of aggression (compare the discretionary language used in Article 33.2 and 34 with the mandatory prescription in Article 39). As the central organ of collective security, the Security Council has typically dealt only with the tip of the iceberg of international disputes, namely those which have crossed the threshold into armed hostilities or are on the point of so doing. The General Assembly has also addressed a range of disputes, but its approach, again, has been by no means comprehensive—rather the Assembly's actions have usually reflected the frustration of states or groups of states which have been unable to have their interests or views pursued through action in the Council.

There is no doubt that, in a great many cases, disputes both can and should be satisfactorily managed and resolved without recourse to the UN, through cooperation at the bilateral, sub-regional or regional level. Local solutions offer such advantages as familiarity of all parties with the parties to the dispute and their interests and sensitivities. Bringing differences before a wider body, and ultimately before the UN membership, can itself be an escalation of a dispute which lessens the margin for its resolution. So, in the area of prevention, the UN's role will often be complementary to more localised efforts, and in many cases secondary to them. All that said, there are still many problems where a preventive response by the UN will be warranted—either because the governments or parties concerned call for it, or because the magnitude of the problem and the absence of any other effective response, cry out for it. And certainly there remains enormous scope for the UN to do better in assisting the resolution of disputes, both those in which it plays a primary role, and those where it can assist in a secondary role through quietly providing expert assistance and experience.

The measures we propose will require the UN to devote more resources to preventive diplomacy. But such cost must be compared with the current high cost of peace making, peace keeping and peace enforcement operations once disputes have erupted into armed conflicts—not to mention the awful cost in lives and property that such escalation usually brings. Currently the UN Secretariat has around 40 staff assigned within the Department of Political Affairs to preventive diplomacy and its companion strategy, peace making, compared to some 82 000 peace keepers in the field. The cost of an individual peace keeper or peace enforcer, taking into account the logistics which support him or her in the field, will far outweigh the cost of individual UN personnel engaged in preventive diplomacy.

Past United Nations practice

The Cold War constrained the development of the UN's cooperative security responses across the entire spectrum: preventive diplomacy was just another one of the casualties. As discussed in Chapter 2, the desire of the superpowers to maintain their influence made them reluctant to have disputes from their domain raised in the Security Council before (or sometimes even after) a dispute had crossed the threshold to armed hostilities. If the UN became involved at all, it was usually at the very point where peaceful methods of dispute settlement were *least* likely to be effective. The crisis orientation of the Council and the slowness of the multilateral political decision-making process not only failed (by providing too little too late) to keep disputes from escalating out of control, but it also eroded the international community's belief in the efficacy of peaceful means of dispute resolution. This loss of faith in peaceful approaches in turn resulted in a self-fulfilling prophecy—too little attention and resources being devoted to the development of such approaches, and further erosion of faith in these methods.

The Cold War also took its toll on the Secretary-General's ability to operate in the peace and security area. As a consequence, the necessary structures to carry out preventive diplomacy within the UN Secretariat were never fully developed. Instead the unrealistic expectation prevailed that the Secretary-General should somehow be able personally to provide good offices and mediation for all emergent situations, while at the same time carrying out the innumerable other functions and duties required of him. While Secretaries-General have historically spent long hours in discussion with parties in dispute, they have not had the necessary infrastructure or personnel to carry out the kind of systematic and sustained effort needed to be effective in dispute resolution.

Over time, and out of necessity, Secretaries-General began assigning senior staff or diplomats to assist in providing good offices and mediation. But these assignments were typically ad hoc in response to crises, and the choice of personnel was usually limited to a very small number of trusted individuals. Frequently, these individuals did not themselves have sufficient resources, in terms of personnel or infrastructure, to back them up. In addition, fact finding missions evolved as a mechanism for gathering information and, in some cases, as a forum for diplomatic initiatives. But once again, fact finding was largely an ad hoc procedure. More often than not staff who had not worked together before were hastily assembled, on short notice, from various parts of the Secretariat and sent off to the field. In some cases, they were unfamiliar with the situation and its political, historical and cultural context. Once staff had reported back, they often returned to their previous posts with little continuity or follow-up.

These ad hoc arrangements for providing good offices and other peaceful means of dispute settlement, together with the Security Council's focus on crisis situations, meant that the Secretary-General and his senior staff were swamped with situations which had deteriorated to the point where they could no longer be ignored—or in many cases, controlled. As the system was structured and practised, handling the conflicts already on the agenda was more than the system could manage.

There is a sense, of course, in which preventive diplomacy can be seen as a continuous behind-the-scenes feature of the UN system, as the Secretary-General and his staff, as well as the diplomatic community, engage in preventive efforts in many different situations through conversations and consultations with a wide range of interlocutors. Without undervaluing these efforts, we believe there is a case for supplementing them with a more systematic and institutionalised approach to assist members in implementing their obligations under Chapter VI of the Charter.

The first significant, although still insufficient, attempt at setting up a preventive diplomacy mechanism in the UN Secretariat occurred in 1987 with the establishment of the Office of Research and the Collection of Information (ORCI). This was established to meet a number of objectives, but among its various sections were two small geographic units, with a total of six professional staff, set up to collect and analyse information, to provide 'early warning', and to suggest options to the Secretary-General.

A second boost for preventive diplomacy came in January 1992 when the Security Council met at the level of Heads of State and Government to consider how the UN could better meet the peace and security challenges of the post-Cold War world. At that meeting there were repeated calls for the United Nations to develop its role in preventive diplomacy, and the Secretary-General was invited to offer his ideas about how this should be done. For the first time, the growing consensus which had been developing about preventive diplomacy was being expressed at the highest levels.

Shortly after Boutros Boutros-Ghali became Secretary-General in January 1992, he acted to initiate a widespread restructuring process intended, among other things, to enhance the Secretariat's capacity to carry out preventive diplomacy and peace making, in particular through geographic divisions set up in the new Department of Political Affairs. These new divisions have certainly provided the basis for a more viable system, but resource shortages and systemic constraints have meant that these reforms are still less than adequate to the task. Even with these initial steps, and even though preventive diplomacy is moving to be now almost universally acknowledged as the most cost-effective approach available, it has remained a vastly underdeveloped cooperative security response.

A new approach: emphasising early prevention

There are two quite different approaches to preventive diplomacy, which might be called 'late prevention' and 'early prevention' respectively. The difference is not between tardiness and timeliness, but rather between different time perspectives and different goals. The distinction has considerable implications for how preventive diplomacy is implemented.

Late prevention

Under a 'late prevention' approach, the UN would monitor situations around the globe, doing little until fairly certain that a particular dispute was about to cross the threshold into armed conflict. If and when this early warning system indicated a problem, the UN would become involved in an attempt to persuade the parties to desist. By this stage, the Security Council would be likely to be the best UN organ for carrying out preventive action, since significant pressure or leverage may well be needed to modify behaviour. Preventive action which the Council might employ could include fact finding missions (in accordance with the 1991 Declaration on Fact-Finding), preventive deployment, recommendation of a specific dispute settlement procedure (Article 36), or a resolution calling upon the parties to desist and warning them of further Council action.

Late prevention action relies heavily on adequate intelligence information, such as the monitoring of troop movements or refugee flows, to indicate that a situation is about to move to a new level of violence. Proposals for obtaining this information have included making arrangements with member states; establishing a UN satellite; converting UN Information Centres into political offices; and improving procedures for alerting the Security Council. Had the UN had an effective system of late prevention in place before Iraqi troops crossed the border into Kuwait, it is likely to have been able to provide better information, and therefore early warning, that Iraqi troops were massing on that border: more such information might have allowed the Council to meet and take action before, rather than after, the invasion.

The last minute, however, will rarely be the optimal time to intervene in a dispute: in fact, the point at which a dispute is just about to erupt into conflict is close to being the most difficult at which the international community could seek to intervene. The dynamics of escalation are usually so strong at this point that it is very difficult to stop or reverse the situation.

Early prevention

A more promising approach to preventive diplomacy is one that involves the UN having the ability to offer, in effect, a dispute resolution *service* to its members to assist them in complying with their obligations under Chapter VI of the Charter. The goal would be to provide skilled third party assistance through good offices and mediation as early as possible in a dispute, when the opportunity for dispute resolution is most ripe.

International disputes rarely develop into full-blown conflicts overnight, at least for those who understand the situation and have been following its development. In many of the situations which have become the object of recent UN efforts, the presence of a serious dispute was well-known to the international community far in advance, even if in some cases, such as the Falklands, few were paying attention. In the case of the Gulf crisis, knowledge of the existence of a border dispute between Iraq and Kuwait was long-standing. It was also well-known for months ahead of time, from rhetoric emanating from Baghdad, that Iraq was becoming increasingly aggrieved and belligerent. Of course, in this case, it is possible that preventive diplomacy of either the early or late prevention type would not have been effective, since the actors might not have cooperated. We will never know, since neither type was seriously mobilised before Kuwait was invaded. (See Box 1.)

Although the United Nations Charter gives primary responsibility for the maintenance of peace and security to the Security Council, the Council is not always, in reality, the best body for carrying out preventive diplomacy, especially at the early stage. Member states are reluctant to bring their disputes to it because they do not wish to relinquish decision-making control over matters of such importance to them, at least until the situation becomes desperate: few third parties will want to pursue the issue under those circumstances. Sometimes there is a perception (irrespective of the justification for this) that Council members are more intent on pursuing their own interests: the frequent discussions about the rights of 'sovereignty' and concerns about 'internationalising' a dispute often reflect, in reality, concerns of this kind. Whatever the reason, member states seldom use Article 35 and Secretaries-General have rarely used Article 99, the provisions enabling matters to be brought to the Council at an early stage.

In addition, the kinds of actions which the Security Council can offer are not particularly well-suited to dispute settlement at this early stage. The notion of the Council as a kind of arbiter causes parties to engage in adversarial debate rather than problem solving. Mutual recrimination and positional arguing by each side to convince the Council of the rightness of its case may further harden positions and inflame a situation. Moreover, to the extent that Council members are forced to declare their sympathies, expressions of support for one side or the other can encourage parties to become entrenched in their positions. In summary, we believe that the Security Council, although it has a role to play at the late prevention stage, is not the ideal structure for carrying out early preventive diplomacy.

Instead, a more professional approach to dispute resolution is needed which can address the problems of timing and control, and offer the right kind of assistance for resolving disputes at the early prevention stage. Establishing such a mechanism in the Secretariat, as we recommend below, with support and assistance from regional organisations and member states, would provide an excellent complement to the work of the Security Council. *The Handbook on the Peaceful Settlement of Disputes Between States* notes that the momentum for such an approach has been gathering:

> The instruments in the field of peaceful settlement of disputes adopted by the international community recently, reflecting the realities of modern international life, clearly indicate the trend toward enlarging

1. Iraq's invasion of Kuwait in 1990: a failure to use preventive diplomacy

The problem: There had been a longstanding but mostly dormant border dispute between Iraq and Kuwait. Iraq's failure to gain access to the Persian Gulf through its eight year war with Iran revived an interest in past claims to Kuwait's Warba and Bubiyan islands in the Gulf. Iraq also claimed that Kuwait had been pumping oil from the Iraqi side of their shared Rumaila oil field. Iraq's war with Iran had been financed by loans from Saudi Arabia and the Gulf States, and some of these States were prepared to forgive the loans in return for the bulwark that Iraq provided against Iran. Kuwait, however, refused to forgive its Iraqi war debt. Short of cash, the Iraqis faced a declining oil market—where Kuwait was helping keep the price down by over-producing on its OPEC quota.

The response: In the months leading up to the conflict Iraqi demands escalated. Both sides became less able to back down. Iraq feared loss of face and Kuwait did not want to give in to intimidation. In modern times no Arab State had invaded another: this caused Kuwait and the international community to discount the possibility of an Iraqi invasion, and this misreading meant a failure to match Iraqi threats with appropriate counter-signals.

In late July 1990 Kuwait suggested to the UN Secretary-General that an Arab Committee examine the Iraq-Kuwait border issue and other Arab states stepped up diplomatic activity for a peaceful solution. These efforts—and a UK suggestion, to which other permanent members were unreceptive, that the border issue be looked at by the Security Council—were overtaken by events, when Iraq invaded Kuwait on 2 August. The Arab League condemned the invasion (in a split decision) but rejected Kuwait's call to have its Defence Pact collective self-defence activated. The international community—including the Arab States, US, France and former Soviet Union—engaged in various peace making efforts over the next six months: Iraq rejected these overtures, and the UN Security Council eventually resorted to peace enforcement, with Coalition forces beginning military operations on 16 January 1991.

The lessons:

At the early prevention stage (before July 1990):

- Although there were long-standing border disagreements between Iraq and Kuwait, there were no real attempts to resolve them: failure to resolve this issue earlier led to later problems.

- In the months leading up to the conflict, there were few concerted efforts to address the specific issues in dispute—ie the oil pricing issue, the Rumaila oil field issue, the Warba and Bubiyan Island issue, and the debt issue—before tensions escalated. Underlying all of these issues was the major Iraqi concern about trying to keep its economy from worsening in the aftermath of the ruinous Iran-Iraq War. In the absence of another solution, invading Kuwait appeared to be an attractive answer to Iraq's financial problems. Early attention to more specific issues may have kept the dispute from escalating to this stage.

At the late prevention stage (July 1990):

- The international community misread Iraqi intentions because they did not take Iraq's threats seriously: threats should be considered to be an important early warning indicator.

- Mixed and confusing messages from the international community aggravated the situation: clear messages are needed in response to threats.

- Member states with satellite reconnaissance failed to provide the UN with early warning: members possessing relevant information have a responsibility to draw it to the attention of the Security Council.

- Neither the Council nor the Secretary-General responded to mounting evidence that a dispute was rapidly escalating: member states should consider exercising Article 35 more readily, and the Secretary-General should use Article 99 to bring escalating disputes to the attention of the Council.

> the role of the Secretary-General in the area of the prevention and
> peaceful settlement of international disputes. (p.171)

Late prevention and early prevention approaches are not mutually exclusive, but giving priority to early prevention has a number of significant advantages:

- *motivation*: parties are more likely to accept assistance while issues are still specific, and before grievances accumulate and the desire for retribution becomes paramount;

- *effectiveness*: prevention is more likely to be effective before issues have generalised, issues and parties have multiplied, positions have hardened and actions have turned into ever-more hostile reverberating echoes of threat and counter-threat;

- *completeness*: since the goal of early prevention is resolution rather than containment, it is more likely that the dispute will be resolved and will not recur; and

- *cost*: early prevention is likely to be more cost-effective in both financial and human terms.

Making UN preventive diplomacy more effective

Discussions of preventive diplomacy have tended to focus more on early warning than on early dispute resolution. Important as it is, however, early warning is merely the first step in preventive diplomacy: what matters even more is acting on such information in an effective and timely manner.

Early warning

The intense focus on early warning stems from the Falklands conflict, which took the UN by such surprise that it is said that there were no maps of the Islands to be found in the UN Secretariat when the invasion occurred. This problem was further highlighted by the Gulf crisis, which also caught the UN unawares since none of its members possessing such information had shared satellite reconnaissance with the Secretary-General or the Security Council.

Currently, the Secretary-General is studying the whole question of improving the UN's early warning capability and will be making recommendations for its improvement to the 1993 General Assembly. While there is little doubt that it is important for the UN to have good sources of information about the whole range of emerging threats, disputes, conflicts and other security crises, the problem is not only the lack of information, but also the system's ability to absorb the enormous amount of incoming information, analyse and apply it it in a meaningful way. It is said that eleven separate warning messages about the deteriorating situation in Somalia were sent during 1991 by the then Office of Research and Collection of Information (ORCI) to the most senior levels of the Secretariat, but these were not responded to because of a combination of under-staffing and preoccupation with other crises.

Not only does the UN need to improve the quality, reliability and speed of information gathering, but it also needs to strengthen its capacity for intelligent and sharply focused political analysis, including in-depth understanding of the real underlying causes of existing and emerging disputes. Part of that needed capacity is the ability to spot not only disputes that may become armed conflicts, but—at an even earlier stage—emerging threats that, if not addressed, may become disputes.

Early dispute resolution

The need to strengthen the UN's ability to *respond* when information is received and analysed has received much less attention than it should have. The organisation of the Department of Political Affairs into a number of geographically-based divisions is an excellent step forward. But the UN still does not have sufficient numbers of senior staff knowledgeable and experienced in conflict resolution. While those appointed to head each of the new geographic divisions are experienced, there are only a handful of staff who can be assigned to such tasks. As a consequence, these small divisions are simply unable to meet the huge demand, and are literally overwhelmed with work.

Another problem is that the infrastructure to support these units is inadequate. Information-gathering processes from the field are cumbersome; there are no research assistants; there is little access to outside consultants; funds for travelling to the region are inadequate; and communication and computer equipment is poor. There is, moreover, no body of documented case histories, and thus no properly recorded or readily accessible institutional memory on fundamental issues or problems.

The system has little means of improving itself within present constraints. There has been virtually no training in dispute resolution for UN staff, and no means of accessing the body of knowledge and expertise which has developed in this field outside the UN over the past few years. Even recently established training programs face the difficulty that Secretariat staff are so overstretched that it is hard for them to be released for training because they are needed on the job. To improve the Secretariat's capacity here, more resources are required.

Preventive diplomacy teams

To develop the various preventive diplomacy capabilities to which we have referred—in particular the need for more sharply focused analysis, and a better response capability when it comes to offering mediation and related services—there will simply have to be significant additions, both at UN Headquarters in New York and in the field, to the present resources available to the Department of Political Affairs. Such increased resources should be devoted to the establishment (or where these already exist in nascent form, enhancement) of regionally focused preventive diplomacy teams or units, staffed by senior professionals expert in dispute resolution and familiar with the disputes on which they work. These individuals should have sufficient experience and stature to be able to negotiate at the highest levels. This may require supplementing existing staff with additional people from the upper echelons of member states' diplomatic corps, from the senior levels of academia, and from experienced professionals who have been practising dispute resolution in other settings—even perhaps, in some cases, from the ranks of the 'World Council of Former Foreign Ministers' inaugurated in St Petersburg in June 1993. As well, each unit should include regional or area experts who are well-versed in the cultural, historical and political perspectives of states and other actors in the region.

Such units would require adequate resources and infrastructure, with appropriate back-up personnel and equipment. This would mean adequate numbers of research assistants; on-line computer facilities with immediate access to wire services, research institutions and data banks; advanced and secure telecommunications equipment, which would allow instant conferencing with actors in the region, with consultants, and with other UN offices in the field; operations rooms with detailed maps and access to cable television; and sufficient funds for regular and routine travel throughout the region, including participation in relevant meetings. Specialised expertise from scholars and practitioners around the world should be available on a consultative basis when required. Better use could also be made of peace research institutes, and similar think tanks, which could be asked to hold special working meetings with expert participants on particular issues.

It would be desirable for preventive diplomacy unit staff to travel to the capitals and 'hot spots' of their region on a regular and routine basis to discuss regional problems with relevant actors, to identify emerging disputes, to track developments in existing disputes, to gain an in-depth understanding of these disputes, to develop a sense of trust and a reputation for fairness, to urge the parties to come to the negotiating table and to offer a range of dispute resolution options where it was deemed appropriate. Such visits could also allow sensitive coordination with other regional or sub-regional groups. Quiet diplomacy could develop in a manner which did not call attention to itself and which did not overtly internationalise any dispute. Routine visits would probably be more acceptable than formally constituted 'fact finding' missions, especially if carried out as standard UN practice throughout all regions.

Preventive diplomacy units should not have to wait for an approach from disputing parties. Once a dispute was apparent, a small preventive diplomacy team could proactively urge the disputants to begin negotiation or mediation without delay. In the past, Secretaries-General have tended to wait to be asked to provide their good offices, because they have not wished to be seen to be interfering. Even though parties are often reluctant to request help since they fear that such action might be viewed by the other side as a sign of weakness, they may be willing to accept assistance which is routinely offered to parties to disputes. Thus a more proactive approach might increase the chance of such assistance. Even if the parties were at first uninterested, they could be urged over repeated visits to take advantage of this service. Indeed, such a practice would be in keeping with the 1988 Declaration on the Prevention and Removal of Disputes, which states that:

> The Secretary-General should consider approaching the State directly concerned with a dispute or situation in an effort to prevent it from becoming a threat to the maintenance of international peace and security.

There are obvious physical and resource limits on the extent to which, in practice, this more proactive role could be pursued. In setting priorities it would be sensible to focus on those situations where the potential for escalation to armed hostilities was most clear, taking into account factors like previous conflict history, evidence of population displacement and weapons flows, and the nature of any threats being made.

Preventive diplomacy units could contribute in a number of different ways, acting as a resource and referral source, as well as providing direct services. Where disputes were uncomplicated, it may be a matter simply of tracking the progress of negotiation by the parties themselves. In other instances, staff might offer their own services as an impartial third party which could facilitate the initial contacts between disputing parties, assist in beginning a dialogue, establish 'talks about talks', or become involved in structuring or guiding talks. Such an approach could be based on newer problem solving methods of negotiation, rather than on traditional negotiation strategies: the goal would be to reconcile the parties' differing interests through innovative solutions, rather than through adversarial bargaining over positions. Using such an approach, the UN intermediaries could encourage and facilitate the discussion of the issues and interests which lie behind parties' positions; encourage and suggest the development of a range of innovative options; study and propose objective criteria or principles of fairness or precedent which might serve as a basis for settlement; package proposals to meet parties' concerns; and rally influential third parties as a source of support.

Through such a process, the aim of the preventive diplomacy team would be to carefully manage the mediation exercise, provide a neutral site, keep emotions under control, encourage acts of goodwill and exclude audiences—recognising always that mediation efforts can sometimes have a 'chilling' effect on negotiations, and that it is crucial that the parties retain full power over the negotiating process and its outcomes. Preventive diplomacy units could also assist parties in making full use of the UN system for resolving their disputes. They could help disputants access, as appropriate, election assistance, constitutional experts, human rights and disarmament specialists who could assist in providing information which might be helpful in formulating agreements. In some instances, preventive diplomacy teams might refer disputants to another third party intermediary for assistance. They might, for example, recommend that the parties approach a regional organisation, a neighbouring state or non-government organisation for assistance with dispute resolution. Staff could assist in making contacts between the disputing parties and an acceptable intermediary and follow through by tracking this process. Should such efforts not succeed, the team could recommend further measures which might be helpful.

In other instances, preventive diplomacy units might assist in setting up an independent dispute resolution procedure, such as conciliation or arbitration, where the third party crafts a substantive decision. Staff could provide standard procedures and assist in finding conciliators or arbiters who would be acceptable to the parties. Preventive diplomacy staff could also advise disputing parties as to whether their case was appropriate for referral to the International Court of Justice, and assist them in approaching the Court and, where necessary, in finding the financial assistance to do so.

Once agreement of any kind had been achieved, staff could assist in monitoring compliance, intervene to prevent slippage, and mediate disputes arising from breaches of the agreement. Preventive diplomacy staff would also provide regular reports, including recommendations where appropriate, to the Secretary-General and the Security Council. In cases where the dispute was of sufficient concern, or was escalating to the late prevention stage, the Secretary-General (under Article 99) could bring the matter to the Council's attention.

Preventive diplomacy units could also very usefully systematically study and analyse the nature and causes of disputes in their region, with such analysis possibly leading to recommendations for changes in international practice. In other instances, the units might point out certain types of situations (such as resource shortages) where conflict could be avoided by ameliorating the source of conflict. Regional units could also support and encourage regional or sub-regional confidence building and peace building exercises, and help promote better preventive regimes within the region.

Finally, those practising preventive diplomacy in this way should be continually refining its methodology through the study of the factors which have evidently promoted or inhibited progress in dispute resolution. By adopting an analytical approach to past and present experience, and evaluating how pitfalls might be avoided in the future, valuable lessons could be learned which would improve the practice of future dispute settlement.

Regional peace and security resource centres

Preventive diplomacy teams performing tasks such as those described above should be based not only at UN Headquarters in New York, as preventive diplomacy staff currently are, but increasingly in the field. By being located on the ground—not just making regular visits to the field—such preventive diplomacy units, which might be called 'Peace and Security Resource Centres', would be able to obtain a truer assessment of situations as they evolved and would be better able to grasp opportunities when they occurred. Such Centres would, desirably, be centrally located in each region, perhaps near the relevant regional organisation itself; they would be under the direction of the Secretary-General, and would need to maintain the closest linkage with UN Headquarters.

To give Peace and Security Resource Centres the necessary political support, they could be established under a mandate by either or both the Security Council and General Assembly, and report to the Council or Assembly on a regular basis on their activities and progress, much as Special Representatives currently do, through the Secretary-General.

Staff from regional organisations might also be seconded to such Centres in order to provide better coordination between themselves and the UN, to contribute a regional perspective, and to give them experience and training in conflict prevention and resolution. This proximity should promote the development of relationships between UN staff and regional actors, thus enhancing the ability to obtain relevant information for early warning, and to develop the range of relationships necessary for all aspects of preventive diplomacy to be fully effective.

At a broader level, Peace and Security Resource Centres might also liaise with appropriate UN institutions to set up training programs for diplomats and government officials from countries in the region.

Training in problem solving methods of negotiation could mean that, over time, local officials would become increasingly effective in resolving their own differences in a more constructive manner.

Preventive diplomacy through other international actors

Regional organisations

The Secretary-General in *An Agenda for Peace* called for greater involvement of regional arrangements and agencies in the UN's peace-related activities, including preventive diplomacy: this was followed up by the Security Council in January 1993, in a Presidential statement (S/25184). Neither the Secretary-General nor the Presidential statement (nor for that matter Chapter VIII of the UN Charter itself, which specifically encourages regional action, where appropriate, on security matters) makes any attempt to prescribe which arrangements or agencies should be so involved. The question of interpretation is deliberately left open for reasons of flexibility. As discussed in Chapter 2, there are many existing regional organisations which play a role here and others, including emerging organisations, that have the potential to do so. In practice, most regional organisations embody agreements among geographically-concentrated groups of states for cooperative action on issues of mutual interest (eg CSCE, ASEAN). Others are brought together by shared experience only partly related, if at all, to geography (eg OIC). All are bound internally by perceived common interest. Yet each is different from the other, in mandate, scope and composition, and in inclination and capacity to take on the functions envisaged under Chapter VIII, whether alone or in cooperation with the UN.

The UN Charter, just as it leaves open the interpretation of arrangements or agencies falling under Chapter VIII, does not define the manner and extent to which regional organisations should develop their security role. Article 52 stipulates that 'local disputes' be addressed in the first instance by regional organisations, if at all possible, but does not elaborate further on what matters are appropriate for regional action. It is for each regional organisation to determine what the parameters of this role should be.

In practice, issues are appropriate for regional action when regional states deem them to be so. This might be because a threat or dispute has multilateral dimensions, with several states involved (eg the South China Sea dispute: see Box 2) or with regional implications going beyond the immediate disputants (eg Cambodia). In other circumstances, states may conclude that there is no longer scope or reason to pursue their local dispute by bilateral means, and may wish

2. The South China Sea since 1990: an innovative regional approach to preventive diplomacy

The problem: The Spratly and Paracel Islands in the South China Sea continue to be subject to disputed territorial claims involving access to resources and control over sea lanes. Most of the friction has been between China and Vietnam, although Taiwan, Malaysia, the Philippines and Brunei have their own territorial claims. The increasing military presence of some claimants has added to concern about the issue becoming a major regional flashpoint.

The response: Since January 1990, a series of 'unofficial' workshops has been sponsored by Indonesia, a littoral non-claimant, and supported by ASEAN (with some resource assistance from Canada). Attended by officials from claimant states 'in their private capacities', and academics and other experts, they promote an informal exchange of views, without putting claimants into any position which could prejudice their respective claims of sovereignty.

The process is an ongoing one, but the workshops have provided a framework for dialogue, the establishment of basic ground rules, the development of working relationships, and the exploration of options (including joint resource exploration zones) which might allow for joint economic gain if sovereignty issues can be resolved or, perhaps more likely, set aside.

The lessons:

- The workshops represent an innovative attempt by an impartial neighbouring state to institute an informal preventive diplomacy process: by redefining the task as a search for options which are of mutual interest to the parties, the process promotes problem solving and the beginning of a cooperative dialogue.

- This kind of 'second track' diplomacy provides an excellent basis for later official talks: such a process takes time, but both the process and the substance of such workshops can systematically build momentum towards a peaceful resolution.

- Joint projects which come from working group proposals develop mutual goals and working relationships: this has been shown to be one of the best ways of reversing a competitive process.

- The workshops provide a positive example of the kinds of thoughtfully-designed regional initiatives which could be undertaken more frequently by regional, sub-regional or unilateral actors.

to place the matter on the regional agenda. This step, while externalising the problem, falls short of the greater symbolism which comes from referring a matter to the UN: so long as the matter is addressed at regional level, and not further 'internationalised', the parties may feel that it has not escalated beyond their control.

There are limitations to what regional organisations can do. For the most part they lack the UN's basic resources, experience and capacity to oblige member states to contribute financially to any dispute resolution activities they might undertake. Accordingly, they rarely have the resources to address problems once they have escalated beyond a certain level. Their mandate may be inadequate to properly address all dimensions of a problem. They may lack the necessary persuasive influence, especially in circumstances where there is political division among member states or where a predominant regional power is closely involved. And, although they will usually be closer to the parties, proximity to a dispute might in fact hamper effective mediation capacity in some cases. To the extent that any generalisation is possible, we agree with the emphasis that has been suggested by Singapore UN diplomat Mark Hong Tat Soon:

> The logical approach for regional organisations is to concentrate on fulfilling their roles in areas where they have comparative advantage. These areas are early warning, information gathering and preventive diplomacy. As neighbours with deep interests in preserving regional peace and stability, regional states would be better informed on incipient conflicts and be able to provide continuous information to the United Nations on developments and dangerous trends.

The unique mandate and composition of each regional organisation impacts directly on its capacity to work with the UN under Chapter VIII. The Secretary-General recognised this with his statement in *An Agenda for Peace* that there could be no formal pattern in the relationship between the UN and regional organisations. The forms of interaction must necessarily be flexible, without rigid division of responsibility, and appropriate to the circumstances of each regional organisation and each issue.

Some mechanisms for cooperation between the UN and regional organisations are already in place. A number of regional organisations, including the OAS, OAU, OIC and Arab League, have standing invitations to participate as observers in the sessions and the work of the General Assembly. Most of these organisations have formal framework agreements for cooperation with the UN, although these framework agreements, while prescribing principles for cooperation, do not always provide concrete mechanisms to achieve it. One exception is the CSCE, which declared itself in July 1992 to be a regional arrangement within the meaning of Chapter VIII. In May 1993, the Secretary-General and the Chairman of the CSCE Council agreed through an exchange of letters on a framework for cooperation and coordination between the UN and the CSCE, including through regular exchange of information in the fields of early warning, conflict prevention and the promotion of democratic values and human rights, and by possible joint fact-finding and other missions relating to the maintenance of international peace and security.

Despite these agreements, there are relatively few instances of practical cooperation on the ground between the UN and regional organisations in preventive approaches. The OAS and the UN have cooperated to restore human rights and democracy to Haiti, through the joint appointment of a Special Envoy by the two Secretaries-General, and the deployment of an international human rights mission comprising contingents of monitors appointed by each organisation (although this is probably better regarded as an exercise in peace building rather than preventive diplomacy). The CSCE and the UN are cooperating closely in observer and mediation missions to potential areas of conflict in the republics of the former Soviet Union, with an agreed division of labour appropriate to each case.

There is no fixed practice as to whether the UN or a regional organisation should take the lead in dispute resolution. The most important point is that any cooperative arrangement between the UN and regional organisations must be sufficiently adaptable to meet each situation as it arises. In some cases, it may be best for the regional organisation to take the lead and carry out preventive diplomacy with consultation and back-up by the UN (perhaps through the preventive diplomacy teams, or more formalised Peace and Security Resource Centres, discussed above); in other cases, it may be more advantageous to have the UN carry out the function with consultation and back-up from regional organisations. In still other instances, both parties acting together may provide the most powerful approach, underlining to protagonists the unanimity of the international community. Coordination of efforts is, of course, essential in order to avoid the diffusion of responsibility which can occur when both the UN and the regional organisation think that the other should be handling a given situation.

States and other actors   The importance of other international actors in such efforts should not be underestimated. Indeed, some of the most important preventive diplomacy efforts have, without doubt, been made by individual states, or individual leaders or their envoys acting unilaterally to try to reduce tensions or to find an acceptable solution to a given situation, eg the Beagle Channel dispute between Argentina and Chile, successfully mediated by the Vatican. Another example may be found in the visits to Senegal and Zambia by South African business leaders to meet ANC representatives, organised in the late 1980s by the prominent white opposition figure, Dr Frederik van Zyl Slabbert, which were an important prelude to the South African Government's change of course on apartheid in 1990. In some cases a single actor may have more influence than the international community as a whole. If preventive diplomacy is to truly succeed, it will be important for the international system to use all of its resources towards this end. Close cooperation with the UN and relevant regional organisations is, however, also desirable in this situation.

Multi-track diplomacy efforts also provide an important part of the spectrum of dispute resolution. A number of 'second track' diplomacy efforts (between influential parties, not necessarily officials, from both sides of a dispute) are under way, sponsored by a variety of governments and unofficial bodies. Such efforts break down enemy image perceptions, open up channels of communication and help all sides to think about new options for old problems. To the extent that such efforts target opinion leaders, they may build a momentum from below for later dispute resolution efforts. The 'unofficial' South China Sea workshops, initiated by Indonesia, are a clear current example of 'second track' diplomacy at work on a specific issue (see Box 2); the Roundtable Seminars on Asia Pacific Regional Security issues, sponsored in recent years by the Malaysian Institute for Strategic and International Studies, offer an example of more generalised communication and confidence-building.

Non-government organisations also play an important role in preventive diplomacy in a variety of ways. One of these is early (as well as late) warning of emerging threats or crises, including the outbreak of hostilities, famine, human rights abuses, refugee flows and the like. Moreover, NGOs are often successful in their attempts to make such threats salient to an overstretched international community, as they have been, in particular, with successive crises on the African continent. As well, NGOs often help to promote problem solving and constructive dialogue between groups.

6

Preventive Deployment

The concept of preventive deployment

Preventive deployment is a new concept for the UN, given prominence by the Secretary-General's advocacy in *An Agenda for Peace* and by its recent application—for the first, and so far only, time—in the Former Yugoslav Republic of Macedonia (FYRM). The essence of this strategy is that it is a preventive *military*, rather than diplomatic, response involving—in the clearest case—the positioning of troops, military observers and related personnel on one or both sides of a border between entities that are in dispute (or where there is an emerging threat of conflict), with the primary object of deterring the escalation of that situation into armed conflict. Associated objectives may be to calm communities in the area by monitoring law and order and general conditions, and to render other forms of assistance to local authorities.

In the case of the FYRM there was a concern (in the context of the deteriorating situation in the former Yugoslavia generally, and its own continuing dispute with Greece) that if the neighbouring Kosovo area of Serbia were to erupt in a conflict between the Serbs and Albanian Muslims, the FYRM—with a quarter of its own population Albanian—could be drawn rapidly into a conflict, with other powers possibly also becoming involved: a clear 'emerging threat' situation. In December 1992 the Security Council authorised the deployment of a small force of 700, plus military observers and civil police, to

81

monitor the FYRM's borders and report developments which could signify a threat to its territory: this was augmented in July 1993 by 300 troops. The forces deployed in the FYRM are clearly too small on their own to handle any actual armed conflict that might erupt in the area. The 'deterrent' here consists in the fact that the Security Council has demonstrated its interest in the situation; all the relevant parties are under close international scrutiny; and there is at least an implication of willingness to take further action if there is any resort to violence. How credible that deterrent is will depend essentially on the weight that potential transgressors give to international opinion, and their assessment of the likelihood in practice of a strong Security Council reaction. A rather clearer deterrent would exist in an overtly 'trip wire' deployment, ie where a small number of military personnel are ranged along a line—the crossing of which would mobilise a larger and more capable 'strike' force held in reserve or out of theatre, clearly armed with both Chapter VII enforcement powers and the capability and will to exercise them.

As already stated, the clearest preventive deployment situation involves a border between disputing entities. The clearest case of such a border, in turn, is an international one between sovereign states; however, the concept of preventive deployment is equally applicable to notional borders *within* states, in situations where lines of one kind or another have been drawn in the context of a dispute—eg one concerning a minority enclave—the crossing of which would escalate it into an armed conflict. One can also envisage cases where preventive deployment might be contemplated, but no immediate 'border' question is involved at all, eg where a dispute is not between immediate neighbours and the threatened action against which troops are preventively deployed is by way of air strike. The essence of preventive deployment, then, goes not so much to *where* troops are deployed as to *why* they are deployed, viz to contain the dispute or emerging threat and prevent it turning into an armed conflict.

In *An Agenda for Peace*, the concept of 'preventive deployment' is taken a little further still, to apply in situations of internal national crisis where, at the request or with the consent of the government or all parties concerned, military personnel are sent in to give humanitarian assistance or create secure conditions. As stated in earlier chapters, however, we think it might help avoid further complications in this already somewhat confused debate if these situations were not regarded as ones of 'preventive deployment'. It is suggested, rather, that if the use of any kind of force is contemplated (other than in self-defence) the deployment is better treated as a form of 'peace enforcement'. And if what is being talked about is in-country help being given by military personnel, in circumstances where the use of force is not contemplated, then that is best treated as a form of 'peace building'.

The legal basis for preventive deployment by the UN, given that no use of force is involved, is Chapter VI of the UN Charter. Such deployment would be authorised by the Security Council. In cases of inter-state disputes consent would be needed from both governments concerned if the deployment were to be on both sides of a border, but a deployment could proceed with the consent only of the requesting country if it were able to persuade the Security Council that this was desirable to deter hostilities. For intra-state situations where the Security Council felt able to intervene, this presumably again would occur only with the consent of the government or all parties concerned: the Secretary-General put it in these terms in *An Agenda for Peace*.

A preventive deployment force has similar tasks to early warning observers, but by deploying in greater strength it performs a greater symbolic role. While the primary object of such a force is deterrence, its task may also include some or all of the following:

- monitoring, observing and reporting on developments which could undermine confidence or stability (including, eg arms flows) in the vicinity of a contested border, or more generally;
- assisting and monitoring local authorities in the maintenance of law and order, including the protection of threatened minorities;
- assisting and monitoring local authorities in the maintenance of essential services (water, power, and the like); or
- assisting local authorities, UN agencies or non-government organisations in the provision of humanitarian assistance.

Making preventive deployment effective

Preventive deployment should only be considered in circumstances in which such a presence will be more likely than any other available method to discourage further escalation of the dispute, or realisation of the emerging threat. Discussion of such deployment, particularly in the absence of support for it from all sides to a dispute, could have the unintended consequence of contributing to escalation of tension. Preventive deployment in isolation from broader diplomatic efforts, even in cases with full consent of all parties, may not defuse tension. It is highly desirable, accordingly, that the decision to deploy a force occur in the context of a comprehensive preventive diplomacy strategy to contain and resolve a dispute.

The addition of preventive deployment to UN strategies for preventive action raises similar problems to those faced in relation to preventive diplomacy, including the need for an enhanced UN capacity for identification of emerging international disputes. It also raises some of the characteristic problems of peace keeping, including the need for the UN to be capable of rapidly assembling and deploying a force; ensuring adequate levels of training and inter-operability so that it can be effective quickly; raising adequate funds (both for start-up costs, eg from the Peacekeeping Reserve Fund, and ongoing costs from assessed contributions); and providing adequate command and control.

A preventive deployment force needs to be more than a symbolic presence. It requires an effective communications capability, including close communications with UN Headquarters in New York; surveillance capacity, linked to an enhanced information capacity at UN Headquarters; and high capacity for mobility. As preventive deployment is not enforcement action, the rules of engagement for preventive deployment forces are, as in peace keeping operations, limited to the use of force in self defence. The UN does not itself have, and is unlikely to have in the foreseeable future, the resources to consider preventive deployment forces with the capacity to repel national forces following the outbreak of hostilities, which would not only require much greater numbers for any such operation, but also a legal basis under Chapter VII. If the UN wanted to have in these situations a stand-by enforcement capacity, this could possibly be supplied by regional organisations with the capacity for collective security action—eg NATO or the WEU, under the authority of a CSCE mandate and with Security Council authorisation.

The preventive deployment task must be clearly defined, in advance, with a specific mandate. There must, moreover, be some clear perception by the Security Council decision makers, even if this is not made fully public at the time, as to what happens next in the event of prevention failing. It is likely to be operationally very difficult, quite apart from anything else, to deploy a lightly armed force by way of preventive deployment, and then—after escalation of the dispute into a conflict—later seek to upgrade that same force into a Chapter VII peace enforcement operation. Unless the force is given from the outset a 'fall back' Chapter VII mandate, and capability, the UN must be prepared to withdraw a preventive deployment force if it has failed in its task; any further military assistance or intervention strategy—by way of regional or UN forces—should be based on different criteria, and structured along different lines, from the original preventive deployment.

While preventive deployment, then, may be a useful option available to the cooperative security system, it is always one that should be very cautiously applied. In cases where there is sufficient good will from all governments or parties to allow preventive deployment, such deployment is arguably not necessary. Preventive deployment at the request of one government or party is more problematic, entailing risks both for the force, if it should fail to deter armed conflict, and with the potential to unwittingly contribute to entrenchment or escalation of the dispute. Too much recourse to preventive deployment as a preventive strategy could erode the UN's position of impartiality, in particular in cases lacking the consensus of all parties.

The financial capacity of the UN is under strain and it is likely any sizeable UN commitment to preventive deployment strategies would meet funding limitations. However, in cases where preventive deployment will contain armed conflict—and better still, assist a political settlement of the dispute in question—the cost to the international community and the protagonists is less than permitting the situation to deteriorate into conflict.

In summary, the UN needs to develop strict criteria for any future use of preventive deployment including clear objectives, clear mandates, a strong likelihood that the deployment will meet its objectives and, desirably, clear linkage to a comprehensive political process for settlement of the dispute. Regional organisations might find preventive deployment practicable, particularly in cases in which they have the consent of all sides and regional actors have a stake in strong preventive measures but, again, any preventive deployment should take place as part of a comprehensive diplomatic process and with Security Council authorisation and broad support from the international community.

IV

Restoring Peace

7

Peace Making

From preventive diplomacy to peace making and keeping

Peace making is a close relative of preventive diplomacy, involving essentially the same range of methods described in Article 33 of the UN Charter—ie 'negotiation, enquiry, mediation, conciliation, arbitration, judicial settlement, resort to regional agencies or agreements'—but applied *after* a dispute has crossed the threshold into armed hostilities. Peace making embraces all the peaceful means applied to resolve armed conflict once it has begun. Its aim is to reduce conflict intensity, separate belligerents, halt bloodshed, put the parties back on a path to peaceful resolution and ultimately to arrive at a durable solution.

Preventive diplomacy, as we said in Chapter 5, works best at early stages of impending disputes because the issues are more limited and specific, there are fewer parties to the dispute, and because the tactics used to persuade the other are still largely rhetorical and do not yet involve large-scale violence with its attendant changes in motivation and perceptions. At this earlier stage, the goal is still to ensure that one's own interests are met rather than to hurt or punish the other. While perceptions of the other side may not be benign, in most cases they have not yet degenerated into a rigid, stereotyped 'enemy image'. Communication is usually still possible and relations between the parties may be ongoing in a broad range of other areas. All this allows a greater opportunity for the acceptance of problem solving methods of negotiation or mediation, and for the possibility of finding a mutually acceptable solution.

After a dispute has crossed the threshold into armed conflict, the process of peaceful resolution—*peace making*—becomes more difficult, demanding and complex. With the eruption of violence, the issues tend to generalise and proliferate. The parties' demands frequently extend far beyond the more circumscribed issues of the original dispute, making a mutually satisfying accommodation nearly impossible to find. As each side experiences physical and psychological injury from the other, motivations expand from meeting one's own interests to the desire to 'hurt' the other and to seek revenge and retribution. 'Enemy image' perceptions by each side are reinforced by hostile interactions and become a reality. The tendency to filter incoming information in terms of the group's established framework and to reject information which contradicts these preconceived ideas (sometimes called group think) is accentuated. Threats and violence become the medium of communication, and the conflict quickly comes to dominate and poison broader relations. As the parties invest ever-greater resources in the conflict, they become increasingly committed to and entrapped in the struggle to prevail. Having persuaded their constituents that the conflict is worth dying for and that the other side is indeed an enemy, leaders often have difficulty (in terms of their public image) in entering into peace making negotiations. Alliances increase the number of parties and further complicate peace making efforts since these third parties often have their own sets of interests.

These are the challenges with which peace makers have to deal. Their task can be thought of as proceeding in two stages. 'Stage I' peace making, which involves trying to bring about an end to armed hostilities, can be thought of as conflict *management*; 'Stage II' peace making, by contrast, is aimed at obtaining a lasting political agreement, and can be thought of as conflict *settlement.* Stage I peace making necessarily focuses on the negotiation of such matters as ceasefires, the freezing in place or withdrawal of troops, the deployment of observer missions of peace keeping forces to separate belligerents and monitor ceasefires, and relief measures for civilians or refugees. Once these measures are in place, peace making efforts may be turned to the equally difficult Stage II task of finding a durable settlement to the dispute or issues which lay behind the hostilities. Methods at this stage may involve rather more of the Article 33 preventive diplomacy repertoire: mediation, arbitration and the like as well as merely negotiation.

Peace keeping, discussed in detail in the next chapter, is often an important adjunct to peace making. In situations where peace makers have already negotiated an agreement to stop the fighting, establish a ceasefire and allow conditions to return to some sort of normality,

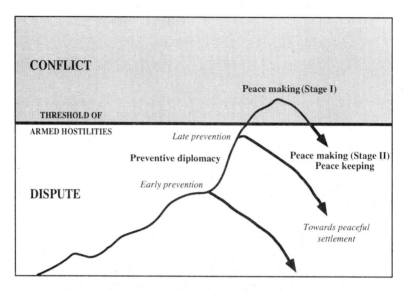

CONFLICT

Peace making (Stage I)

THRESHOLD OF
ARMED HOSTILITIES

Late prevention

Preventive diplomacy

Peace making (Stage II)
Peace keeping

Early prevention

DISPUTE

*Towards peaceful
settlement*

**Chart 4 The relationship between preventive diplomacy,
peace making and peace keeping**

peace keepers can be introduced to monitor, supervise and verify those agreements, and, generally, assist in further cooling off, so that Stage II peace making—the negotiation of the underlying issues—can proceed. In other situations, the peace making process may have gone further than a ceasefire, and made some headway into elements of Stage II peace making with agreements achieved among the parties to a settlement process. It might be decided that the insertion then of a peace keeping operation—particularly of a 'multi-dimensional' or 'expanded' kind (extending to election supervision, human rights monitoring and the like)—is necessary to hold that process together.

Careful consultation and coordination between peace makers and those who are planning and carrying out peace keeping activities is essential to the success of both missions. While peace makers negotiate problems at the larger political level, peace keepers are often called upon to negotiate or mediate disputes or conflicts which occur in the field in the course of their everyday operations: in these cases, they may also need to draw on the problem solving techniques used by peace makers. The overall relationship between preventive diplomacy, peace making and peace keeping—as successive responses to a dispute escalating into armed conflict—is sketched in the accompanying Chart 4.

Peace making through the United Nations

United Nations peace making efforts in the past have not always been successful in achieving the vitally important Stage II conflict settlement. As a consequence, many conflicts persist and fester at a lower level of intensity, occasionally re-erupting into violations of ceasefires, skirmishes, incursions and, in some cases, resurgence of full-scale hostilities. In such cases, UN involvement can be protracted and expensive, and may even unwittingly contribute to sustaining the problem by creating a status quo that is more comfortable for both sides than the changes that would have to be made if an negotiated settlement were to be achieved. Cyprus (see Box 3) is one example: the fighting ceased and a demarcation line in the form of a buffer zone was established for policing by a UN peace keeping force, but further progress has not been possible on a settlement to the underlying problem. Kashmir is another: the peace keeping mandate given to UNMOGIP in 1949 was not tied to a stipulated outcome, nor to progress toward a negotiated settlement, and in effect absolved the parties from negotiating their own cooperative arrangements to avoid further incidents along disputed boundaries.

While some situations are bound to be intractable, UN peace making efforts generally could be significantly strengthened by providing high calibre staff to devote their energies on a full-time basis to peace making over a prolonged period, with adequate support and back-up for their efforts. Most of the UN's successful peace making efforts in recent years have involved such sustained attempts over long periods of time by senior staff travelling frequently to the region of the conflict. Often the most effective peace making practitioners are those with experience in preventive diplomacy. There may be a few skills specific to peace making which do not apply to preventive diplomacy—such as expertise in how to establish ceasefires and de-escalate military conflict—but the UN should be able to strengthen its peace making and preventive diplomacy skills through the same institutional structures.

In this respect, permanent UN Secretariat peace making units located in the regions could be an effective support mechanism for peace making. The creation of UN Peace and Security Resource Centres within each region, as suggested in Chapter 5, might provide one means of accomplishing this goal. The establishment of such permanent structures, rather than ad hoc ones as currently occurs whenever a major peace making effort is required, would permit the

3.   Cyprus since 1964: keeping but not making peace

The problem: The Republic of Cyprus was granted independence from the UK in 1960. Its Constitution assured a government structure for the co-existence of the island's Greek Cypriot and Turkish Cypriot communities. The UK, Turkey and Greece were established as guarantor powers of the Constitution. It was a difficult relationship from the start, and after three years, conflict broke out between the two groups.

The response: The guarantor powers responded initially, in December 1963, with a small peace keeping force which, while establishing a 'green line' in Nicosia, failed to prevent inter-communal fighting. In 1964, the Security Council established a peace keeping force (UNFICYP), and in 1967 its mandate was, at the request of the Cyprus Government, strengthened. After a pro-Greek coup and the subsequent invasion and occupation by Turkish forces in 1974, the mandate was again expanded. UNFICYP was able to secure a buffer zone between the parties across the width of the island, maintain the de facto ceasefire, and deliver humanitarian assistance.

The ceasefire has held, but repeated UN-sponsored peace making initiatives have not succeeded in bringing the parties to agreement; there is an almost total divison of the island along ethnic lines; and there is still no agreement on reciprocal arrangements for disarmament.

The lessons:

• UNFICYP, operating with the consent of the parties, has been relatively successful in conflict management, by effectively policing a dividing line and providing humanitarian assistance. As a force with only a peace keeping mandate, it had no capacity to prevent the intervention of a third party.

• UNFICYP may nonetheless have inadvertently undermined the peace making process by assuring an indefinite status quo which has to date been more acceptable to both sides than the compromises needed for settlement.

• UNFICYP's mandate did not link it to progress in negotiations on a resolution of the conflict, and provided for no incentives or penalties for actions by the parties likely to enhance or detract from prospects for a settlement.

Secretariat to build and retain institutional experience and memory as an important aid to its peace making efforts. An in-depth knowledge of the region, and established networks and relationships with actors in the regions, would give permanent staff an advantage over staff assigned on an ad hoc basis. A greater regional presence, and more developed structures of cooperation with regional and sub-regional bodies, would have the advantage of making it easier for peace makers to communicate and coordinate with peace keepers on the ground. Peace makers could more easily visit a conflict zone, while at the same time having an adequately resourced home base and a neutral venue for talks with the relevant parties. Contact with the Secretary-General and others at Headquarters could be maintained through fully developed telecommunications networks, as occurs now in foreign ministries. Access to the parties would be easier than if talks took place only at UN Headquarters in New York. And by conducting talks in the region, regional and sub-regional organisations and other influential third parties could more easily become involved in the settlement process where it was useful for them to do so.

Where the situation requires it, the practice of appointing Special or Personal Representatives of the Secretary-General could still be employed. Regionally based units would provide them the necessary support services which have so often been lacking in the past. Being closer to the action, peace makers would have easier access to in-depth background information and continuing evaluation of developments relevant to the particular peace making process. A wider range of first-hand information and interlocutors would be available and opportunities could be more quickly seized as events evolved. Being on the spot would give peace makers a chance to achieve successive small successes, establishing momentum and building trust over time. Access to local research institutes and a world wide network of outside consultants—backed up by the headquarters resources of the Secretariat—could develop a flow of innovative ideas, many of them locally grown, for a more effective peace making process. There has been some use of creative ideas and processes in recent UN peace making efforts: an example is the brainstorming session in the El Salvador peace process, involving members of the human rights community in generating new ideas for tackling human rights problems.

Regional units would not, of course, preclude talks in New York or Geneva, or the Secretary-General's personal involvement in cases where that was deemed important. Modern communications work both ways, and there may be stronger arguments in some cases for staging talks further from, rather than closer to, the action, eg to work in a less emotional environment.

Peace making through other international actors

Regional organisations

These have an important role to play in peace making activities, and often this can usefully be in coordination with the UN. The role of ASEAN in the Cambodian settlement, the role of the Organization of American States (OAS) in El Salvador (with five Central American Presidents, the 'Friends of the Secretary-General', assisting senior UN officials), and the role of the Organization of African Unity (OAU), the Organisation of the Islamic Conference (OIC) and the Arab League in Somalia all demonstrate the ways in which regional bodies can contribute to peace making.

Against this, regional organisations can also play a less then helpful role in the peace making process in cases where member states within the organisation are divided about what should be done or are encouraging one or more sides to the conflict to pursue coercive means to achieve their aims. Divisions within the various European regional organisations (as within the UN itself) have not made it easy to effectively tackle the problems of the former Yugoslavia, and divisions in the Arab League inhibited its attempts to respond to the Gulf crisis. Just as regional organisations have to weigh and balance whether or not to become involved in local peace making efforts, so too will it be important for UN peace makers to examine ahead of time the pros and cons of involving a regional organisation in the peace making process, and to give careful consideration to how this might be done in a manner which does not bring into play the various risks of doing so.

States

Individual states have made important contributions to peace making. In the Middle East, the United States has been able to play a role where the UN has been unable to act (see Box 4). In addition to direct involvement, there are a number of indirect roles that states can usefully play. The use of the 'Friends of the Secretary-General' in the El Salvador peace making process is a notable and creative example. Others include Australia's contribution of the 'Red Book' Cambodian peace proposal in early 1990. Informal behind-the-scenes roles can be very useful, such as those played by a number of Middle East states in the Iran–Iraq peace process in the 1980s. In some cases again, however, involvement by third parties, even when they are trying to be helpful, can be detrimental to peace making. This tends to occur most often when the third party has its own set of interests. Since larger powers are frequently seen in this light, peace making is sometimes

4.   The Middle East since 1991: seizing the peace making momentum

The problem: At the end of the Gulf War, and with the profound change in the political landscape of the region following the end of the influence of superpower rivalries, there was renewed international interest in seeking a negotiated settlement to the Arab/Israeli conflict. The challenge was to devise effective architecture for the negotiations. The framework had to accommodate an ambiguity on Palestinian participation, as Israel believed that the Madrid process should exclude the Palestinian diaspora.

The Response: Recognising the opportunity, the United States sought the cooperation of the Soviet Union as a co-sponsor and secured the concurrence of all principal regional parties to participation in negotiations: Israel, Syria, Lebanon, Jordan and the Palestinians. The first step, an international conference held in Madrid in October 1991, established a framework for negotiating a settlement predicated on UN Security Council Resolutions 242 and 338. The negotiations were to proceed in two mutually reinforcing phases: a bilateral phase comprising talks between Israel and the Palestinians and Israel and its neighbours Jordan, Lebanon and Syria, and a multilateral phase dealing with broader regional issues, and involving countries both within and outside the region. The United States became a full partner in the negotiations in February 1993.

The lessons:

- While progress remains slow, the establishment of a framework for peace negotiations exemplifies a working post-conflict peace making initiative.

- The peace process, being based on Security Council resolutions, enjoyed an indirect UN mandate, but direct sponsorship by the US and the Soviet Union (later Russia) was crucial in getting the process off the ground. The US decision to become a full partner in the process has also played a pivotal role in ensuring that the negotiations remain alive. In a situation as complex as this, direct UN involvement may not always be the best solution, and influential and trusted actors from outside the region may need to take the initiative in launching and sustaining a given peace making process.

- The framework for the peace process reflected various competing interests and was shaped by the compromises necessary to accommodate these, in particular the exclusion of the Palestine Liberation Organisation (PLO) from direct participation in the process-although the lack of any structured, clearly representative delegation has reduced the Palestinians' negotiating authority and has made progress more difficult. All principal parties to a conflict should be included as equal partners in the negotiating process.

- The separate but simultaneous track of bilateral talks allows sufficient flexibility for each of the parties to pursue their own objectives, but retain the coordinated focus for progress towards a comprehensive settlement; the multilateral phase helps maintain momentum by generating a sense of purpose even when bilateral talks encounter difficulty, and also involves post-conflict peace building.

- Despite continuing violence, and other destabilising actions, the peace process has endured. Although progress is painfully slow, all participants remain committed to a negotiated settlement, as the best prospect for their long term peace and security: peace making has to be interest based.

- There may come a point when, if key issues are to be resolved, skilful mediation will need to supplement the structured negotiation approach central to this peace making effort. But the present process is well designed to show the limits of what is possible through direct negotiation between the parties.

more successful when pursued by small and medium powers able to win trust quickly and be seen as acting more altruistically.

Where states take on a peace making role it would be helpful for them to discuss their approaches and ideas with the Secretary-General and to keep him informed of progress or problems along the way. The Falklands is a case in point. US Secretary of State Alexander Haig played an intermediary role, initiated without consultation with the UN but which effectively precluded UN involvement until the United States concluded its efforts. When the UN then took up the intermediary role, it appears that there was no sharing of information by the United States administration about what progress had been obtained or what obstacles had been confronted. Some commentators have suggested that valuable time was lost for UN mediators and that the military imperative for armed conflict had in the meantime grown to such an extent that UN efforts were overwhelmed by events.

The logical corollary to the possible helpful role of states is that individual states can also hinder the peace process for their own self interested reasons. A member state may supply massive arms or finance war efforts in a manner that is not helpful to peace making. In such cases, the international community—the UN and regional organisations—can bring pressure to bear upon parties undermining a peace making effort—whether they are small, middle-sized or large powers. By acting together, inconsistencies in rhetoric and behaviour of individual states can be disclosed and brought into line by pressure and suasion from the international community.

Other actors

As with preventive diplomacy, there are a number of cases where other actors, or combinations of them, have made a difference in conflict resolution situations. Three diverse examples make the point. The Commonwealth played a crucial role in the Rhodesia/Zimbabwe peace settlement, in particular through the 1979 Lancaster House constitutional conference. In the case of the Mozambique General Peace Agreement, concluded in Rome in October 1992, the Catholic St Egido Community, the Governments of Zimbabwe and Botswana, and British businessman Tiny Rowland of Lonhro, all played significant roles in the negotiations. And the Carter Center played a helpful role in the final resolution of the long running Ethiopia/Eritrea conflict.

8

Peace Keeping

The evolution of United Nations peace keeping

Peace keeping involves the deployment of military or police personnel, and frequently civilians as well, to assist in the implementation of agreements reached between governments or parties who have been engaged in conflict. Although neither defined nor described in the UN Charter itself (although implicitly authorised by Chapter VI), peace keeping has been fairly claimed as an invention of the UN, certainly one which has won it deserved credit—not least in the Nobel Peace Prize awarded to United Nations Peace Keepers in 1988.

Some residual confusion exists here, as elsewhere, about terminology, but it need not. Peace keeping deployments occur after armed conflict; preventive deployments occur before that threshold is crossed. Peace keeping is about ensuring that agreements are implemented; peace making is about reaching them in the first place. Peace keeping is premised on cooperation, and, except for self-defence, its methods are inherently peaceful; peace enforcement presumes resistance by one or more parties, and its methods are as forceful as they have to be.

Peace keeping can be thought of as an option available to peace makers to assist the parties in bridging the gap between the will to peace and the achievement of peace. It is an external, impartial mechanism, which peace makers can propose to encourage the parties

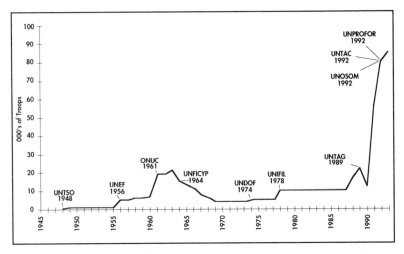

Chart 5   UN peace keeping personnel deployed 1946-1993

to agree to a ceasefire. In its implementation, peace keeping can assist the maintenance of a ceasefire, the building of confidence and the establishment of suitable conditions for a lasting resolution of the conflict. Conversely, peace keeping has been known to be used by one or more parties to create a situation to its or their advantage: peace keeping is not, in itself, a solution to conflict but only one mechanism to assist the on-going peace making process.

Since 1946 there have been 28 separate UN observer missions and peace keeping forces, collectively referred to here as peace keeping operations, fifteen of which have been established since 1988. Chart 5 indicates the scale of the deployments involved and Chart 6 lists all these operations and their purpose. (It should be noted that UNOSOM II is wholly, and UNPROFOR partly, a Chapter VII peace *enforcement*, rather than Chapter VI peace keeping, operation, but both are treated as if they were peace keeping operations for UN budgetary and administrative purposes). The early peace keeping operations were conceived, during the Cold War, as one method by which the UN could pursue conflict management, but a lack of political will by the major powers represented on the Security Council limited that role to regions outside the initial zone of superpower confrontation. Few of the early peace keeping experiments resulted in conflict resolution.

With the new international climate following the end of the Cold War, the major powers have demonstrated a greater political will

Chart 6   UN peace keeping operations 1946–1993

Peace Keeping Operations	Dates	Mandates and Numbers Deployed
UNTSO (UN Truce Supervision Organization)	1948–	Supervise the truce in Palestine; supervise the observance of armistice agreements between Israel and Egypt, Jordan, Lebanon and Syria; observe ceasefires in the Golan Heights and the Suez Canal; assist and cooperate with UNIFIL and UNDOF (600)
UNMOGIP (UN Military Observer Group in India and Pakistan)	1949–	Monitor ceasefire line between India and Pakistan in the state of Jammu and Kashmir (100)
UNEF I (UN Emergency Force)	1956–67	Supervise ceasefire and withdrawal of forces from Egypt; separate Egyptian and Israeli forces in the Sinai (6,000)
UNOGIL (UN Observation Group in Lebanon)	1958	Monitor infiltration of arms, troops and materiel into Lebanon from Syria (600)
ONUC (UN Operation in the Congo)	1960–64	Ensure withdrawal of Belgian and other forces; assist law and order; maintain Congo's territorial integrity; provide technical assistance (20,000)
UNTEA (UN Temporary Executive Authority)	1962–63	Administer W. New Guinea in the transition to its transfer to Indonesia; including a UN Security Force to maintain law and order (1,500—UNSF)
UNYOM (UN Yemen Observation Mission)	1963–64	Monitor disengagement agreement between Saudi Arabia and the United Arab Republic (200)
UNFICYP (UN Peacekeeping Force in Cyprus)	1964–	Maintain law and order; from 1974, secure a buffer zone, monitor the *de facto* ceasefire and provide humanitarian assistance (6,500)
DOMREP (Representative of the Secretary–General in the Dominican Republic)	1965–66	Observe the ceasefire between two *de facto* authorities (also monitored by OAS Inter-American Peace Force) (4)
UNIPOM (UN India–Pakistan Observation Mission)	1965–66	Monitor ceasefire along border, except the state of Jammu and Kashmir; supervise withdrawal of all armed personnel to positions held by them before 5 August 1965 (100)
UNEF II (UN Emergency Force II)	1973–79	Supervise the ceasefire and redeployment of Egyptian and Israeli forces and control buffer zone in the Suez Canal sector and later the Sinai (7000)
UNDOF) (UN Disengagement Observer Force)	1974–	Supervise the ceasefire between Israel and Syria in the Golan Heights; supervise disengagement and separation of forces (1,500)
UNIFIL (UN Interim Force in Lebanon)	1978–	Monitor withdrawal of Israeli troops from southern Lebanon; assist restoration of Government authority (7,500)
UNGOMAP (UN Good Offices Mission—Afghanistan and Pakistan)	1988–90	Monitor withdrawal of Soviet Forces from Afghanistan and non-interference and non-intervention by the parties in each other's affairs (50)
UNIIMOG (UN Iran–Iraq Military Observer Group)	1988–91	Supervise the ceasefire; monitor withdrawal of all forces to recognised boundaries (400)

UNAVEM I (UN Angola Verification Mission)	1988–91	Monitor withdrawal of Cuban forces (70)
UNTAG (UN Transition Assistance Group)	1989–90	Supervise transition of Namibia to independence; organise and supervise election (8,000)
ONUCA (UN Observer Group in Central America)	1989–91	Monitor arms flows and infiltration of troops in Central America; monitor demobilisation of Nicaraguan contras; monitor Nicaraguan ceasefire and separation of forces (1,000)
UNIKOM (UN Iraq–Kuwait Observer Mission)	1991–	Monitor buffer zone along the Iraq–Kuwait border (Ch VII mandate, but not itself an enforcement operation) (1,440)
MINURSO (UN Mission for the Referendum in W. Sahara)	1991–	Conduct referendum on independence or integration with Morocco (500)
ONUSAL (UN Observer Mission in El Salvador)	1991–	Monitor human rights and verify implementation of the peace accords (1,000)
UNAVEM II (UN Angola Verification Mission II)	1991–	Monitor ceasefire and creation of new joint armed forces; observe and monitor elections (1000)
UNAMIC (UN Advance Mission in Cambodia)	1991–92	Advance mission for UNTAC
UNTAC (UN Transitional Authority in Cambodia)	1992–	Supervise government functions and elections; supervise disarmament and demobilisation of rival armies; supervise repatriation and rehabilitation of refugees; monitor human rights (22,000)
UNPROFOR (UN Protection Force) Croatia, Bosnia–Herzegovina (B–H), and Former Yugoslav Republic of Macedonia (FYRM)	1992–	Monitor ceasefire in Croatia; supervise withdrawal of Yugoslav forces; ensure UN Protected Areas demilitarised and inhabitants protected. Support UNHCR delivery of humanitarian relief in B–H, ensure security and functioning of Sarajevo airport; protect UN personnel including in the six safe areas in B–H (Ch VII mandate). Preventive deployment in FYRM (26,500)
UNOSOM (UN Operation in Somalia)	1992–93	Monitor the ceasefire; assist provision of humanitarian relief (1000)
ONUMOZ (UN Operation in Mozambique)	1992–	Verify demobilisation and disarmament of forces, and withdrawal of foreign troops; assist and monitor organisation of elections; coordinate humanitarian assistance (7,000)
UNOSOM II (UN Operation in Somalia II)	1993–	Ensure maintenance of secure environment for humanitarian relief operations (authorised under Chapter VII), including by disarmament; foster national reconciliation and restoration of national institutions (25,000)
UNOMUR (UN Observer Mission Uganda–Rwanda)	1993–	Monitor the Uganda/Rwanda border; verify non-transit of military assistance to Rwanda (105)

Notes: • Numbers deployed are indicative only, and data on civilian elements is not available in all cases. • UNOSOM II has a Ch VII peace enforcement mandate, and part of UNPROFOR's mandate is explicitly based on Ch VII, but both are treated as if they were peace keeping for UN budgeting and administrative purposes. UNIKOM, established after the Gulf War, has a Ch VII mandate, but is deployed as a peace keeping, not enforcement, operation. • As at mid-August 1993, further UN peace keeping operations were in prospect for Georgia and Liberia.

to use the Security Council to seek solutions to conflicts, and indeed less inclination to support former Cold War combatants, from Afghanistan to El Salvador. The conditions have been ripe for relatively more successful UN peace making. Diplomatic breakthroughs, with UN assistance, in South-Western Africa, between Iran and Iraq, and in Central America and Cambodia, among others, have all utilised the peace keeping option. There has been a qualitative change in the nature and function of a number of the recent peace keeping operations, in an attempt to utilise peace keeping for more than conflict management—to assist in more ambitious attempts to reach conflict resolution. Mandates have become more complex and the number, size and make-up of these peace keeping operations are of quite a different order to that experienced for the first forty years of the UN.

'Traditional peace keeping'

This has as its principal role the positioning of forces between or among combatants, to monitor, supervise and verify ceasefire and related agreements: the goal is to contain or prevent further conflict. From the beginning of peace keeping there were variations on this role, for example the sending of unarmed observers to monitor cross-border external support for one or more of the parties. Some elements of early peace keeping mandates also anticipated more complex modern roles: for example, the United Nations peace keeping force in Cyprus (UNFICYP) developed a humanitarian role in cooperation with the UNHCR and the ICRC, assisting the moment of people in both directions across the buffer zone and providing emergency medical services.

Certainly the great majority of the mandates of earlier UN peace keeping forces were less complicated and less extensive than has been the norm in recent years. The one significant exception was the UN force in the Congo (ONUC), which was sent in 1960 with a limited mandate to provide military assistance to the new government, following the country's achievement of independence, until its own security forces could meet the task, and to ensure the withdrawal of Belgian troops; following the secession of Katanga province, ONUC became a considerably more intensive undertaking, with a revised mandate including the use of force as a last resort to prevent civil war.

Since its foundation, the UN through the Security Council has been the main—almost the only—organisation developing peace keeping as a cooperative security response. Notable exceptions were the Commonwealth, which played a major role in ending the conflict in Rhodesia in the 1970s through both peace making and peace keeping, and the OAU, which has been involved in peace keeping in Chad and Liberia. The dominance of the UN in this field reflected historical circumstances as well as its mandate and standing to play such a role: most other forums for international security cooperation tended to be organised around the opposing nodes of Cold War rivalry.

Over the years, a reasonably clear set of principles—based on those originally articulated by Secretary-General Dag Hammarskjöld —has evolved to govern UN peace keeping operations. While not being fully descriptive of all the considerations which are, or should be, taken into account in deciding upon any particular operation, these at least describe certain conditions now accepted as basic:

- all parties to the conflict consent to, and are prepared to fully cooperate with, the UN's role;

- the operation has the full backing of the international community, as expressed through the support of the Security Council and broad willingness among member states to contribute troops and to finance the costs of the operation;

- the force is under UN command, with control vested in the Secretary-General acting under the authority of the Security Council;

- the force is multinational in composition, selected in consultation with the Security Council and the parties to the conflict (traditionally the permanent members of the Security Council have provided contingents only infrequently to peace keeping operations);

- peace keepers do not use force except in self-defence and carry only defensive weapons; and

- peace keepers remain completely impartial.

'Expanded peace keeping'

This describes the considerably broader, more activist, multi-functional character that peace keeping has assumed in recent years, essentially in recognition of the reality that traditional peace keeping was in the past often not enough to achieve a lasting peaceful settlement. Expanded peace keeping seeks to go far beyond traditional peace keeping by assisting the parties in implementing the settlement that they have arrived at in Stage II peace making, assisting them to bring about a genuine and durable solution. It goes well beyond those previous mandates which sometimes had the unfortunate effect of preserving a hot dispute along a ceasefire line.

The first substantial—and highly successful—expanded peace keeping operation was UNTAG in Namibia; in 1993 similar operations were in place—with varying degrees of success—in Cambodia (see

Box 5), Angola, El Salvador, Mozambique and Western Sahara. The range of functions carried out in these kinds of operations has been conveniently summarised by the UK House of Commons Foreign Affairs Committee in a recent report:

> *Military:* monitoring ceasefires, cantonment and demobilisation of troops, location and destruction of weapons, de-mining, reform and retraining of armed forces, protecting borders, investigating claims of the presence of foreign forces, providing security for elections and helping rebuild infrastructure.
>
> *Police:* visiting police stations, monitoring police activities, investigating alleged human rights violations by national police forces, training new police forces, enforcing arrests of suspected criminals and protecting the electoral process.
>
> *Human rights:* monitoring human rights, conducting human rights education programs and investigating human rights violations.
>
> *Information:* explaining the peace settlement, the reasons for the UN deployment and the opportunities for the future of the country.
>
> *Elections:* the UN's involvement can range from simple observation and verification, through supervision and control of nationally conducted elections up to the organisation and conduct of elections by the UN itself.
>
> *Rehabilitation:* the UN has helped in many cases to rehabilitate and reconstruct a state, both in the short term and through longer-term development projects.
>
> *Repatriation:* the UN has arranged for the return and resettlement of hundreds of thousands of refugees.
>
> *Administration:* supervising or controlling the administration within states. The UN Transitional Authority in Cambodia (UNTAC), for instance, was mandated to control foreign affairs, national defence, public security, finance and information in an attempt to create, sustain and monitor a neutral political environment for elections to take place. (Para. 35)

The more recently established peace keeping operations have frequently been involved in facilitating the resolution of intra-state conflict—domestic conflicts or civil wars—stemming either from ethnically-based disputes, internal political struggle or the collapse of state institutions, with restoration of stable democratic government being in several cases an express aim. Although each one of these conflicts has arguably had at least some international implication to justify UN involvement, there is no doubt that since the end of the Cold War the UN has been much more involved than in the past in what are primarily internal conflicts.

A significant consequence of the different nature of the conflicts in which UN peace keepers now play a role is that they are often keeping the peace between non-state actors such as armed factions and political movements, or a combination of governments and such actors. This is more challenging, in part because of the complexity of multi-sided disputes and conflicts, but also because it is harder to influence, let alone compel, non-government parties to respect the UN's role. Not only do such actors feel little or no obligation to observe the principles of the Charter and the letter of Security Council resolutions, but they are often less disciplined than government forces. The commitment of their leaders to agreements can therefore have less effect on what happens in the field. Local groups may not abide by ceasefire, cantonment or other agreements or arrangements reached by their nominal leaders.

The result is that the environment for peace keeping is no longer benign. Mandates may include protecting civilians in an area of conflict rather than simply aiming to prevent or contain the conflict; and peace keepers increasingly work in a climate of continuing armed conflict, sometimes where there are no defined borders or ceasefire lines and no guarantee of respect for their safety or role.

These considerations, together with the ever-growing pressure on scarce UN resources, make it more imperative than ever to think clearly about *when* and *how* the UN should become involved in peace keeping operations. It is to these questions that we now turn.

When peace keepers should be deployed

There are those who fear that setting out criteria for deciding when to deploy peace keepers may hinder flexibility in determining the best response to each situation. There is, however, a strong case for doing so given the burgeoning demand on the UN for peace keeping and the much greater complexity of situations in which the UN is willing to consider peace keeping. At the same time, it has to be acknowledged that no list of criteria can be so complete or precise as to give unequivocal and universally acceptable guidance in every situation. There will always be a strong ad hoc element in the international community's response to particular conflicts, and it is pointless to pretend otherwise.

In particular, the question of how much of an 'international' character intra-state conflict should have in order to justify UN involvement is almost impossible to answer. Whether the Security Council will require evidence of direct external involvement with the conflict (as in Cambodia); 'spill-over' effects (usually in the form of refugee flows to neighbouring countries, as in Cambodia, Somalia and with the Kurds in Iraq); or more generalised 'regional destabilisation', as in Somalia and the former Yugoslavia; or something even less than that, will depend essentially on the balance of interests at stake, and

5. Cambodia 1992–1993: a flawed but successful expanded peace keeping operation

The problem: Hitherto tranquil Cambodia had suffered grievously since 1969 through a cycle of war, civil war, genocide, invasion and civil war again. Following Vietnam's invasion in December 1978, the international community was faced with a country under an externally imposed administration, opposed militarily by three factions—one of them the Khmer Rouge—operating from Thailand. The civil war that ensued, and related economic hardships, caused the exodus of nearly 400,000 Cambodians. The situation had particular international significance because each of the factions had powerful external backing. The situation had the potential to destabilise the region. Vietnam withdrew its military presence from Cambodia in late 1989, at a time of global geopolitical realignment. Meaningful negotiations between the factions began at this time.

The response: During the late 1980s, several international meetings were held in an attempt to resolve the conflict, culminating in the First Paris Conference in mid-1989. While this failed to achieve a comprehensive settlement, it mapped out a broad strategy, which subsequently faltered on the proposed four-faction composition of the transitional administration. To break this impasse, Australia put forward the 'Red Book' peace proposal which advocated that the UN itself assume direct control of the civil administration during a transitional period enabling elections to be held, a constitution adopted and a new government formed. The plan was taken up by the Permanent Five. After a hiatus, agreement on the plan was reached in mid-1991, with the final agreements signed at the Second Paris Conference in October 1991.

The UNTAC mission was the UN's most ambitious and complex peace keeping operation. During the eighteen months of the operation, repatriation of nearly 370,000 displaced persons from the Thai border was completed successfully, all political prisoners were released, and political parties were established and were able to operate and campaign widely and with a degree of security. The UN-organised elections were held without serious incident and with massive popular participation, leading to the establishment of a provisional government linking all parties who won seats. Cantonment, disarming and demobilisation did not take place because of the refusal of the Khmer Rouge to participate in the peace process after June 1992.

The success of the elections has given Cambodia its first real chance in over twenty years to escape from civil war and political repression and to build a stable and prosperous country. But there were unquestionably flaws in the UNTAC operations: tardy deployment undermined the aims of the mission from the outset; a neutral political environment was never really established; civil administration 'control' over key areas of government was by no means fully achieved; the civilian police element was, with some conspicuous exceptions, ineffective; and prosecution of human rights abuses proved impossible.

The lessons:

- Senior staff, both civilian and military, must be chosen early and involved with the planning of the operation. The Secretariat needs to establish or strengthen planning units for specific components—police, human rights, electoral, military—and achieve a greater integration between planning and operations.

- Deployment must take place as soon as possible after the parties to a conflict have reached agreement so as to build confidence and show that the UN is serious.

- The UN and member states must ensure that they provide the best qualified personnel: pre-deployment training to a common UN standard, where this is lacking, is essential.

- The UN must develop efficient, streamlined administrative procedures to support peace keeping operations particularly with regard to budget allocation.

- Communication between the force and the UN Secretariat must be strengthened with the Secretariat responding rapidly to force recommendations or requests.

- The operation again highlighted the risk to a peace keeping operation if one of the parties to a settlement reneges on its commitments, although in the event this was not enough either to abort or seriously deflect the achievement of the operation's basic mission.

the general mood of the moment. As with the question of the 'right of humanitarian intervention', which we shall address in detail in a later chapter, one factor which will undoubtedly in practice influence judgement—although it does not have much to do with the 'international' character or otherwise of the conflict—is the scale of the suffering that has been involved in the conflict, and that is likely to be alleviated by a successful peace keeping operation: the 'conscience shock' factor. At the end of the day, however, it has to be frankly acknowledged that, in the context of peace keeping as elsewhere, what is a matter of 'international' peace and security is what the Security Council is prepared to regard as such.

But if there are limits to how much certainty can be injected into some decision-making criteria, so too is there scope for being rather more precise than we have tended to be in the past in defining the necessary conditions for a peace keeping operation to be effective. The decision to deploy a peace keeping force should never be one made just for the sake of doing, or being seen to do, something: at the very least a hard-headed assessment should be made as to whether what the operation is supposed to be doing is worth doing, and whether it is capable of doing it. (This consideration applies, of course, with even more force to peace enforcement operations, where the stakes are higher still.) Although it is not always possible, in the real world rush of events, to analyse or predict with certainty, it should be possible at least to avoid embarking upon operations which are manifestly likely to be ineffective, and as such put at risk the most crucial UN resource of all—its credibility.

Conditions for effective peace keeping.

There are seven basic conditions for ensuring an effective peace keeping operation: clear and achievable goals; adequate resources; close coordination of peace keeping with peace making; impartiality; local support; external support; and a signposted exit.

Clear and achievable goals   These are essential, not least to avoid unrealistic or ill-founded expectations of the UN's role as peace keeper.   In practice, disagreement within the Security Council has sometimes resulted in vagueness or ambiguity about the purpose of deploying peace keepers. If there is no agreement among decision-makers on goals, peace keeping commitments should not be made. It is sometimes argued that precise language is not the friend of diplomatic compromise. Yet for peace keeping, as for any military operation, force commanders need clearly stated goals, translated into precise and practicable mandates capable of implementation.   The willingness of governments to commit personnel may well depend on the feasibility of mandates. More generally, it has to be constantly remembered that the credibility of the Security Council as an authoritative body will progressively be undermined by passing unachievable mandates to satisfy political imperatives.

Adequate resources   The UN is being called on to undertake more peace keeping than ever before, often in the more complex expanded type of operation. At the same time the UN faces increasing reluctance, or incapacity, on the part of member states to contribute money and troops. Demonstrable will, and capacity to deploy sufficient peace keepers in strength, should be a precondition for any decision to establish a new peace keeping operation. Tasks such as containment or the disarming of belligerents, for which demonstration of authority is essential, require significantly more military strength than traditional peace keeping. An early display of strength, moreover, may well obviate the need to resort to force to maintain peace keeping and peace making authority. There may also be a case for adding capacities which were not called upon in traditional peace keeping, such as more sophisticated forms of surveillance.

UNTAC's experience in Cambodia identified one area where, in some operations, more resources may be needed than have been provided in the past, ie the provision of a functioning criminal justice system (not only during the peace keeping process, but indeed beyond it, as we have suggested already in our discussion of post-conflict peace building). What may be required here are any or all of the following: a body of applicable law; an effective police force; an independent judiciary; prosecutors and defenders; correctional facilities; and gaolers. The point is simply that if a peace keeping force is given a mandate to guard against human rights violations, but there is no functioning system to bring violators to justice—even those who violate others' right to life—then not only is the UN force's mandate to that extent unachievable, but its whole operation is likely to lose credibility.

Close coordination of peace keeping with peace making activity
This is required if peace keeping is to play its role in helping achieve a lasting settlement. Effective peace making can establish a ceasefire, at which point peace keepers may enter to play either a traditional or expanded peace keeping role. The task of the peace makers has not, however, ended. With peace keepers stabilising and cooling the situation further, they can work with the parties to negotiate additional agreements and arrangements to bring the conflict even closer to settlement. The peace keepers may extend their role to cantonment, disarmament and demobilisation of belligerents if the parties have agreed to any or all of these additional steps. Throughout, the peace keepers may be protecting aid workers as the peace makers secure agreements to the provision of humanitarian assistance. If the peace makers fail to secure a lasting settlement, the peace keepers may become trapped between the parties.

Impartiality   This is an essential requirement for peace keepers. In some recent peace keeping operations, conventional understandings about impartiality and the use of force have been challenged and attenuated, in part as a result of the more active role peace keepers are playing. The more complex the situation, the more difficult the challenge of retaining the confidence of all the parties. In many situations the parties may try to use the UN's presence to advance their own goals, particularly in the absence of a clear process of reconciliation or when the parties have differing interests in the outcome of such a process. The elections which peace keeping forces have helped make possible produce winners and losers. Recent experience has shown that those who have entered a political agreement often overestimate the extent of their popular support: the reaction of the loser all too often is to depict the UN as favouring the other side.

It is not only a matter of peace keepers working hard to *be* impartial; they must be *seen* to be. It is increasingly important that, where peace keepers are involved in an intra-state conflict, the UN work on its image of impartiality in the eyes of local populations by explaining clearly the role of the peace keepers when they first arrive and by giving priority to developing the best possible relations with local communities. An active and imaginative public information effort is an essential tool in this task.

Local support   This is crucial to the success of a peace keeping force within any country. Consent and full cooperation may be qualified, especially in the case of multi-sided internal conflicts. In these cases majority support among the population and leadership is the best that may, by definition, be achieved. But significant local support must still be a condition for the deployment of a peace keeping force. If all parties are to remain committed to an agreement on which deployment of a force has been based, they will need to believe that their interests are served by that agreement. The UN has much experience in assessing this with unequivocally international agreements, but is very much less experienced when it comes to conflicts which have few if any international dimensions, like that in Somalia.

There are several recent examples of the problems faced by a peace keeping force when local support for peace keeping is in question from the outset, or, as happens more often, when one of the major parties to an agreement has turned against the presence of the force: Cambodia, Somalia, former Yugoslavia and Angola have all confronted the UN with this kind of problem. There has been much debate about whether the mandate for the peace keeping force, which would normally be under Chapter VI of the Charter, can continue to be adequate in these circumstances. What is the appropriate role for peace keepers in the resulting grey area between peace keeping and peace enforcement?

If a UN peace keeping force finds itself losing support from one or more parties to the extent that it is clearly unable to fulfil its original purpose without going on the offensive militarily, then the UN has crossed the line from a peace keeping to a potential peace enforcement situation and must re-evaluate its response by reference to the criteria appropriate to the latter. Sometimes the situation will be more ambiguous—as in Cambodia after the withdrawal of the Khmer Rouge from the peace process. The basic options, in either event, will be, first, to change the peace keeping nature of the force's mandate to peace enforcement, recognising that any mid-stream change of this kind is likely to cause major problems for the troop contributors; secondly, to soldier on in a peace keeping role, re-emphasising the peace making function, at the risk both of physical danger to the peace keeping force and of the peace process becoming bogged down indefinitely; or, thirdly, to withdraw.

The UN has usually been reluctant to withdraw, preferring to adjust the nature of the peace keeping operation and its mandate: Cambodia is a clear and (as things turned out) successful example of soldiering on. The trouble is that the adjustments made to peace keeping operations have sometimes been more political or diplomatic than of a practical kind enabling the peace keeping force to effectively meets its goals: in Bosnia–Herzegovina, for example, the strengthening of UNPROFOR's mandate in May 1993 to protect six 'safe areas' seems to have had more to do with symbolism than any realistic military assessment of practical efficacy. In the face of multiple international demands for peace keeping resources, and the cost to the UN's credibility of continuing indefinitely an ineffectual involvement, the UN needs to give serious thought to pulling out of certain situations, ie where a peace keeping force has lost local support to the extent that, even if the force is not in physical danger, it is unable to fulfil its purpose.

Whether withdrawal is the best option in these cases depends essentially on whether a renewed effort at peace making is likely to be productive. It may be that a complete reappraisal of the conflict is required at this stage, with new thinking about the kinds of incentives that may be necessary to make resolution of the complaint attractive to all parties: both the original peace makers and the peace keepers have an important contribution to make in this exercise, not least in doing everything possible to win back support for the international process from all those it is designed to help. In most cases, there is probably a limit to the number of times the peace making 'well' can be productively revisited. The stakes will be so high in some conflicts—eg that between Israel and its neighbours—that there is probably no alternative to soldiering on indefinitely. But elsewhere there will come a time when the UN, to preserve its credibility and conserve its resources, may simply have to acknowledge failure and withdraw.

External support   There must be evident support for the peace keeping process from those external powers—whether major powers, regional powers or neighbours—who may previously have been involved in supporting one side or another in the conflict in question. For peace keeping to be a viable option, there must be some guarantee that the outside backers and suppliers of the warring parties will end their support for non-peaceful actions. In Cambodia, one reason for the success in holding elections was that the external backers of the various factions pressed the parties not to return to violence. In contrast, the failure of elections in Angola to end the conflict there appears to have been in part the result of continuing external support for one of the parties, and lack of pressure on the leader of one of this group from his external backers to accept a democratic outcome.

The express endorsement by regional organisations of a particular peace keeping operation will provide important political reinforcement from countries which are likely to be most directly affected. States which contribute troops to a given peace keeping effort, whether within their own region or elsewhere, will obviously also draw strength from an express declaration of regional support wherever they are operating.

The existence of the veto power in the Security Council has in practical terms meant that the interests of the five permanent members of the Council must also be satisfied, or at a minimum not be threatened, by UN involvement. Since the end of the Cold War, however, and the increasingly good working relationship among the five permanent members, this has become less of a problem and should allow future Council deliberations to come closer to the ideal of consistency of response discussed in Chapter 1.

Signposted exit   Every peace keeping mandate should have a clearly designated termination point, or set of termination criteria. In the interests of maintaining the effectiveness and credibility of its total peace support effort, the UN has to know not only when and how to get into peace operations, but when and how to get out of them. As peace keeping forces become larger and take on more challenging roles, it becomes more and more important that there be consideration from the outset as to when and how the operation will end. The valid concerns of troop contributors about open-ended commitments are a factor. So that mandate renewal does not come to be routine, as it largely has been in the past, mandates could include an explicit sunset clause, or at least identify 'milestones' to be observed in the process of reconciliation and dispute settlement to allow for the scaling down and then withdrawal of a force. The staggered deployment of peace keepers to Namibia—and as planned for MINURSO—is one way of tying steps in the commitment of peace keepers to successful steps in the peace making process, testing and demonstrating along the way the continuing willingness of the parties to reach a solution.

In establishing when and how a peace keeping operation should end, it may be necessary to do more than identify a single event which will signal the departure of the force. As Angola (see Box 6) demonstrated, staging a model election is not sufficient if the parties do not accept the outcome. Peace keeping in many situations has assumed the role of supporting a process of internal national reconciliation. In these situations, the UN and its peace makers must not only ensure follow through on the ceasefires, elections, referendums or acts of self-determination which the peace keepers are mandated to administer or observe, but have a keen eye for the arrangements being contemplated for institution rebuilding and general national reconstruction.

Without such arrangements being negotiated and put in place, peace keeping may not have any enduring effect. In the case of Angola, there was little attempt to give the party which had lost the election a stake in the new government. In contrast, in Cambodia the parties which contested the election have worked out arrangements which give the strongest factions reason to remain committed to peaceful means of pursuing their goals within a new Cambodian state.

The UN cannot always guarantee such outcomes but it can encourage reconciliation. Timely plans for post-conflict peace building should complement the role of peace keeping forces and will facilitate their timely withdrawal. In this sense, decisions about creating a peace keeping force should be linked from the beginning, if at all possible, not only with peace making but also with the securing of commitments to post-conflict peace building, eg the creation of a functioning criminal justice system. Unless a comprehensive and integrated approach is adopted, there will be a high risk of failure.

Who decides?

The *Security Council* has the responsibility under the UN Charter for maintaining international peace and security and it continues to be the central body for determining when peace keeping is the appropriate response to an international security problem. While the UN Charter does not refer expressly to peace keeping, the practices developed under it have established the Council's authority in this area. Of the 28 UN peace keeping operations, about a quarter were the result of a direct Council initiative. The rest were responses by it to requests for UN assistance by the parties to a conflict or arose from agreements brokered by third parties which sought UN and Security Council assistance in implementing them. The Council's role is therefore not in question. What is at issue is whether the Council's composition and decision-making procedures should be reviewed, and whether there

6. Angola since 1991 : peace keeping under strain

The problem and UN response: Angola has long suffered civil war, with rival factions supported by external powers, Cuba/Soviet Union and South Africa/United States respectively. Improved superpower relations in the late 1980s provided the conditions for progress in the peace process and in 1988 UNAVEM was established to verify the agreed withdrawal of Cuban troops. In the 1991 Bicesse Peace Accords, the parties agreed to a ceasefire, demobilisation of troops and multi-party elections, and a relatively small peace keeping operation, UNAVEM II, was established to monitor and verify the implementation of the ceasefire, demobilisation and confinement of troops and selection of troops for the new Angolan Armed Forces. In 1992, UNAVEM II was further mandated to observe and verify the elections. The opposition movement, UNITA, was not committed to fulfilling the agreements under the Accords and refused to disarm or withdraw from occupied areas. The elections were held in September 1992 and the ruling MPLA was elected. UNITA has refused to accept the election result and has resumed the civil war. Since the resumption of civil war, the mandate for UNAVEM II has been periodically renewed but the operation remains in a reduced holding pattern, concentrated in Luanda. An enlarged UNAVEM II has been proposed by participants in negotiations to assist re-establishment of the Bicesse Accords following a ceasefire.

The lessons:

- UNAVEM II was inadequately resourced to fulfil its mandate. With only 350 military observers, 90 police, a civilian air unit, a medical unit, 90 international and 120 local civilian staff, it was unable to monitor and verify the demobilisation/confinement process. The addition of 400 election observers and 36 police was equally inadequate to establish a credible presence for the UN during the election (UNTAG in Namibia had 6,000 elections observers), although there was international acceptance that the election was free and fair.

- Even with adequate resources, UNAVEM II could not have achieved what the peace making process had not. Years of external support for UNITA probably contributed to its unwillingness to accept the election result. More pressure on UNITA by its former international backers to cooperate may have made the peace process more effective. Agreement in the peace process to form a Government of National Unity may have been more workable than proceeding with an early election.

- The failure of the peace process has left UNAVEM II without a role and the UN with diminished credibility in Angola. An expanded UNAVEM II would need to be based on a more sustainable peace agreement, with the UN putting significant effort into peace making as well as peace keeping.

are other bodies which could also legitimately participate in decisions on peace keeping.

Increasing attention is being focused on the Council's representativeness. Effectiveness and legitimacy are closely inter-related in considering the Council's role in peace keeping. Its decisions ultimately depend for their effect on the extent of international support, which will in turn be influenced by the degree to which the Council is perceived to be adequately representative of the overall UN membership and to reflect the realities of global and regional power. To retain its legitimacy, the Council must be seen to have a global range and to be willing to turn its attention to conflicts and threats to international peace and security whenever the situation requires, rather than in accordance with the dictates of the national interests of individual Council members. Peace keeping remains a multinational enterprise, and broad support from all regions is essential for the UN to continue to assemble and fund peace keeping forces.

Security Council reform should address not only the issue of representativeness, but also the need to enhance decision-making procedures. The Council's decision-making must be prompt and effective, as required by the Charter and by the exigencies of responding to situations of armed conflict. There are practical limits therefore on the efficient size of the Council. If it is too large, the timeliness of its responses could suffer. The ability of the Security Council to respond effectively to demands for peace keeping must also be built upon several layers of consultation: most intensively among all the Council members themselves; regularly with member states outside the Council and regional groups whose interests are affected by a particular issue before it; and broadly from time to time with the whole membership of the United Nations. In the case of issues which have a peace keeping dimension, troop contributing countries should be consulted as a matter of course on all matters which have a bearing on their contingents.

Individual governments and groups of governments have occasionally established multinational peace keeping operations without reference to the UN. This has not displaced the UN as the key peace keeping body and reflects historical factors, including the inability of the Security Council to reach agreement on some issues at certain periods. For example, the United States-organised Multinational Force deployments (MNF I and II) in Lebanon from 1982 to 1984 and the Multinational Force and Observers (MFO) in the Sinai from 1982 to the present were devised partly because of the difficulty of acting through the Security Council. In a few cases, regional countries have acted either from a wish to deal with a problem without recourse to the

UN or because they have judged the UN response inadequate or likely to be so. It would unnecessarily restrict the margin for constructive responses to security problems if all peace keeping operations were required to be under the UN's umbrella. They should, however, be consistent with UN actions.

There is no consistent pattern amongst *regional organisations* in their capacity for undertaking peace keeping. A few, such as the Organization of American States (OAS), have both a mandate and some experience in mounting peace keeping operations. Others such as NATO have the capacity, but it is not clear that all their members want the organisation to develop a peace keeping role. Most face serious limitations in taking peace keeping initiatives as a result of a variety of constraints, including cost, mandate and authority, aversion to military responses and the difficulty of being accepted as an objective neutral actor. The fact that the UN can levy assessed contributions towards peace keeping costs, and has the demonstrated ability to assemble multinational peace keeping forces, is itself sufficient reason to expect that regional organisations will continue to look largely to the UN to organise most peace keeping forces.

Nonetheless, given that the UN is already overstretched in meeting peace keeping demands, there is a case for regional organisations carrying out more peace keeping, especially in some cases where their capacity to do so is not in question. In *An Agenda for Peace* the Secretary-General notes the potential for joint undertakings so that regional organisations would be assured of international support. He also points to the option, provided for in Article 52 of the Charter, of the Security Council authorising a regional arrangement or organisation to take the lead in promoting peaceful settlement of local disputes.

Who pays?

It has long been accepted that it is the collective responsibility of all member states to fund UN peace keeping. This should continue to be the guiding principle for reasons of equity and efficiency. Peace keeping has developed as one of the UN's core tasks and its costs should be met as expenses of the organisation under Article 17.2 of the Charter and hence be met by assessed contributions of all member states. The system since 1960 of adjusting levels of payment to take account of the greater capacity to pay of wealthier countries remains relevant for the 1990s and should continue.

There may be cases where the parties to a conflict could reasonably be expected to contribute to the costs of a peace keeping force either immediately or over time. Kuwait, for example, has offered to voluntarily contribute two-thirds of the costs of UNIKOM and in the case of UNFICYP, the Governments of Cyprus and Greece have agreed to voluntarily fund half the cost of the operation. Asking parties to a conflict to contribute to the costs of peace keeping may even be a way of bringing more pressure on the parties to a conflict to move to a peaceful settlement. This could be done by creation of a scale of gradually increasing contributions by the parties to the cost of peace keeping. It would be difficult to apply this as a general rule, given the possible incapacity of some states to pay a higher amount than their assessed contributions. There will also always be a need to avoid creating excuses for the parties to back away from previous ceasefire agreements on the grounds that they cannot meet a greater share of the peace keeping costs.

Applying burden-sharing to the peace keeping operations of regional bodies is more problematic. There will be some understandable reluctance on the part of the collectivity of UN member states for the UN to subsidise peace keeping measures decided upon and pursued by countries in a particular region. The guiding rule could be that the cost of peace keeping mandated by the UN, or mounted by a regional organisation at the UN's request, should be borne by the UN. Other operations should be financed by the members of the organisation or coalition which has agreed to establish the peace keeping force.

The question of who pays for peace keeping should be kept in context. The peace keeping bill must be compared with the potential much larger cost of *not* undertaking peace keeping. Conflict not only has direct financial, human and infrastructure costs which are likely to outweigh considerably the UN's peace keeping budget in a particular situation; it also brings significant indirect costs in terms of lost economic opportunities and the generation of refugee flows. It is useful to compare what states are prepared to spend on armaments with their UN peace keeping costs. It has been estimated that, in the late 1980s, the five Security Council permanent members spent about $2,400 to buy arms for every dollar they spent on UN peace keeping; the Group B (industrialised) countries spent an average of $750 on arms for every peace keeping dollar; the Group C (developing) countries averaged $20,000 for each dollar; and the 78 least developed countries in Group D averaged $40,000 expenditure on arms for every dollar they contributed to UN peace keeping costs.

The biggest problem facing the financing of UN peace keeping is that member states are constantly in arrears in meeting their assessed contributions, which are mandatory, under Article 17 of the Charter. In August 1993, the UN peace keeping budget had over $1 billion outstanding. This, in turn, causes a backlog of some years in UN reimbursements to member states for the costs of contributing forces to peace keeping operations, which is beginning to erode the ability of member states to agree to UN requests for troops. The problem has arisen in part because of the dramatic increase in financing requirements for the significant increase in the number, size and complexity of peace keeping operations in recent years. The total cost of peace keeping has risen from $400 million in 1991 to an estimated $3.7 billion in 1993, a considerable sum in comparison with the size of the UN's regular budget of just over $1 billion for 1993 and total assessed contributions for the specialised agencies of around $1.7 billion.

But peace keeping remains less expensive than peace enforcement. The enforcement operation against Iraq in the Gulf War, funded by a coalition of member states, is estimated to have cost well over $70 billion. When the UN establishes operations with a peace enforcement mandate, it does not have resources of that scale. UNOSOM II, the only comprehensive UN peace enforcement operation (but which is grouped here with the peace keeping operations as it is also financed by assessed contributions) will cost an estimated $1.2 billion in its first twelve months, but this is an operation which does not require the deployment of massive force on the scale of an enforcement action against an aggressor state, such as in the Gulf War.

The financing of peace keeping needs to be put on a firmer and more predictable footing, consistent with the contribution it makes to the UN's role of maintaining international peace and security. The new consensus in the Security Council and throughout the UN membership on an enhanced security role for the UN should allow the financial question to be seriously addressed. The only completely satisfactory solution to the financing deficit is for all member states to pay their contributions in full and on time, but there are other options which could also enhance the efficiency of peace keeping financing and streamline costs.

Delays in start-up financing have set back the timetable of deployment for peace keeping operations, as in the recent case of ONUMOZ. Such delays are undesirable both for the implementation of peace agreements and in ensuring adequate safety of UN personnel. To better assure rapid deployment, the Peace Keeping Reserve Fund, which is currently called upon heavily by 'borrowing' from on-going peace keeping operations, should be dedicated to the start-up costs of new peace keeping operations, which was envisaged to be its primary role when the Fund was established. Given the rapid increase in peace keeping costs, there is also a good argument for an increase in the size of the Reserve Fund, from $150 million to closer to the $400 million proposed by the 1993 Volcker-Ogata Report on *Financing an Effective United Nations*. It has been proposed that the Secretary-General should have discretion to spend a greater proportion of the estimated cost for each operation before the General Assembly's approval of its budget is finalised.

A more comprehensive solution for streamlining financing of peace keeping would be to establish a unified budget for UN peace keeping, with separate line items for each peace keeping operation. A unified budget would allow the Secretary-General much more flexibility in financing the rapid deployment, as well as on-going funding, of peace keeping operations. It would remove the current problems caused by delayed approvals. It would save considerably on the administration of numerous and diverse peace keeping operation budgets. While the budget of each peace keeping operation would still require financial scrutiny and dedicated management, a unified budget would allow the Secretariat to replace the current multi-billing process with an annual billing system for member states' assessed contributions. Unanticipated costs could be met by one annual supplementary assessment mid-year; unanticipated savings could be reimbursed or credited against future assessments. The expansion of one operation could be offset by the contraction of another. The present system of assessments arriving at unpredictable intervals is inefficient and causes problems for member states in providing the required funds in the requested period, as the assessments do not coincide with national budget processes. A unified budget may therefore encourage better national budget planning and more prompt payment. Mandate periods, which are currently six months in most cases, would not need to be affected by an annual unified budget but there may be a case for annual budgetary planning for some peace keeping operations which are clearly expected to remain in place over more than a twelve month period.

A number of other proposals have been made, in an attempt to address the peace keeping financial problem: the endorsement of commercial borrowing by the Secretary-General; a levy on arms sales as listed in the Arms Register; a levy on international air tickets; tax exemptions for private contributions to the UN; and changes to the assessments scale. All of these warrant careful study—but the greatest need is for member states to accept their collective responsibility to meet their share of the costs of peace keeping, and to pay their contributions in full and on time.

The organisation and management of peace keeping operations

The United Nations currently faces a daunting task in organising and managing peace keeping operations at a time when demands for peace keeping have never been higher. It is widely recognised that the United Nations is, as a result, badly overstretched and that its organisational structures and systems, resources and procedures are no longer adequate to meet the demands of the increased number, size and complexity of such operations.

Improving headquarters organisation and planning

In response to these challenges, the UN Secretariat has already undertaken some significant changes. A new, enlarged Department of Peace Operations has been established, bringing all UN field missions, including relevant elements of logistics and procurement, under the one coordinating wing; there has been a modest expansion in overall staffing levels; a 24-hour situation room has been established; a start has been made with dedicated military planning staff; experts in training, mine clearance and civilian police operations have been recruited; steps have been taken to improve the flow of information between the Department and member states, in particular troop contributors; some countries have posted military representatives to New York to liaise with the Secretariat on peace keeping; and work has begun to develop a comprehensive UN manual on logistics policies and procedures. All this is very positive.

Much more is nevertheless required to equip the UN to organise and administer peace keeping operations effectively to meet present day demands and challenges. This will be necessary whether or not there is more selective resort to peace keeping. The overall numbers of peace keepers in the field, and the complexity of mandates, is not likely to fall to pre-1990 levels. There is now enough recent experience—particularly from Namibia, Cambodia, Somalia, the former Yugoslavia and Angola—to make sensible choices about the most practical and effective ways to organise peace keeping. We must ensure that the implementation of peace keeping works according to plan, in support of the peace process, and that problems associated with means do not become confused with ends.

Given the spotlight that continues to play on these issues, there is a case for a thorough review of the way that the UN Secretariat is resourced and organised to meet its peace keeping responsibilities. This might best be commissioned externally, given the huge day to day time pressures on senior UN personnel. Such a review could examine, in particular, whether the current centralised system for managing and supporting peace keeping operations is still appropriate or effective given their increased number, size and complexity. An alternative is a more decentralised system in which broad political, operational, administrative and financial direction and oversight is provided from New York while Special Representatives and force commanders would be given the funds, the staff and the day to day authority to run their missions in a more autonomous manner. The Headquarters Secretariat could then divest itself of much of the detail which threatens to overload New York personnel and concentrate instead on developing policy focused guidance for the field, and effective policy oversight of operations.

Such a review could also examine ways of simplifying the multiple lines of authority from individual peace keeping forces to different senior officials in the Headquarters Secretariat; integrating closely-related functions such as recruitment of civilian and military components which are currently handled by distinct areas of the Secretariat; more closely coordinating those planning and implementing peace keeping operations with the peace makers in the Secretary General's Office and the Department of Political Affairs; and creating an enhanced capacity for professional military assessment, advice and planning in the Secretariat.

The UN for the most of its history has been diffident about developing the military aspects of the Charter. In the field of peace keeping it has been cautious in the extreme about divesting any control to force commanders in the field. The challenges of contemporary peace keeping require that a greater place be found for professional military advice in decisions about peace keeping deployment and in operating the forces. A priority is to secure military staff with specific skills in areas such as planning and logistics. Military familiar with the countries and situations—and languages—where forces are currently deployed are also necessary. While the strengthening of the Secretariat's military capacity can come through recruitment to new posts, its military expertise can be further strengthened by short-term secondments from member states, particularly from those countries which are current or prospective troop contributors.

There has been a rapid growth in the size of the civilian components of recent peace keeping operations. This means that the Secretariat will also need to strengthen civilian functions when planning and implementing peace keeping, and to give priority to obtaining civilian as well as military contingents from member states. In particular, key civilian staff need to be selected early and should be involved in pre-deployment planning. This could be assisted by greater coordination between the planning personnel in the Department of Peace Operations and the Department of Administration and Management, responsible for civilian recruitment. To strengthen the civilian functions of peace keeping, there is scope to do more to exploit expertise outside the UN system, eg through commercial service contracts, as well as that in the specialised agencies and other developmental bodies. There will also be a reserve of expertise in non-government organisations (NGOs) with programs operating in countries to which the UN plans to send peace keepers. NGOs should be consulted and, where this is possible without compromising their impartiality, their advice and capacities should be utilised by peace keeping operations.

A particular issue arises with civilian police personnel. We have already emphasised how the deployment of police with training as well as law enforcement responsibilities can play a crucial role in peace keeping and post-conflict peace building exercises in countries where the rule of law, and the institutions needed to support it, have manifestly broken down. However, the UN has found it difficult to recruit sufficient police personnel for its operations in the past and there is no standardised training for police personnel in peace keeping operations. UN police must be trained in international service, as there will be significant differences between local situations and the often relatively anarchic situations in which expanded peace keeping operations are now deployed. In order for UN police to exercise full police powers in such circumstances they will also have to be deployed in substantial numbers. The UN should seek to develop a roster of national police capabilities available for these various operations and develop standardised training material.

The capacity of the UN Secretariat to plan peace keeping operations has been under great strain. By necessity planning has been reactive as the Secretariat has responded to a rapidly evolving agenda and a large and growing number of conflict zones in which peace keeping is contemplated. The need for planning to be comprehensive and to integrate fully all aspects of peace keeping deployment highlights the need for a central planning office in the Secretariat. The challenge is to establish the capacity to develop timely plans which coherently combine political, military and logistic aspects.

Recent experience has shown how inadequate planning for logistics and procurement has hampered the timely deployment of peace keeping operations—Namibia and Somalia are two examples of slow deployment causing serious problems. Sometimes peace keeping operations have been deployed without adequate logistics systems in place for weeks and even several months. Imprecise planning has also often led to major revisions of plans and budgets as the result of later changes of mind or revision of costings by the Security Council and budgetary bodies. One reason for this has been the lack of information about the situation into which peace keepers are to be deployed. There is equally a need for the UN to develop the capacity to evaluate and learn from the experience of previous peace keeping forces and to feed this analysis back into planning for present and future forces. Giving planning staff first-hand experience of peace keeping operations could help to improve both planning and execution.

We support, as a first step, expanding the small planning cell that has been established under the Under Secretary-General for Peace Operations to a larger office, combining military and civilian planners, with sufficient staff to be able to meet simultaneous demands promptly and to plan for the multi-dimensional operations characteristic of expanded peace keeping. This office should include financial experts with the experience and standing to ensure that the plans presented to the Security Council and for budgetary approval through review bodies and the General Assembly stand up to scrutiny; we do not think it is appropriate to continue to rely on the UN Budget Office for the preparation of the financial aspects of operations, the cost of which in total greatly exceed the UN's regular budget.

In order to give the UN a sustainable capacity to plan and manage peace keeping, a more long term solution would be the creation of a UN General Staff for Peace Operations, selected from middle and high-ranking officers from member states' military forces and civilians with suitable expertise. Members of the General Staff would comprise permanent UN officers, officers seconded from governments and, in times of greater demand, a 'surge' capacity of officers provided by governments, who would work according to high professional standards and create in the Secretariat and in field headquarters a larger pool of expertise and experience.

Improving Implementation in the Field

Assembling forces With the increase in the number of peace keepers in the field, from about 11,000 at the beginning of 1992 to some 82 000 in 1993, the problems facing the Secretariat in assembling new peace keeping forces are of a different and far greater order than in previous years. In *An Agenda for Peace*, the Secretary-General pointed to the increasing difficulty of obtaining specialised forces, such as air and ground transport, logistics, communications, engineering and medical units, to meet commitments being made by the Security Council. A characteristic problem of peace keeping has been one of timely deployment. This has a political aspect, in that decisions to deploy peace keepers have sometimes been taken too late. There are also practical problems limiting the capacity for timely deployment of peace keeping forces, to which there are a number of possible solutions. The scale of the new problems requires exploration of new approaches.

Each operation has its own force requirements but a more standardised approach to putting together peace keeping operations would help improve planning for future peace keeping. A UN Stand-by Forces Planning Group has been working on designing a basic force structure for future peace keeping operations. Traditionally, the identification of a force commander and identification of countries able to contribute civilian and military contingents have been pursued separately. The UN has traditionally sought equitable geographic representation in peace keeping operations, and must also take into account, in assembling the force, differences in language, training, command procedures and compatibility of technology and equipment.

The inevitable delays make even more difficult the task of pre-deployment planning, and the integration of the peace keeping with the peace making function.

It might be more effective if peace keeping forces could initially be formed from groups of contributing countries which have already established cooperative arrangements between their armed forces (for example, the Five Power Defence Arrangements between Malaysia, Singapore, Australia, New Zealand and the United Kingdom). Effective planning requires the early identification of a force commander and headquarters staff, and this could be done in association with the identification of an early deployment contingent if the initial force was made available by one country or a group of countries. The headquarters staff and an early deployment contingent could be drawn from the region in which the force is to be placed, and would then have the additional advantage of some familiarity with the situation: the UN could later add supplementary headquarters staff or forces from other countries. Such an early deployment contingent would have the advantages, not only of significantly assisting planning and rapid deployment, but of a force commander, headquarters staff and forces with familiar command and control procedures, already established levels of inter-operability and its own logistics system. The only real downside risk to be weighed in these kinds of arrangements is that, if it is deployed in its own region, such a force might be too close to one or more of the parties involved for it to be, or at least seen to be, impartial.

The Secretary-General has made a number of proposals, in *An Agenda for Peace*, to allow rapid deployment of peace keeping forces. The proposals range from establishment of a standing UN rapid deployment force to national ear-marking of forces for peace keeping. The UN Stand-by Forces Planning Group has been investigating member states' willingness to ear-mark specific forces to be placed on stand-by for deployment. There is as yet little readiness among member states to pre-commit military forces to a standing UN force (or, for that matter, to encourage or even allow volunteers for this purpose). Some governments may, however, now be in a position to enter into agreements under Article 43 of the Charter to designate forces, assistance and facilities available on stand-by. Others will prefer to retain the discretion to identify and commit available national forces on a case-by-case basis.

An expanded UN data base on national capacities for contributions of personnel and equipment to peace keeping is a more immediate measure which, with cooperation from contributor countries, could assist UN planning and rapid deployment. Such a data base would need to draw together and keep up-to-date standardised information on national military and non-military capacities ear-marked for peace keeping or available on a case-by-case basis, together with information on force structures and logistics requirements relevant to their use in peace keeping. Such a data base could help in the development of standardised systems for logistic support and the supply of equipment to UN operations. It should include lists of individual civilians with professional and technical skills who are available on stand-by for deployment to peace keeping operations.

Pre-positioned equipment stocks, established in key regional centres, of standard items such as motor vehicles, non-perishable disaster relief materials and field accommodation could reduce supply delays for new peace keeping operations. While there is a range of equipment which will rapidly become obsolete if stockpiled, the number of new missions mounted by the UN in recent years suggests that it is no longer sufficient to aim to recycle equipment from previous or continuing missions, or to plan equipment purchases for each peace keeping operation as a separate exercise.

There is an emerging consensus on general principles required in training personnel for peace keeping. Training can play an important role in ensuring generalised understanding and application of procedures in the field. The UN's role should be primarily to promote approaches to training which ensure that peace keepers can work together and that, notwithstanding the great variety of national differences, essential common standards in training are observed. Actual training should be left primarily to member states, individually and collectively, and the UN should encourage the existing and new training centres established in a wide range of countries. The development of standard UN training materials would be a most useful input to national and regional peace keeping training. Training the trainers and officer training, possibly through the establishment of an International Staff College, would be an effective way to establish common standards and to provide training for force commanders and headquarters staff. Options for funding from outside the UN might need to be explored for such a Staff College: while standard military training remains the basic requirement for military contingents for peace keeping, military as well as non-military peace keepers require training in negotiation skills, cultural awareness, specific operation-related matters and, sometimes, language, in order to carry out their tasks effectively.

Command, control and information   Effective command, control and information arrangements are a prerequisite for effective and efficient peace keeping operations. Command and control relationships need to be clearly defined within agreed peace keeping doctrine, and supported by an effective UN communications system (both from UN Headquarters to the field missions and within the missions themselves) for the UN to have access to timely and accurate information both at Headquarters and in the field. Peace keeping operations involve three levels of command, ie strategic, operational and tactical. It is essential that the unique roles and tasks of each of these levels of command are recognised and that resources allocated to each level are sufficient for it to carry out its tasks.

The UN Secretariat is a strategic level headquarters and as such is required to provide the resources and effective political, operational and administrative oversight to operational commanders in the field. But operational commanders need, on the face of it, to be given more authority in the operational, administrative and financial fields so that they have more control over the running of the operations on a day-to-day basis, allowing UN Headquarters to divest itself of much of the minutiae which currently threatens to overload it.

There is a trend for contributing countries to become more involved in operational decisions as the UN increasingly becomes committed to more complex and dangerous situations. This situation is threatening to undermine the effectiveness of the peace keeping operations themselves as well as the credibility of the UN. The importance of unity of command at all levels must be recognised by the Secretariat and contributing countries alike to ensure that all personnel and units are working towards common goals and so that commanders can rely upon subordinate staff and units to follow their commands. The need for unity of command has to be understood and accepted by contributing governments: only in the most extreme and exceptional circumstances should national political jurisdiction over contingents be exercised in a way that cuts across that command, eg where there is clear reason to believe that the command is over-reaching its mandate.

Special Representatives and force commanders should not be put in the position of having to interpret uncertain mandates, as has occurred in the past. The need for the Security Council to articulate clear and unequivocal mandates, and for the Secretary-General to provide precise direction to field commanders in relation to the mission's objectives and tasks, are prerequisites to overcoming many of the problems that are presently emerging, including defining clear rules of engagement.

If UN Headquarters is to effectively manage and coordinate peace keeping operations and involve itself in preventive diplomacy, peace making and peace building, then it is axiomatic that the Secretariat must have access to accurate and timely information and assessments. Due recognition must also be paid to the increasing information requirements of field commanders involved in complex multi-dimensional operations. There is a need, as we have said elsewhere, not only for a better communications system, but to establish within the Secretariat an enhanced capacity to gather, receive, analyse and disseminate information. This requires a more systematic approach to information gathering and analysis, with an appropriately professionally dedicated support unit in the Secretariat.

The UN has taken steps recently to improve its command and control procedures, including by establishing improved communications between New York and the field. The planned extension of the 24-hour situation room for monitoring UNTAC (Cambodia), UNPROFOR (former Yugoslavia) and UNOSOM II (Somalia) to cover all operations is very much to be welcomed. Liaison officer posts for all field operations should also be established in Headquarters in New York.

The quality of information available to the UN, both in the field and at Headquarters, would be assisted by greater reliance on new technology and less reluctance on the part of member states to supply sensitive information. Ground acoustic sensors and surveillance radars have already been used by the MFO in the Sinai as well as by some UN peace keepers. Technologies such as satellite imagery, surveillance drones and night vision devices can also assist, for example, in monitoring disarmament agreements or troop cantonment.

The main barriers to greater use of modern techniques appear to be cost and political sensitivity to use of equipment which might be seen as having 'espionage' potential. Until some of this equipment becomes widely available, the UN may have to rely on the support of the major powers to provide sophisticated technology and the know-how to operate and maintain it. The most effective way of allaying local concerns may be to educate the parties as to the use and limitations of such equipment, and demonstrate its constructive role.

Safety of peace keepers

UN peace keeping operations have always involved risk for the peace keepers. The risk is increasing as peace keepers are increasingly asked to operate in situations of intra-state conflict. In assessing acceptable levels or risk for peace keepers, it is important to distinguish clearly between peace keeping and peace enforcement. The former relies on peaceful means of achieving its goals and assumes the consent of most, if not always all, parties; the latter assumes the need to use force for its ends. Because their methods, processes and objectives are peaceful, the UN must assume a special responsibility for the safety of its peace keepers.

Hostile acts against UN personnel should be subject to universal jurisdiction. This approach, and the clear resolve of all member states not to tolerate such behaviour, are the most effective way of dealing with such groups. This is particularly so when those responsible are typically non-state actors who are not accountable in the community of states, have little if any interest in preserving their international respectability, and hence do not respond to standard forms of international pressure.

The Special Committee on Peacekeeping Operations is considering, on New Zealand's initiative, the development of a new international legal instrument which would create legal obligations on state parties to protect peace keeping personnel and punish those responsible for attacks on UN peace keepers. This proposal should be supported and pursued; there should be no hesitation by UN members in demonstrating solidarity with peace keepers assigned to carry out UN mandates.

Of course, not every situation will be susceptible to remedy through a legal regime of this kind, and the options canvassed in *An Agenda for Peace*, for Chapter VII protective or retaliatory action in appropriate circumstances, is not one that should be excluded in extreme cases: the issue of peace enforcement in support of peace keeping operations is considered further in Chapter 10.

V

Enforcing Peace

9

Sanctions

Sanctions and peace enforcement

The enforcement provisions in Chapter VII of the UN Charter are not an afterthought, but in many ways at the heart of the reason for the UN's existence. A capacity to respond decisively and effectively, with military force if need be, to 'threats to the peace, breaches of the peace and acts of aggression' is exactly what one would have expected the UN's founders to emphasise, coming together as they did in the wake of World War II, by far the most destructive conflict in history.

But it is also clear from both the letter and spirit of the Charter that enforcement strategies—and in particular military force—were seen as very much last resort measures, to be contemplated only when peace making efforts have demonstrably failed to end a conflict. Enforcement measures are by their nature drastically intrusive, overriding (as Article 2.7 makes clear) the principle of non-intervention in matters within the domestic jurisdiction of states. Unlike all the rest of the UN's response repertoire—in peace building, peace maintenance and peace restoration—measures which may be taken here are *not* premised on the consent of all relevant governments or parties. And, again unlike all those other measures, they may involve the active (as distinct from merely self-defensive) application of military force. So Chapter VII of the Charter sets out not just one permissible enforcement response, but a series of graduated steps, in which sanctions are poised midway.

In the first place, Article 40 envisages the adoption of 'provisional measures' which do not 'prejudice the rights, claims or position of the parties concerned', and which are designed essentially 'to prevent an aggravation of the situation'. While the Security Council does not often explicitly invoke this article, such measures can include calls for the withdrawal of armed forces, calls for a ceasefire, calls for a party to comply with an agreement, requests for a decision to be suspended pending an advisory opinion from the ICJ, and calls upon a party to rescind certain measures in an occupied territory. In situations where it is thought premature, or perhaps unduly provocative, to move immediately to the imposition of sanctions, it is possible to use Article 40 to indicate that sanctions will be imposed in the event that certain actions are not taken.

The next step is sanctions, described by Article 41 as 'measures not involving the use of armed force' which 'may include complete or partial interruption of economic relations and of rail, sea, air, postal, telegraphic, radio and other means of communication and the severance of diplomatic relations'. The object of applying sanctions in any form is either to compel a course of conduct against the will of the state in question, or to bring an end to certain conduct. Sanctions are designed to achieve their objective by depriving the state concerned of the military and economic means to maintain the offending behaviour; by bringing domestic pressure to bear on the government concerned, either through general popular resentment of resulting deprivation or pressure from commercial interests; and by bringing moral pressure to bear globally by making the government or state concerned feel that it is an international pariah.

Finally, 'should the Security Council consider that measures provided for in Article 41 would be inadequate or have proved to be inadequate', then Article 42 provides that the Council 'may take such action by air, sea, or land forces as may be necessary to maintain or restore international peace and security.' We discuss the scope and operation of peace enforcement under Article 42 in the next chapter.

Past United Nations practice

Experience of all Chapter VII measures was very limited in the UN's first 45 years, but has grown rapidly with the Security Council cooperation that has proved possible since the end of the Cold War. Just as three of the only five military peace enforcement operations explicitly or implicitly authorised under Chapter VII have occurred since 1990 (ie the Gulf War Coalition, UNOSOM II, and parts of the UNPROFOR and related operations in Bosnia–Herzegovina; the earlier operations being the Unified Command in Korea and the latter stages of the ONUC operation in the Congo), so too have five of the seven instances of sanctions in the UN's history been imposed since 1990 (ie Iraq, former Yugoslavia, Somalia, Libya and Haiti; the earlier cases being Rhodesia and South Africa).

The actual sanctions measures imposed have varied from case to case. Some measures envisaged under Article 41—interruption of telecommunications and severance of diplomatic relations—have not been utilised by the Security Council. Other measures not specifically mentioned in Article 41, such as restrictions on sporting, scientific and technical cooperation, have recently been imposed in the case of Serbia and Montenegro. Medical supplies are usually exempted from sanctions, as is food (although Security Council Resolution 661, in relation to Iraq, exempted food only 'in humanitarian circumstances'). The most favoured single sanction measure, recurring in every one of the UN cases mentioned above, is an arms embargo—the attraction being its clear demonstration of international concern, if not always its efficacy in reducing the actual level of conflict or human rights violations. The most common specifically *economic* sanction has been an oil embargo, for reasons both of impact and enforceability.

UN sanctions resolutions have usually imposed mandatory obligations on member states, but there have been exceptions. In the case of Cambodia in 1992, for example, the Security Council, relying on the provisions of the Paris Agreements and decisions of the Supreme National Council, merely requested states to implement various economic measures targeted at the Khmer Rouge following its non-compliance with the military provisions of the Paris Agreements (SCR 792): while the possibility of further measures against the Khmer Rouge was not ruled out, a move to Chapter VII action could have encountered stiff resistance from some Security Council members and key regional players whose cooperation in enforcing such sanctions would have been essential. The General Assembly's powers are only recommendatory, so while the 1977 Security Council arms embargo against South Africa was mandatory, the 1985 General Assembly Resolution (UNGA 40/64I) on an oil embargo and other economic measures sought only voluntary compliance, as did the 1975 General Assembly Resolution on apartheid in sport (UNGA 34/11E).

It is self-evident that sanctions require adherence by all relevant states and parties—ie those neighbouring or dealing with the target state or party—if they are to have the maximum chance of success. Unilateral sanctions, even when imposed by as powerful a neighbour as the US is to Cuba, can be relatively easily circumvented. But it has to be acknowledged that even when mandatory sanctions have been applied by the UN in the past, the record of success has been at best mixed. A review of the various situations where the UN has imposed mandatory sanctions reveals some of the strengths and weaknesses of the mechanism.

The comprehensive sanctions regime imposed by the Security Council against *Rhodesia* in 1966 (SCR 232), following its unilateral declaration of independence, is generally held to have had little effect on the Rhodesian authorities. Many states took no action to prevent their nationals from trading with Rhodesia. Portugal provided Rhodesia with access to the port of Beira in its then colony of Mozambique and South Africa also provided rail access to Rhodesia. Sanctions coverage as a consequence was quite porous. Sanctions only began to be effective after Portugal withdrew from Mozambique, the Carter Administration ceased United States' purchases of strategic minerals and pressure began to be imposed on Rhodesia by South Africa.

The record of sanctions against *South Africa* bears more detailed examination because it illustrates many of the factors which can determine the effectiveness of a sanctions operation. The embargo on arms trade with South Africa, imposed by Security Council Resolutions 418 (1977), 558 (1984) and 591 (1986), was the only application by the UN of mandatory sanctions against the apartheid regime, and appears by itself to have had little practical impact either on attitudes or on military capacity. But this embargo, and other voluntary sanctions proposals adopted by the Security Council and General Assembly from 1975 to 1986 on oil, sporting, cultural, technical, trade, investment and financial contacts were accompanied by a comprehensive range of economic sanctions adopted between 1973 and 1986, albeit in a relatively uncoordinated fashion, by a whole range of other national and international bodies, including the Organization of Petroleum Exporting Countries (OPEC), the OAU, the Commonwealth, the EC and United States Federal, State and municipal legislatures.

Trade sanctions generally were an unwelcome impost on South Africa's economy but, because they were not universally applied, their overall effect was not decisive. The oil embargo, particularly that applied by OPEC, certainly imposed a significant burden on the economy, but it also accelerated South African development of coal to oil technology. 'People to people' sanctions, especially restrictions on sporting contacts, undoubtedly had a considerable psychological impact on the white South African population and created great pressure to end racially based sports competition. Whether their overall impact, however, was more to stimulate progressive reform, or to provoke defiance and a laager reaction, is still open to debate.

Unquestionably it was the threat, and then subsequently the imposition, of *financial* sanctions that eventually had the most significant impact. The informal sanctions imposed by banks and the private sector during the late 1980s significantly increased the economic costs of apartheid, dramatically reducing the country's capacity to grow. It was as a result of financial sanctions that South African industry over time began to press the government to dismantle apartheid. These various layers of sanctions, supported by a broad coalition of diverse interests in the international community, helped over time to isolate South Africa and created a cumulative burden which, as acknowledged with increasing frankness by government and financial sector spokesmen in the late 1980s, was ultimately too great for South Africa to sustain.

Comprehensive sanctions imposed on *Iraq* by the Security Council in 1990 (SCRs 661 and 670), following its invasion and purported annexation of Kuwait, were unsuccessful in reversing Iraq's aggression. Nor has their continued implementation yet succeeded in forcing Iraq's full compliance with the conditions imposed on it by the Security Council after the Gulf War. While deprivation has been felt by the people of Iraq, particularly internal opponents of the regime, the regime itself appears to have been largely untouched. Sanctions have provided it with a focus for popular resentment and provoked a degree of international humanitarian concern about their possible impact on Iraqis' health and welfare. There has been some continuing commerce with Iraq through neighbouring states. The effects of sanctions have also been attenuated because of Iraq's substantial domestic production capacity in agriculture and manufacturing, although this is at well below pre-conflict levels. On the other hand, there can be no doubt that the imposition of sanctions, together with the activities of the United Nations Special Commission (UNSCOM), have severely limited Iraq's ability to rearm. As intended by the Security Council, Iraq's capacity to renew its threat to peace and security in the region has thus been circumscribed by the sanctions regime.

Sanctions imposed by the United Nations against the constituent republics of the *former Yugoslavia* in 1991 to 1993 have been essentially in two parts: an arms embargo, applied against all of the former Yugoslavian republics (SCR 713); and economic sanctions against Serbia and Montenegro of successively increasing stringency (including prohibition of access of goods along the Danube and through other points of entry, and a ban on the provision of financial and other services to any business: SCRs 757, 787 and 820).

The arms embargo has been controversial from the outset because of its potentially discriminatory burden on Bosnian Muslims, but the prevailing view has been that it has helped restrict the overall scale of fighting. Economic sanctions have certainly disrupted life in the Federal Republic of Yugoslavia, but this disruption has not been severe enough to cause a major change in Serbian policy. Part of the problem has been that, despite attempts at a full-scale blockade, the application of the arms embargo and economic sanctions has been far from watertight.

As part of its involvement in seeking to end the hostilities in *Somalia*, the Security Council in 1992 imposed an embargo on all deliveries of weapons and military equipment to Somalia (SCR 733). Given the extensive weapons stores in Somalia, the arms embargo has had, at least as yet, little effect on dampening the fighting in Somalia. Efforts have instead concentrated on means to disarm the warring factions.

Sanctions imposed by the Security Council on *Libya* in 1992 (SCR 748), following evidence of its involvement in two terrorist attacks against civil aviation, were limited to an air embargo, an arms embargo and restrictions on diplomatic staff. These have no doubt caused some discomfort to the Libyan people, but they have so far been insufficiently stringent as to cause the Libyan Government to comply with the UN's demands to hand over the suspects in the Lockerbie Pan Am bombing and to cooperate with the French investigation of a UTA bombing.

Sanctions recently imposed by the Security Council on *Haiti* comprise an oil and arms embargo and the freezing of overseas assets of the de facto authorities (SCR 841). The sanctions were imposed as a means of putting pressure on the de facto authorities to negotiate conditions being brokered by the Special Representative of the Secretary-General and the OAS for the restoration of democratic processes in Haiti and the return of President Aristide. Sanctions may have an unusually direct and early impact in the case of Haiti. They can be enforced by a naval blockade along its relatively limited coastline: road links to the Dominican Republic are poor and Haiti has limited natural resources.

Making sanctions more effective

The record reveals that the impact of sanctions has been patchy at best. They generally require a longer period of time to have any significant impact, are too often porous, and can have effects opposite to those intended, eg rallying domestic support for the regime being targeted and encouraging new industry and growth, at least temporarily, inside the target country. To be effective, sanctions must have clearly defined and achievable objectives and be implemented rigorously.

Defining achievable objectives

As stated earlier, the basic objective of applying sanctions in any form should be to compel a course of conduct against the will of a state

(Libya, Haiti) or to bring an end to certain conduct (Iraq, South Africa, Federal Republic of Yugoslavia). Sanctions introduced simply in order for the international community to be seen to be doing something—perhaps in a situation where the only action likely to be successful is full scale military peace enforcement, but where there is insufficient support for this course—may be better not introduced at all. If, having been introduced in these circumstances, sanctions are enforced only half-heartedly, the problem is compounded.

That said, there may still be cases in which sanctions—even though unsuccessful in achieving their primary aim—can still be justified on the basis of sending a clear signal to all members of the international community about the unacceptability of the conduct which led to their imposition. Thus, for example, in imposing sanctions against Libya in relation to its involvement in terrorist attacks against civil aviation, several Security Council members explicitly pointed to the sanctions action as a means of deterring state-sponsored international terrorism generally.

Such cases apart, if sanctions are to maintain their credibility and play an effective role in the graduated response to threats to international peace and security they should aim at achieving specified, realistic objectives within a broadly specified, but again realistic, time frame. One way to do this is to introduce a broad range of sanctions measures and undertake to lift them progressively as particular targets are achieved. This has been the Commonwealth approach to its South African sanctions. Four 'tranches' of sanctions have been identified (viz the sports boycott and other 'people to people' sanctions; trade sanctions; financial sanctions; and the arms embargo); each has a different 'trigger' for its lifting—from the abolition of apartheid in sport for the first tranche, to installation of a fully-elected government for the last. The joint action by the UN and OAS in response to the political crisis in Haiti is a good example of a similar strategy: in an agreement brokered by the UN and OAS between the de facto authorities and the legitimate government, a series of steps was established to restore democratic processes and return President Aristide, with specific triggers to allow for the suspension and eventual lifting of sanctions.

Applying appropriate disciplines

To be effective, sanctions have to be appropriate in scope and properly enforced. One clear lesson from the application of sanctions in the former Yugoslavia was that the initial set of measures was too limited for the primary objective in question, namely doing enough damage, and quickly enough, to the Serbian economy to ensure compliance with the Vance–Owen peace plan. We agree, in this context, with the UK House of Commons Foreign Affairs Committee:

> [I]f the UN wishes to use sanctions as an effective weapon they need to be accompanied from the start by a blockade, by land, sea and air, and by a sophisticated range of controls over commercial, financial and trading mechanisms. (Para. 130)

To ensure that sanctions are observed, it will sometimes be necessary to employ armed force. The naval patrols in the Red Sea to interdict possible illicit shipments bound for Iraq are one example of this category of action. For the most part, such actions may be portrayed as monitoring compliance rather than enforcement, but there is always the possibility that force will be required to prevent a violation of sanctions. In such actions, the principle of proportionality should be observed strictly.

If sanctions are to be effective in actually achieving results—as distinct from merely expressing disapproval—*concerted* action by states, especially neighbouring states and significant trading partners, is required. Unilateral sanctions can have little effect, even when imposed by a dominant trading partner, and the same is true of sanctions observed in practice on a less than totally solid basis.

It is only in the recent cases of Iraq and the former Yugoslavia that the Security Council has made rigorous attempts to apply its sanctions. UN sanctions are administered by committees of the Security Council. Their procedures are now quite detailed and complicated, but this has not always been the case. The committee to administer the application of sanctions on South Africa meets only to consider complaints from member states about violations of the regime, and its procedures are relatively unspecific. The committee established to deal with the sanctions regime on Iraq, however, is quite active and has established detailed guidelines to govern its activities. Detailed procedures have likewise been developed by the committee dealing with the sanctions applying to the former Yugoslavia. Leakage, nonetheless, has been a major inhibitor of the effectiveness of most sanction regimes. Despite the sanctions committee procedures, it has proved extremely difficult to prevent leakage, short of the threat of military force. Warships continue to patrol the Red Sea to check cargoes bound for Iraq and a maritime blockade of the Federal Republic of Yugoslavia has been necessary, but even with these measures, it is clear that the sanctions regimes remain porous.

It has often been suggested that one means of ensuring better adherence to sanctions regimes would be to apply sanctions to 'sanctions busters'. One possible approach to discourage violations of sanctions would be for the Security Council to decide at the time it imposes sanctions that violations would result more or less automatically in a flow-on of the sanctions to the violator. An additional paragraph to this effect could be included in the original resolution. All that would be necessary, to trigger the application of sanctions against the violator, would be for the relevant sanctions committee to find that a certain country was in violation of the regime and for this finding to be upheld by the Council. Already the Council has found it necessary on occasion when taking enforcement action to remind member states of their obligation under Article 25 'to accept and carry out' the Council's decisions.

It must be recognised that some states will have more difficulties than others in enforcing sanctions. Assistance should be made available to those states, as was the case with EC and United States assistance to the riparian states (on the banks of the Danube) in enforcing the further sanctions against Serbia and Montenegro (pursuant to SCR 820) which were introduced to strengthen implementation of earlier sanctions under SCRs 713, 757 and 787.

Being fair

If sanctions are to be enforced as rigorously as possible, some better means of mitigating the effects on third parties have to be found. The Secretary-General has said that this is a question of pressing importance which must be pursued as a matter of urgency. Article 50 of the Charter provides for no more than consultation between the Security Council and those states which suffer 'special economic problems' as a result of the Council's actions. It is not much consolation for those countries recognised as having qualified under Article 50, as a result of the sanctions imposed on Iraq, to have had the Sanctions Committee making a request to member states, UN agencies and international financial institutions to lend assistance to them where possible.

One remedy would be for those countries adversely affected by sanctions to obtain compensation from levies on the target country. While this might be practical in the case of target states with substantial economic resources such as Iraq, there would be little point to such action in the case of poorer targets. This is especially the case when the effect of sanctions is to impoverish the target. Moreover, even if a target state were able to pay, it would scarcely do so while still defying the Security Council: countries adversely affected would therefore have to wait until sanctions had succeeded before they could hope to receive any compensation. If such a system were, nonetheless, to be introduced, it would be important to put in place an objective method of assessing member states' claimed losses as a result of sanctions, and to ensure a consistent approach to such claims.

Other proposals are under consideration in United Nations forums for the establishment of permanent or specific funds from which compensation payments could be made. Such a fund could be established by special assessment by the General Assembly following the imposition of sanctions. Such an approach does, of course, require a broad consensus if it is to work. Alternatively, a permanent fund might be established with disbursements to be made on the recommendation, from time to time, of sanctions committees.

10

Peace Enforcement

The peace enforcement option

When all other strategies to deal with armed conflict or a major security crisis have failed, and the situation threatens to produce continuing bloodshed and destruction—or an unopposed triumph for aggression—the active use of military force by the international community is an option that must be contemplated. Article 42 of the UN Charter makes clear that such an option is available: when the Security Council, in response to 'any threat to the peace, breach of the peace or act of aggression', considers that lesser measures have been or would be inadequate, 'it may take such action by air, sea, or land forces as may be necessary to maintain or restore international peace and security'.

Intervention of this kind by the UN has been, however, extremely rare. In 1950 the Security Council authorised enforcement action against North Korea. Notwithstanding the Cold War, the Council was able to act in this instance due to the temporary absence from its ranks of the Soviet Union over the issue of Chinese representation. Acting swiftly in a series of resolutions, the Council recommended that member states 'furnish such assistance to the Republic of Korea as may be necessary to repel the armed attack' (SCR 83), created the

Unified Command to which member states contributed troops, requested the United States to designate the commander and authorised the Unified Command to use the UN flag (SCR 84). Although the Security Council never explicitly invoked Chapter VII provisions, it based its response on Chapter VII, determining that North Korea's action constituted 'a breach of the peace' (SCR 82).

In July 1960 the Security Council constituted the UN Operation in the Congo (ONUC) to assist the newly independent government in maintaining law and order, and to provide technical assistance (SCR 143). In February and November 1961 the Security Council went on to authorise ONUC to undertake enforcement action to prevent civil war (SCR 161) and to complete the removal of mercenaries (SCR 169). As in Korea, the Council did not explicitly invoke Chapter VII but based its actions squarely on Chapter VII criteria, being 'deeply concerned at ... the threat to international peace and security' (SCR 161).

But while there were only these two Chapter VII enforcement operations in the whole of the Cold War years, since 1990 the United Nations has already approved three more. The first was in November 1990 (SCR 678) in response to Iraq's continued occupation of Kuwait. The second was the Council's authorisation in December 1992 (SCR 794) of the US-led Unified Task Force (UNITAF) to restore order in Somalia, and the subsequent creation of UNOSOM II in 1993 (SCR 814). The third instance was in the former Yugoslavia, where in 1992–93 Chapter VII mandates were assigned to aspects of the UN Protection Force (UNPROFOR) peace keeping operation to ensure, particularly in Bosnia–Herzegovina, the safe delivery of humanitarian aid (SCR 770), the security and freedom of movement of personnel (SCRs 807, 815, 819 and 824) and the protection of safe areas (SCRs 836 and 844); the Security Council also authorised Chapter VII action to enforce the 'no fly zone' in Bosnia–Herzegovina (SCR 816). (It should perhaps also be noted, for completeness, that the UN Iraq–Kuwait Observation Mission (UNIKOM), although a traditional peace keeping operation, was also given its mandate under Chapter VII (SCR 689): this simply reflected its genesis as part of the comprehensive ceasefire provisions to end the Gulf War in 1991.)

While the level of activity has thus increased in recent years, there has also been, in a number of member states, some questioning of UN military peace enforcement. This has reflected, in particular, the substantial number of troops required, the enormous costs associated with that, and the considerable risk to military and civilian personnel involved in such enforcement operations. The killing of 24 Pakistani UNOSOM II troops in June 1993 constituted the largest number of UN troop deaths on one occasion since the killing of 44 Ghanaian troops in the Congo in April 1961. The action taken in response to that and related provocations has led in turn to criticism that UNOSOM II has become a partisan antagonist in the internal hostilities in Somalia. More generally, there has been some criticism directed toward the United States government, from both home and abroad, for the leading role it has taken in peace enforcement operations under UN auspices.

In responding to criticisms of peace enforcement, it has to be acknowledged at the outset that it is certainly consistent with the aims of the Charter, and the structure of Chapters VI and VII, that the use of force should be a 'last resort' (the phrase actually used by the Security Council when it realised some distance down the track that it was involved in enforcement action in the Congo (SCR 161)). While it is true that on a strict reading of Article 42, enforcement action can be set in train in response to a 'threat to the peace' which has not yet spilled over into actual armed hostilities, it is extremely unlikely in practice that a full-scale peace enforcement operation would be initiated on this basis. We certainly take the view that a military enforcement response (as distinct from sanctions) would be likely to be quite inappropriate in any situation falling short of a 'breach of the peace, or act of aggression'. But equally, we strongly agree with the Secretary-General in *An Agenda for Peace* that, when such a situation does arise, the international community cannot turn away from its responsibilities:

> While such action should only be taken when all peaceful means have
> failed, the option of taking it is essential to the credibility of the
> United Nations as a guarantor of international security. (Para. 43)

A further general question that has to be faced in all these cases is not only whether military force should be used, but how much. Local and international support for an enforcement operation—which is crucial for the continued credibility of UN-authorised enforcement action, and of UN operations more generally—will be undermined if the public perceives UN-authorised troops to be using excessive force, especially against civilians. While considerable force may be required in response to cross-border aggression, where the aim is to repel an invading army, force should be far more restrained in enforcement operations in support of peace keeping operations or humanitarian objectives, where the aim is to achieve strictly pacific objectives. It goes without saying that in all peace enforcement questions, the Geneva Conventions should be strictly observed.

Yet another question that needs to be faced (and at the threshold of an enforcement action, not after the event) is the likely longer term consequences. It has to be borne in mind that any UN member state which has been the object of a peace enforcement operation will need to be reintegrated as soon as possible into the family of nations upon completion of such an operation. Those deciding upon an enforcement action may often not be able to plan in any detail that far ahead, but they should certainly bear in mind the importance of ensuring that the transition from peace enforcement to post-conflict peace building can occur as quickly and as smoothly as possible.

What all this comes down to is that it is important, for international peace and security, that 'last resort' UN peace enforcement operations maintain their credibility and broad international support. This means, in particular, that the circumstances in which the peace enforcement option may be used must be better defined—so that the measures used are appropriate, proportionate, meet the objectives set for them, and maintain the widest possible, mutually reinforcing national, regional and international support.

It is not, however, easy to define with precision the circumstances in which peace enforcement may be appropriate. The clearest case is cross-border aggression by one state against another, but even here questions of definition and consistency of response arise. A second case, where questions of fine judgement are always likely to be involved, is where peace enforcement is called in aid in support of a peace keeping operation. The third kind of case, least clear of all, is where an essentially internal conflict or crisis—involving significant human suffering and clearly requiring some kind of forcible intervention to quell—has become a matter of international concern: it is being increasingly claimed that, in such cases, there is a 'right of humanitarian intervention'. It is necessary to consider each of these situations in more detail.

Peace enforcement in response to cross-border aggression

It is the fundamental right of member states of the UN to be secure from cross-border aggression, invasion and occupation, and it was indeed essentially for this purpose that the role of the Security Council was conceived. Article 1 of the UN Charter defines the UN's primary purpose to include taking 'effective collective measures for the... suppression of acts of aggression or other breaches of the peace'. Chapter VII of the Charter provides, in Article 39, for the Security Council to determine the existence of a breach of the peace or act of aggression. The General Assembly reached agreement on what constitutes aggression in consensus Resolution 3314 (XXIX) on 14 December 1974, which refers to aggression as the 'use of armed force by a state against the sovereignty, territorial integrity or political independence of another state, or in any manner inconsistent with the Charter of the United Nations'. Certainly, the use of force by the UN in response to cross-border aggression is the most readily justified of any such action. Two of the five enforcement operations authorised so far by the Security Council have been actions of this type—those in response to North Korea's attack on South Korea in 1950, and Iraq's invasion of Kuwait in 1990.

It is crucial that the willingness of the UN to continue to respond to such aggression be unqualified, both as an assurance to member states and as a deterrent to potential aggressors. This was not possible during the Cold War, but it should be possible now. The first test of clear-cut, naked aggression since the end of the Cold War was Iraq's invasion and occupation of Kuwait, which resulted in the UN authorising peace enforcement action (SCR 678) and that action, undertaken by a coalition of member states, achieving the restoration of Kuwait's territorial integrity (see Box 7). There could have been few more stark and indisputable cases of the very kind of action, so often taken in the 1930s, that the UN's collective security framework had been developed to counter. There was also a buoyant mood of international cooperation, no doubt at least partly born of the feelings that the UN was no longer a venue for the playing out of superpower rivalries; that this was a chance to use the Charter provisions exactly as had been intended; and that it was, moreover, a perfect opportunity to demonstrate to other potential aggressors that actions of this kind were not tolerable and that the international community had both the will and the means to respond to them.

Some have been moved to suggest that this kind of response may not easily be able to be repeated in the future, and that the invasion of a banana producer might not have quite the same resonance as an attack on a major oil producer. It would be deeply unfortunate if any such impression were to become conventional wisdom. There are few bottom lines in international affairs, but this is one of them. If there is ever another case of naked aggression as clear-cut as Iraq's against Kuwait, the Security Council must act totally consistently with its authorisation of peace enforcement in that case, and the international community must act just as swiftly, decisively and effectively.

It has to be acknowledged, however, that there may well be in future less clear-cut cases, eg where low level hostilities are continuing across a border or where for some other reason the cross-border character of the aggression or breach of the peace is not as manifest. (Certainly the situation in Bosnia–Herzegovina, for example, has been generally treated as one of internal civil war—albeit with considerable external involvement—rather than as involving cross-border aggression.) The Security Council may wish in these situations to consider responses other than enforcement, ie peace making, with the option of peace keeping as well, but with the credible threat of peace enforcement should the conflict be escalated by an aggressor state.

7.   The Gulf War coalition 1990–1991: peace enforcement in response to cross-border aggression

The problem: Iraq invaded Kuwait in August 1990, then purported to annex the country despite almost unanimous international condemnation and the imposition of comprehensive sanctions. Concern mounted over reported atrocities by the occupying forces.

The response: SCR 678 authorised member states cooperating with Kuwait's legitimate government to use 'all necessary means' to compel Iraq to comply with the Security Council's resolutions, including the call for immediate and unconditional withdrawal from Kuwait (SCR 660) by 15 January 1991.

Despite efforts by a number of member states and the Secretary-General, Iraq remained unmoved. A military coalition, assembled and led by the United States, began military operations on 16 January 1991. Thirty-eight countries participated directly in the action and another four (including Germany and Japan) contributed major financial and logistic support. In six weeks of intensive air and ground action, the enforcement operation successfully expelled the Iraqi forces from Kuwait. As part of the ceasefire, Iraq agreed to the elimination of its weapons of mass destruction and a reduction of its conventional weapons capacity.

The lessons:

• The United States built the military coalition by acting through the Security Council. Such endorsement provides an enforcement operation with crucial international legitimacy. However the US was perceived to be setting the operation's objectives and assessing when they had been met. If objectives need to be revisited as an enforcement operation proceeds, this should be done formally by the Security Council: the Council should maintain, and be seen to maintain, overall policy control of the enforcement operations it authorises.

• The speed with which the enforcement operation achieved its goals demonstrates the operational advantages of a coalition operation led by a major military power. Enforcement operations, especially in response to cross-border aggression, should realistically continue on the basis of national or coalition command for the foreseeable future.

• Iraq's defeat led to rebellions of its minorities, stimulating internal crises in Iraq which required humanitarian intervention and a continuing commitment by the Coalition not originally intended: the international community should be prepared to deal with the aftermath of a peace enforcement operation.

• Even the speediest and most successful peace enforcement operation of this type is extremely expensive: it is estimated that US costs alone were some $61 billion, and the overall cost well over $70 billion.

Peace enforcement in response to cross-border aggression is likely to involve—as it did in the Gulf War—a scale and intensity of operations which surpass that of any other UN operation. It is important that the UN deploy a force capable of carrying out its tasks in the shortest possible time and with the minimum number of casualties. The enforcement response must be timely. There will therefore be a need for significant numbers of well equipped, well trained forces. Contributing governments will need to have confidence in the command and control arrangements and the intelligence and administrative support systems of the force. Where several nations contribute forces, their national units will need to have a high level of inter-operability: the likely use of sophisticated weaponry and technology increases the importance of this. Contributing countries holding such technology may well want to restrict its use to their own nationals or close allies: the UN itself could not afford to obtain or maintain stocks of such weapons.

Enforcement in response to cross-border aggression is, for these various reasons, likely to continue to involve very strong pressure for the operation to be under national or coalition, rather than UN, command. But to ensure that the UN is not seen to have abdicated its responsibilities in such circumstances, and to give it the basis for effectively asserting ultimate authority, the Security Council should consider upgrading its reporting requirements from commanders. In the case of the Korean operation it asked the United States to 'provide the Security Council with reports as appropriate' on action taken by the Unified Command. When action was taken against Iraq, Security Council Resolution 678 asked participating countries to 'keep the Security Council regularly informed'. Reporting requirements should include, as a minimum, full analysis of action taken with reference to the Council's objectives. If the UN, and the Security Council in particular, are to maintain credibility, then the Security Council must retain full policy control over the operations it authorises.

Peace enforcement in support of peace keeping operations

The concept of using force in support of peace keeping operations is relatively new, the only instance being the Security Council's authorisation of force to protect UNPROFOR troops and the safe areas, and to enforce the 'no fly zone', in Bosnia–Herzegovina (see Box 8). Its use is envisaged in *An Agenda for Peace*, where the Secretary-General suggests that circumstances in which force might be required could include compelling the observance of ceasefire agreements (Para. 44).

8. Bosnia–Herzegovina since 1992: enforcement in support of peace keeping operations

The problem: Absence of cooperation from all parties has made it increasingly difficult for UNPROFOR to fulfil its mandate of meeting pressing humanitarian needs and protecting threatened civilian populations. Peace keepers have come under direct military attack.

The response: The Security Council adopted a Chapter VII resolution (SCR 770) calling on member states acting nationally or through regional organisations 'to take all measures necessary' to facilitate, in coordination with the UN, the delivery of humanitarian aid, following which it took the unprecedented step of renewing UNPROFOR's mandate under Chapter VII to 'ensure the security of UNPROFOR' (SCR 807) and to 'ensure its freedom of movement for all its missions' (SCR 815). Chapter VII was similarly invoked in relation to safe areas protected by UNPROFOR (SCRs 819, 824, 836 and 844), and in authorising enforcement of the 'no fly zone' (SCR 816) in Bosnia–Herzegovina. Breaches of the 'no fly zone' significantly decreased following adoption of SCR 816. No enforcement action has been carried out to date, although NATO has made plans for this, as well as for aerial strikes to support UNPROFOR in the safe areas. Some UNPROFOR troop contributors are concerned that such military action might endanger their forces by provoking a retaliation.

The lessons:

- Peace keepers are vulnerable to determined attack. When physical safety is involved, rapid decisions are required, allowing the Security Council little time to consider the consequences: one option is to incorporate guidelines for the protection of peace keepers in the Rules of Engagement for the peace keeping operation (with appropriate resources to match) rather than invoking Chapter VII on a case by case basis.

- There has been an unhelpful lack of clarity about the scope of enforcement action in Bosnia–Herzegovina (to protect UNPROFOR troops or the safe areas themselves) and who should decide to take such action (NATO or the UN): the Security Council must enact clear mandates for enforcement action, ensure that the commander reports to it regularly, and maintain clear policy control of the operation.

- If in a peace keeping operation there are obviously major risks to UN personnel and a danger of the UN becoming a party to the conflict if enforcement action is taken, these risks must be weighed, balanced and clear decisions made at the outset: ambiguity and uncertainty about what the UN will do will rarely be helpful to those engaged in ongoing peace making and peace keeping.

The appropriateness of enforcement measures in support of peace keeping may be more precisely assessed by separating this category of enforcement into two: first, the use of force to ensure the physical protection of peace keepers; and secondly, the use of force to enable a peace keeping mandate which is being frustrated, to be carried out.

As to the first question, it has to be acknowledged that peace keepers are vulnerable to determined attack. They are usually at best only lightly armed, often travel in soft-skinned vehicles, and may only exercise their right to self-defence in circumstances which have been narrowly defined since the Congo operation. It is the Security Council which must decide whether to authorise peace enforcement in response to sustained attacks on peace keepers. When physical safety is involved, rapid decisions are required, allowing little time for the Council to consider the issues involved. Some member states have reservations about adopting Chapter VII measures for such operational reasons given issues of sovereignty and reservations about the major task of moving to enforcement action. China and some non-permanent members of the Security Council, for example, expressed reservations when the Council authorised a Chapter VII mandate for UNPROFOR in Bosnia–Herzegovina for protection of its members.

These considerations suggest that, while the option of considering Chapter VII measures to protect peace keepers on an ad hoc basis, as problems arise, should not be excluded (particularly in the most serious cases of armed assault), it may be preferable for the Security Council to adopt separate general guidelines for incorporation in the confidential Rules of Engagement issued by the Secretariat to each peace keeping force commander.

The second question is whether peace enforcement is appropriate when the level of threat or obstruction to a peace keeping operation prevents, or may prevent, the operation from fulfilling its mandate: usually this situation arises as a result of a party to an agreement subsequently backing away from it. In these circumstances the Council would need to consider whether the frustration of the peace keeping mandate was a sufficiently grave threat to international peace and security as to justify a move to peace enforcement to achieve the mandate. The Council must take into account the risk to UN personnel, the increased costs, the substantial additional numbers of troops likely to be required, and the danger of the UN becoming a party to the conflict in the event that the enforcement action is taken against one or more of the parties to the conflict. If these factors, taken together, suggest that the UN may not be successful in achieving the objective of enabling the peace keeping operation to carry out its mandate, then (as discussed in Chapter 8) the Council may decide, if 'soldiering on regardless' is not a realistic option, to withdraw the operation or change its mandate to a more achievable objective.

So far as possible, again, decisions about these matters should be made before, rather than after, the peace keeping operation has commenced. Bosnia–Herzegovina is as clear an example as one could find. If there are obviously going to be major risks to UN personnel, and a real danger of the UN effectively becoming a party to the conflict if enforcement action is taken, these risks must be weighed and balanced, and clear decisions made at the outset. Ambiguity and uncertainty about what the UN will do will rarely be helpful to those engaged in peace keeping—and in ongoing peace making.

In principle, it would be desirable if an enforcement operation taken in support of a peace keeping operation were able to be kept clearly separate from the latter, so that resentment of any lethal force employed in that connection does not carry over into opposition to the peace keeping operation itself and compromise its effectiveness. In practice, however, such a distinction would be very difficult to achieve, not least at times when emotions are running high. If, at the time of deciding a peace keeping mandate, it is clear that events may require peace enforcement in support, then it is preferable that the necessary authority, and the resources and flexibility to employ it, be granted to the force commander from the outset.

Overall, where peace enforcement is used in support of peace keeping, the following criteria should be applied:

- the enforcement action should remain fixed on the basic objective of enabling the peace keeping force to carry out its mandate, and should avoid becoming involved in escalating retaliation against a party or parties;

- the enforcement operation should have a short-term mandate and when its expiry approaches, the Security Council should review whether its objectives have been achieved, or are achievable, and whether the enforcement operation should be prolonged or concluded;

- there should be full and clear public explanation of the objectives of the enforcement action and the conduct of operations; and

- the commander of the enforcement action should report regularly to the Security Council, enabling the Council to continue to clearly exercise policy control.

A role for civil police?

There have been suggestions that, as the UN expands its peace keeping functions, and increasingly has to contemplate the possibility of employing peace enforcers in support, greater attention should be given to using civil police instead of, or to supplement, military personnel. Civil police are particularly suited to basic law and order functions such as crowd control, criminal investigation, arrest and detention. It may be that they would also be distinguishable, to at least some extent, from the military peace keeping personnel, thus doing something to advance the desirable principle of separation between peace keeping and peace enforcement activity. Certainly the use of military peace keepers for what are essentially police operations can contribute to local resentment (synthetic though it may sometimes be) at 'heavy handed' UN actions. Generally speaking, however, one could only contemplate the deployment of civil police as an alternative to military enforcement personnel in low-level conflict situations (including possibly some of the humanitarian intervention situations dealt with below), not where a major enforcement exercise is required.

Peace enforcement in support of humanitarian objectives

Peace enforcement in support of humanitarian objectives is a relatively new concept in the United Nations, and attitudes to it are still evolving. There has long been broad agreement on the right of peoples to receive humanitarian assistance: indeed there is already a well established body of international law (under the Geneva Conventions of 1944 and Additional Protocols of 1977) which obliges states not to prevent people, whose lives and health are endangered, from receiving assistance from international organisations: this is applicable to both international and non-international armed conflict situations. But what has *not* previously been accepted is that there is any basis for that assistance being forcibly rendered, in reliance on the security provisions of the UN Charter.

The debate as to whether there is a new international 'right of humanitarian intervention', in response to suffering caused by conflicts or other major crises, was set running by the Security Council's 'Operation Provide Comfort' decision in 1991 in the aftermath of the Gulf War (SCR 688), when it determined that Iraq's repression of Kurds threatened 'international peace and security in the region', demanded 'that Iraq end this repression' and insisted that it 'allow immediate access by international humanitarian organizations to all those in need of assistance in all parts of Iraq and make available all necessary facilities for their operations'.

What broke really new ground, however, was the action taken in December 1992 (SCR 794) to authorise the deployment of US forces in Somalia (see Box 9). The mandate was unambiguously humanitarian, expressing 'grave alarm' at 'widespread' violations of

9. Somalia since 1992: enforcement in support of humanitarian objectives

The problem: A bitter civil war led to the overthrow of President Siad Barre in January 1991 and the collapse of the Somali state. The country was divided between warring factions. By 1992 the Somali people faced mass starvation. Mounting concern over the famine saw limited UN intervention early in 1992 (UNOSOM, SCR 751) which failed to maintain a ceasefire or to protect relief supplies.

The response: In December 1992 the UN Security Council authorised intervention by a US-led coalition, UNITAF, with a mandate to establish a secure environment for relief operations (SCR 794). In 1993 a new UN operation, UNOSOM II, was established to continue the work of UNITAF and undertake rehabilitation and reconciliation (SCR 814).

UNITAF and UNOSOM II have ensured that most Somalis are no longer starving. But the implementation of a political settlement, agreed by the Somali factions in April, is slow and UNOSOM II challenged militarily in Mogadishu by General Aideed. Most of the UN's attention and resources in Somalia are being thus absorbed. Enforcement actions against Aideed have led to criticism of UN methods and a decline in international public support for its objectives.

The lessons:

- Interventions in situations of unresolved internal conflict under narrow short-term goals, ie the use of armed forces to establish secure conditions for delivery of relief supplies, are unlikely to be capable of early successful termination.

- UN forces should not be introduced unless it is agreed that they will remain as long as necessary for the establishment of conditions allowing for sustained relief, rehabilitation and reconstruction activities to continue on their withdrawal.

- Before deciding on coercive measures specifically to prevent loss of life and prevent human suffering, which should be a rare last resort, the Security Council should receive independent outside advice that the humanitarian situation is such that coercive measures are essential.

- The Rules of Engagement of UN forces introduced for humanitarian purposes should be carefully considered for each situation from the perspective of minimising the impact of the use of force on the civilian population.

- The public dispute between one troop contributor and the UN over the appropriate role of UNOSOM II forces highlights the importance of a clear mandate for enforcement operations.

international humanitarian law and 'dismay' at the 'continuation of conditions that impede the delivery of humanitarian supplies to destinations within Somalia'. Shortly afterwards the Security Council established UNOSOM II (SCR 814), the first Chapter VII military operation unequivocally under the direct command and control of the UN Secretary-General. It should also be noted that in 1992, and again in 1993, the UNPROFOR peace keeping operation in Bosnia–Herzegovina was given some specific Chapter VII enforcement authority to assist in the delivery of humanitarian relief and the protection of safe areas—but the most clear-cut example of a humanitarian rationale for peace enforcement remains Somalia.

There is no evidence of meticulous attention having been paid to threshold criteria for intervention before the UN plunged into Somalia. The situation was manifestly extreme, and with Somalia by that point lacking almost any recognisable characteristic of a viable state, the voices one might normally have expected to hear on the question of protecting national sovereignty were conspicuously silent. At the end of the day, what proved decisive was the pressure on the industrialised countries from non-government organisations and public opinion, stimulated by television pictures of the dead and dying, especially children—combined with the perceived feasibility of intervention in terms of military risk.

However, the subsequent course of events in Somalia has prompted some second thoughts. A number of relief agencies, both official and non-governmental, have queried whether the humanitarian objectives of the whole exercise could not have been more substantially met by a better coordinated relief effort from the outset (with, among other things, greater amounts of food on the ground reducing the incentive for looting and banditry), or at least by a more modest military operation. These concerns gained further momentum in mid-1993 with the retaliatory cycle of violence triggered by the killing of UNOSOM soldiers and subsequently pursued by military operations targeted against General Aideed. The Somali operation has proved neither as quick nor as clean as had been hoped by most of those appalled at the suffering which gave it birth.

Another question being widely asked in the light of UNOSOM II is why has the UN been involved in this way in Somalia, when in recent times comparable suffering has been occurring on a comparable scale in comparable countries. Why was a peace enforcement operation not set in train in Rwanda? Or in Liberia? Or in the Sudan? Or in Mozambique? And, as justified as the US military contribution in support of the Kurds in Operation Provide Comfort may have been, how does one weigh the cost of $800 million dollars that was involved, when this amounted to more than the entire global UNHCR budget in support of refugees in the year in question?

These considerations all mean that it is important to try and define clearer criteria for humanitarian-motivated peace enforcement operations in the future. If there is to be a 'right of humanitarian intervention' recognised—and we think that, in extreme cases, it should be—perhaps this should only apply when the following conditions are satisfied:

- there is a consensus that not just any human right but the most basic, the right to life, is under direct and widespread threat;

- there is no prospect of alleviation of the situation by the government—if there is one—of the state in question;

- all non-force options have been considered, and all non-forcible means to alleviate the situation have failed;

- there is a report from an impartial and neutral source, such as the International Committee for the Red Cross (ICRC), that the humanitarian crisis can no longer be satisfactorily managed;

- there has been consultation reflecting not only a wide spectrum of expert advice but, so far as possible in the circumstances, the views of external and internal parties involved. Those consultations would include regional organisations and other inter-governmental bodies; UN specialised agencies; non-government organisations, particularly the ICRC; and the internal parties concerned, including major contenders for power. Many examples now exist of UN consultation at a high level with such movements, for example the Afghan Mujahadeen factions, the Polisario Front and the Eritrean Liberation Front: such consultations would need explicitly to avoid any implication of recognition, and be limited to considerations relevant to success of the humanitarian objectives;

- there is a high degree of consensus on the issue between developed and developing countries; and

- hard-headed assessments have been made about the international community's capacity, in terms of human resources, finance and organisational skills, to follow through from addressing an immediate crisis to helping the affected state regain its viability as a functioning sovereign state able to take care of its own citizens. Long term international peace and security will not be advanced by ineffectual use of military force which overrides sovereignty in the name of humanitarian objectives, but which may, through subsequent neglect, leave the affected state in no better, or even worse, humanitarian circumstances.

In addition to these threshold criteria, going to whether the intervention should be contemplated at all, a further question has to be addressed as to how that intervention should occur, and whether it can be viable. General Colin Powell has identified a set of questions that will always be relevant for proposed UN peace enforcement operations, not just in a humanitarian-support context:

> Is the political objective we seek to achieve important, clearly defined and understood? Have all other non-violent policy means failed? Will military forces achieve the objective? At what cost? Have the gains and risks been analyzed? How might the situation that we seek to alter, once it is altered by force, develop further and what might be the consequences?

Certainly, in deciding to intervene in humanitarian crises with a show of force, the international community should bear in mind that there is a hierarchy of measures that can be used. One measure used with relative success in Iraq, ie the provision of 500 essentially symbolic UN guards, might be an appropriate first response in some crisis situations. And, as discussed earlier in relation to peace keeping, greater use of civil police rather than military personnel could also assist the UN in these circumstances. Effectively functioning police units may lessen the need for military back-up and unrestricted use of force to keep the peace.

These considerations might be translated into a set of guidelines for intervention along the following lines:

- the objectives for intervention should be clear and based solely on humanitarian considerations;
- the intervention and all its operations should be justifiable and necessary in terms of these objectives;
- the command structure and personnel should, so far as possible in the circumstances, be clearly separate from the UN military and civilian personnel involved in the humanitarian relief operations;
- the Rules of Engagement of UN forces introduced for humanitarian purposes should be carefully considered for each situation from the perspective of minimising the impact of the use of force on the civilian population;
- a substantial effort should be made to present the UN's reasons for intervention to the local people and all relevant local parties as well as to the international community;
- there should be a requirement for frequent reporting to the Security Council, to enable the Council to maintain effective policy control of the operation; and
- the Security Council should schedule frequent consultations with interested states and organisations, and regular briefings of troop

contributing countries, to ensure that the maximum degree of consensus is maintained.

The question of humanitarian intervention opens up a number of related issues for discussion. Two in particular that deserve brief attention here are the question of the UN playing a trusteeship role in 'failed state' situations, and the general problem of UN humanitarian relief coordination.

A new UN trusteeship role?

Somalia's status as a classic 'failed state', characterised by the complete breakdown of all civil authority, has led to suggestions that it—and others like it—might appropriately come under a form of UN 'trusteeship' or 'conservatorship' to enable reconstruction to take place in an orderly way with the support and assistance of the international community.

In principle it is difficult to argue against this notion, involving as it does such a logical extension of the concept of peace building. It is not being suggested that states like Somalia come under the authority of the Trusteeship Council, or in any other way within the formal ambit of the UN's existing Trusteeship system: Article 73 of the UN Charter clearly restricts that system to those territories which have not become members of the UN. It may be, however, that, with its original functions now largely exhausted, the Trusteeship machinery could somehow be utilised for this new purpose. No doubt there would be argument against any such proposal, on the ground that it represents another possible kind of intrusion into internal affairs, but at the same time it will be widely acknowledged that 'failed states' are quite likely to generate situations which the international community simply cannot ignore, just as happened in Somalia.

The strongest argument against the proposal is probably practical. If the international community is to establish, and sustain over time, a civil administration in order to recreate civil society and rehabilitate the infrastructure necessary for that society's economic functioning, the expense is likely to be greater than that sustained even in Cambodia over the short life of UNTAC ($1.8 billion)—and there must be real doubts about the willingness of governments to provide those kinds of resources, other than on a very infrequent and ad hoc basis.

Humanitarian relief coordination

There are widely acknowledged inadequacies in the present UN international system, and structural reasons lie at the heart of them. In the first place, the post-Second World War UN relief system evolved from a structure created for different purposes. Apart from UNHCR and UNICEF, all the main agencies now involved in emergencies—ie WFP, UNDP, FAO and WHO—acquired that role as a secondary function, the main role being seen as the promotion of economic and social development. Notwithstanding the dramatic upsurge in their humanitarian relief work in the 1980s, the organisation of the agencies underwent no fundamental change.

Secondly, it is not clear that the recent establishment of the Department of Humanitarian Affairs is going to be capable of resolving the coordination problems that flow from this multiple-agency, multiple-function structure. In the UN system the specialist agencies are linked only in the loosest way with the central UN organs, and the functional programs—including UNICEF, UNDP, UNHCR and WFP—although legally less independent, operate with much the same autonomy. Separate agencies are inevitably in competition for scarce funds and want to be seen to be making a major contribution to any problem exercising donor governments, not least any headline-catching major humanitarian disaster. This competition, and the conflicts between (and gaps in) mandates of agencies, prevent the kind of swift and purposeful action required to come to grips with complex, rapidly evolving humanitarian emergencies due to armed conflict, sudden natural disasters or the like. The coordination problem is compounded by the extraordinary number of voluntary aid agencies now working in developing countries and responding in their own ways to humanitarian emergencies.

Given that the problem is largely structural in origin, it seems to cry out for a structural solution. A number of models have been suggested, but our own preference is for the creation of a single UN disaster response agency under the aegis of the Secretary-General, working to a new Deputy Secretary-General for Humanitarian Affairs. This would be an operational body, taking over the relief and related basic rehabilitation work of the current major players—UNHCR, UNICEF and WFP. To the extent that the skills of other agencies were required, they would be provided under contract on a fee for service basis; the necessary skills could also be purchased elsewhere from non-government organisations and national governments. All this would leave UNICEF and WFP continuing with their development work, and UNHCR concentrating on its protection work. While this model does involve major change—and such change in the UN system is always controversial—we believe it should be seriously considered, perhaps in the context of the General Assembly's foreshadowed review of the future of the Department of Humanitarian Affairs.

The organisation and management of peace enforcement operations

The infrequency of, and varying degrees of UN responsibility for, peace enforcement operations has meant that, in contrast to peace keeping operations, no body of doctrine or operational guidelines has as yet evolved. To the extent that a peace enforcement operation is under direct UN command, as with UNOSOM II, then most of the considerations relevant to the planning, implementation and command of peace keeping operations are equally applicable here: these were discussed in detail in Chapter 8 and need not be repeated. But the two largest peace enforcement operations that have occurred to date—in Korea and the Gulf—were both under national or coalition, rather than direct UN, command and a number of additional questions arise as a result. What is the case for national or coalition, rather than UN, command of forces assembled on an ad hoc basis? How should forces under national or coalition command be managed in the field? Is it possible to create a standing UN military capability for peace operations, and in particular peace enforcement purposes?

The case for national or coalition command

The scale of the situations confronting the UN has been important in dictating command and control arrangements. Because of the need to use superior force and the usual lack of available local logistic support and supplies, enforcement operations need to be much larger than peace keeping operations. Both in Korea and the Gulf, there was a need to mobilise large forces quickly: North Korean forces had invaded the South and Iraq had occupied Kuwait. It was simply impracticable in both cases to consider the establishment of a UN command structure, whether under the Military Staff Committee or not. A singular advantage of moving to national command is that such structures are available 'off the shelf'.

Moreover, national or coalition arrangements allow commanders to select and deploy partners where the advantages of practised cooperation and inter-operability can be maximised. Coalition action in the Gulf demonstrated the value of these procedures. The problems which have been obvious in a number of peace keeping operations, with differences of training and doctrine between constituent units in a force, are magnified in an enforcement action.

Of course, none of this should be read as derogating from the duty of all member states to be ready to support the UN in all of its responsibilities. Article 2.5 requires all members to 'give the UN every assistance in any action it takes in accordance with the present Charter'. This duty was underlined in Security Council Resolution 678 which requested all states to support the action taken by the coalition against Iraq.

One of the basic problems associated with direct UN command of major military operations is that the Military Staff Committee —established under Chapter VII of the Charter as the body 'responsible under the Security Council for the strategic direction of any armed forces placed at the disposal of the Security Council'—has been moribund since its inception and seems likely to remain so. Suggestions for reviving the Committee have been made from time to time but to no avail. The chief difficulty lies in the Committee's role of advice and assistance to the Security Council in all of its military activities. The wider membership is unlikely to be enthusiastic about contributing forces to any enforcement operation in effect commanded by the fifteen member governments of the Council. The risks involved with peace enforcement are significantly greater than for a peace keeping operation, and there is an understandable concern to retain some control. The decisive authority of one powerful member state, or a small coalition exercising clearly delegated authority, is likely to be much more reassuring in such circumstances.

Although operational control of enforcement actions will therefore generally best be vested in a national or coalition commander, the basis for that control should always lie in the mandate from the Security Council. In the case of Iraq (SCR 678) this mandate consisted of the specific objectives in previous resolutions together with a general reference to the need for restoration of international peace and security in the area. The discretion allowed as a result of this formula was operationally useful. Iraq could not calculate with confidence how far to press its defiance. At the same time, however, there was some lack of clarity about objectives, which did not assist public presentation of strategy. Clarity of objectives is required by the principles of collective responsibility and the Council's responsibility to the wider UN membership. If, as the conflict proceeds, there is a need to revisit the objectives, this should be done formally by the Security Council.

Field management under national or coalition command

In the case of an enforcement operation under national or coalition command, a primary consideration is to retain the Security Council's ultimate political control to ensure that the operation does not overstep its mandate. Regular reporting from the field will assist in this. In both cases, clear Rules of Engagement, a vital aspect of the control of any use of force, should be derived from the mandate for an operation. They should reflect fully the context in which force is used and provide maximum flexibility to the force commander.

The scope for communication with forces in the field, and the degree to which national command is exercised, are key issues for potential contributors to enforcement actions and will be a major consideration in deciding contributions. In national and coalition forces, where the chain of command extends through a national structure or structures, governments are likely to preserve more or less unrestricted access to their contingents.

Blue helmets—the symbol of UN command—signify an expectation that their wearers will offer the UN their primary allegiance in the same way as their civilian counterparts do. Access by contributing governments to their troops is limited, and only informal arrangements are manageable. There have indeed been problems for governments and the UN in peace keeping forces where the UN is in command. When forces are engaged in peace enforcement under UN command the problems can be even more pressing and immediate, as shown by differences between the Government of Italy and the UN over the role of Italy's contingent in UNOSOM II deployed in Mogadishu in 1993. There is much scope for improving this situation, through greater consultation between the UN and contributing countries, but it is unlikely that the needs of the UN and of governments can be fully reconciled.

Good intelligence is important to the success of any military operation. Even in peace keeping, the quality of intelligence information can determine tactical decisions and ultimate success or failure: with enforcement action, the stakes are much higher. The need is for reliable information to be collected and disseminated to all who require it. When an operation is under national command, this can usually be achieved by employment of national means of collection and assessment since those countries likely to be given command of an operation are likely to possess sophisticated intelligence capabilities. Controlling the product, the nation in command has to decide only how to disseminate it beyond its own nationals. Experience shows that this can probably be achieved without great difficulty.

For the UN, access to useful information is a continuing problem. A major area of difficulty is sensitivity in the Secretariat to acceptance of possibly self-serving information and assessments from member states, although this might be overcome in part by the cultivation of different sources. (This was attempted to some extent in the past with the creation of the now abolished Office of Research and the Collection of Information (ORCI)). The Secretariat will remain vulnerable until it has its own professional assessment capability.

If the Secretariat's military planning and operations staff is sufficiently augmented, the organisation's capacity for collection and assessment of field intelligence may be enhanced. Useful overhead imagery is now available from commercial sources and saturation media coverage of certain events will often provide data which can be profitably analysed for military purposes. In relation to its responsibilities in Iraq, the United Nations Special Commission (UNSCOM) has been able to use a U2 aircraft for its own purposes. Even if the Secretariat were to solicit intelligence information, it would encounter some reluctance on the part of potential providers. The Secretariat makes every effort to safeguard sensitive information but security in the UN cannot be as tight as some providers would wish. In these circumstances they are unlikely to provide the UN with highly sensitive or large quantities of intelligence information. One proposal that may be worth further examining in this respect is that a group of professionals from various countries with expertise in intelligence and satellite reconnaissance be recruited and approved by the Security Council to be the select group which is given access to classified information, and then asked to transmit an independent opinion (as international civil servants) to the Council.

As always, of course, access to information is only part of the problem. Here as elsewhere the Secretariat needs to dramatically improve its capacity to process, analyse and act on the information that is already available to it. This applies across the board to all of the UN's activity in preventive diplomacy, peace making, peace keeping and peace enforcement.

The case for a standing UN military capability

Shortly following World War II, there was extensive discussion and planning towards the possibility that military forces would be made available to the Security Council 'on its call' as member states undertake to do in Article 43. Very large numbers of troops and many aircraft and ships were to be included. Before agreement could be reached, the Cold War intervened and the plans were abandoned. Although current political circumstances are more favourable, there is still substantial resistance by member states to abrogating their right to national decision-making on whether or not to commit military forces to any particular operation. The current widespread complaints about the scale of UN demands for peace keeping imply that member states would also resist this further substantial requirement on resource grounds.

More recently there have been calls, including in *An Agenda for Peace*, for attachment of smaller numbers of troops to the UN for limited enforcement action: the Secretary-General proposes their use as 'peace enforcement units'. To date there has been no explicit response from member states to this proposal, although at the Summit meeting of the Security Council in January 1992 President Mitterrand volunteered a French quick reaction force to be made available at short notice when required.

The UN has always found it difficult to obtain more than the most general indications from most member states of possible future contributions even for peace keeping, let alone firm nominations of units to be made available to the Secretariat on call for enforcement duties. The 1989 survey of member states on peace keeping produced results which were so limited as not to warrant their use as the basis for a Secretariat data base. While there may have been a strengthening of interest in and support for the UN's role in promoting international peace and security since then, it remains unlikely that the Secretariat would be successful now in asking states to nominate forces to be employed as peace enforcement units. The United Kingdom, for example, argued that it would remove the required flexibility which contributors need in deciding the best combination of officers, troops and equipment to contribute.

Governments of several member states, including some which have frequently provided highly-regarded components of UN peace keeping operations, have constitutional or political constraints and requirements for legislative consultation regarding commitment to enforcement operations. These are likely to prevent them nominating on-call units for these purposes. Most military authorities would oppose such a proposal on the grounds that it would limit their capacity to develop and deploy the services under their command. And governments would certainly not agree to nominate units for peace enforcement under UN command unless they retained full rights to decide, case by case, whether troops would actually be made available. Even if this were possible, it is unlikely that many governments would accept the obligations implicit in nominating units. At the same time the Secretary-General may well be right in believing that there would be an enthusiastic response to calls for volunteers from within the military forces of member states.

The most specific recent proposal for a new standing military capability for the UN has come from Sir Brian Urquhart: as a long time observer of the delays and uncertainties which attend the deployment of military units on behalf of the UN, whether for peace keeping or peace enforcement, his views command respect. Urquhart has suggested that a volunteer force of about 5000 strong be recruited, essentially from former service personnel around the world. Such a force would be under the authority of the Security Council and the operational control of the Secretary-General. He sees the force as being available both for peace keeping and preventive deployment, as well as for peace enforcement, but as having a particular utility in being able to forcibly intervene to 'break the cycle of violence at an early stage in low-level but dangerous conflicts'.

It may be that there would still be political difficulties for member states in embracing this idea, even though the 'volunteer' concept is, on the face of it, an easier option for them to contemplate than the commitment of whole units on an on-call basis. It will take a deal of persuasion to make a number of developing countries, in particular, give up their reservations about vesting power in the Security Council to call up its own force without having to put together the usual balanced multinational group. And quite a few countries are bound to be concerned about accepting any standing force under the day to day direction of the Secretary-General and Secretariat.

But the real problems are practical. While at first sight a useful addition to the UN's response capacity, such a force could only—at the size envisaged—be deployed on a very short term basis, as a rapid deployment unit subject to early replacement by national forces. If needed for longer than this, questions of rotation of personnel—not to mention demands for their availability in the field elsewhere—would mean that, in order to keep 5000 troops in the field at any one time, a force much larger than that (closer to 15 000 or even 20 000 in total) would be necessary. And to recruit, train, house, equip and deploy a standing force of this order of magnitude could well cost over $1 billion annually.

Moreover, there is a real question, going back to the original rationale for such a force, as to whether it could really have made a decisive impact on the kind of larger conflicts with which the UN is currently trying to deal. In Cambodia, it took 16 000 troops to run a base-line peace keeping operation, without any enforcement role at all. In Somalia, tens of thousands of troops were necessary to deal with the relatively straightforward problem of the 'technicals'. And how many UN volunteers would have been needed to make a difference, even at the infancy of the crisis, in the Balkans?

At the end of the day, there seems little realistic alternative to continuing with present arrangements, viz the ad hoc assembling from member states of particular forces for particular purposes as occasions arise—but with the delays and difficulties of the past being comprehensively addressed, as is occurring at the moment, by a major enhancement of the Secretariat's military planning and operational support capability.

VI

Cooperating for Peace

11

Reforming the United Nations

The need for further reform

It is a miracle, in many ways, that the UN has done as well as it has in responding to the peace and security challenges unceasingly hurled at it since the end of the Cold War. Given an organisational structure reflecting past rather than present priorities, an ongoing funding crisis, personnel resources littered with a good deal of accumulated debris from the post-Cold War years, and expectations accelerating beyond *any* institutional capacity to meet them, it should be a matter of enormous pride to Secretaries-General Perez de Cuellar and Boutros-Ghali that they have not only kept the United Nations in the game, but have ensured it remains the continuing focus for the hopes and aspirations of so many governments and peoples around the world.

Since coming to office in January 1992, Secretary-General Boutros-Ghali has committed himself firmly and unequivocally to a process of major institutional change. He has shown himself to be well aware of the problems crying out for attention, has already implemented significant reforms on many fronts, as has been acknowledged throughout this study, and in *An Agenda for Peace* has made a major contribution to stimulating new thinking about the particular changes needed to re-equip the UN for its peace and security role. But much more remains to be done, and it has been part of the purpose of this study to identify the crucial priorities, as we now see them, in this respect.

In the discussion of these priorities that follow, we have not attempted to describe the whole range of issues that remain to be addressed—including in the economic and social areas of the UN system—for the UN to make a completely successful transition from the Cold War wings to the post-Cold War centre stage. But we have tried to list, in some order of immediate importance, the main changes we think are necessary for the UN to play its peace and security role with both the confidence and competence the international community now expects of it. Of course the UN is not the only actor in the international community with a contribution to make towards maintaining and restoring international peace and security: we have been at pains to stress this throughout, and will again in the concluding chapter. But the UN is unquestionably, these days, the *main* player—and as such it, and the member states whose organisation it is, have special responsibilities to ensure that it performs with maximum effectiveness.

Priority 1: Restructuring the Secretariat

While the Security Council has the critical role of decision-making on measures to maintain and restore international peace and security, it is the Secretary-General who must not only implement its decisions but anticipate its needs and service its ever more lengthy and complex deliberations. A considerable burden has therefore fallen on the Secretariat as expectations of the UN, and requirements for new responses, have grown extraordinarily over the past four years. There is huge pressure upon it to adjust to dramatically changed circumstances and priorities, rationalise old structures, drop non-essential activities and develop new functions and structures.

Secretary-General Boutros-Ghali has taken welcome steps to restructure the top levels of the organisation to better reflect the post-Cold War demands being placed upon it. He has created a new Department of Peace Operations, bringing together elements which were previously spread among various departments. He has taken other steps to rationalise the senior Secretariat structure, to improve coordination within the Secretariat and with the specialised agencies, and to make necessary changes to personnel and to management systems. That the Secretary-General has had time to focus on any of this, and make any systematic organisational changes at all, should be a matter of considerable appreciation by member states, given the almost unimaginable pressures upon his time: not only has he a larger and more complex diplomatic brief than any foreign minister in the world, but he is the executive head of a vast, sprawling system in which over forty departments, agencies, representatives and offices report directly to him.

The question arises as to whether, in these new circumstances of the 1990s, the Secretary-General should have the assistance of a group of very senior deputies, as is the case with most other very large organisations. There have been various proposals in recent years for the appointment of Deputy Secretaries-General—with a consequent restructuring of the organisation into appropriate functional groups under each—and we believe the time has now well and truly come to grasp this nettle. We find it inconceivable that the Secretary-General's own status or effectiveness could be in any way diminished by such an innovation: he or she would retain all the stature and prerogatives of a chief executive but at the same time have a much enhanced capacity to ensure effective performance of individual elements in the system, and effective coordination of the whole.

Overall policy direction would remain the ultimate responsibility of the Secretary-General, as would the capacity to give directions—as occasion demanded, as at present—to any component of the system in a line relationship with him or her. The creation of an appropriate number of deputies—who would ideally be co-located with him or her, on the same floor at UN Headquarters in New York, and with whom he or she would, ideally, meet collectively at least once a week—would free the Secretary-General to concentrate on priority tasks, delegating day to day management, coordination and policy implementation to officials with sufficiently high status to deal at appropriately high levels with member states, regional organisations, the specialised agencies and relevant non-government organisations. The size and complexity of the job to be done by the UN has grown to the point where its resources simply have to be expanded at its most senior levels.

Our preference would be for four Deputy Secretaries-General to be appointed, covering respectively peace and security affairs, economic and social affairs, humanitarian affairs, and administration and management (see Chart 7). Some of the organisational implications of this are spelt out in a little more detail under other headings later in this chapter, but the main elements of the proposed reorganisation are summarised below. In order to keep attention focused, for present purposes, on the crucial issues of the appointment of deputies and the appropriate division of broad functional responsibilities to go with that, we refer here simply to each deputy being responsible for a particular 'functional area', and describe simply as 'elements' the particular functions exercised within each such area and the organisational units that might exercise them. In other words, we do not on this occasion feel it necessary to step into the minefield

Chart 7   Proposed reorganisation of UN Secretariat

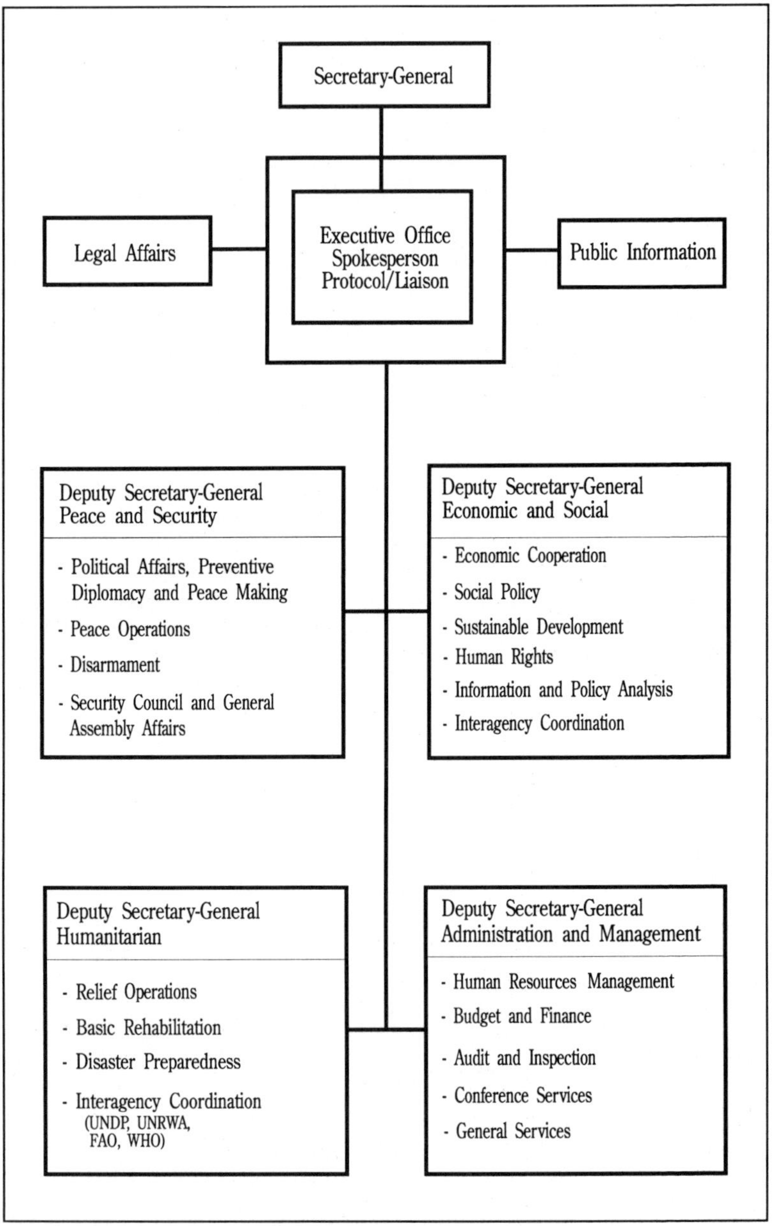

```
                    ┌─────────────────────┐
                    │  Secretary-General  │
                    └─────────────────────┘

┌──────────────┐    ┌─────────────────────┐    ┌──────────────────┐
│ Legal Affairs│────│   Executive Office  │────│ Public Information│
└──────────────┘    │     Spokesperson    │    └──────────────────┘
                    │   Protocol/Liaison  │
                    └─────────────────────┘
```

Deputy Secretary-General Peace and Security	Deputy Secretary-General Economic and Social
- Political Affairs, Preventive Diplomacy and Peace Making - Peace Operations - Disarmament - Security Council and General Assembly Affairs	- Economic Cooperation - Social Policy - Sustainable Development - Human Rights - Information and Policy Analysis - Interagency Coordination

Deputy Secretary-General Humanitarian	Deputy Secretary-General Administration and Management
- Relief Operations - Basic Rehabilitation - Disaster Preparedness - Interagency Coordination (UNDP, UNRWA, FAO, WHO)	- Human Resources Management - Budget and Finance - Audit and Inspection - Conference Services - General Services

Source: Adapted from Erskine Childers and Brian Urquhart, *Towards a More Effective United Nations*, Dag Hammarskjöld Foundation, 1992

of distinguishing between 'departments', 'divisions', 'commissions', 'offices' and the like, or of notionally allocating 'Under Secretary-General', 'Assistant Secretary-General' or other such job designations to particular elements.

Peace and Security Affairs

This functional area would encompass the present Departments of Political Affairs, Peace Operations and Disarmament Affairs. Its Deputy Secretary-General would have two primary objectives: ensuring comprehensive coordination of UN peace operations, delivering effective planning and implementation; and achieving appropriate balance in peace and security priorities between, on the one hand, peace operations and, on the other hand, what we have argued to be the crucially important, and hitherto under-nourished, areas of preventive diplomacy, peace making and peace building.

Economic and Social Affairs

This functional area would embrace the present economic and social Departments, and the ECOSOC group of organs, programs, commissions and agencies. Its elements would include economic cooperation, social policy, sustainable development, information and policy analysis, and strong interagency coordination arrangements. Whether the human rights element should continue to have its home in this part of the UN system as at present, or whether it might be more appropriately relocated, is a question that will need to be addressed after the General Assembly considers, in accordance with the recommendation of the 1993 World Conference on Human Rights in Vienna, whether a new post of Human Rights Commissioner should be established. The Deputy Secretary-General for Economic and Social Affairs would have, among his innumerable coordination and management tasks, a special responsibility for developing—in cooperation with his or her colleagues in Peace and Security Affairs and Humanitarian Affairs—effective peace building strategies.

Humanitarian Affairs

There is a strong case to be made for elevating the coordination of humanitarian affairs to Deputy Secretary-General level, given the diversity of players in humanitarian relief operations, both within the UN system (at both specialised agency and internal commission or program level) and outside it, and the often unproductive competition that has gone with that. Only someone with the clout that an appointment at this level could bring is likely to be able to maximise the UN's capacity to direct, rationalise and coordinate humanitarian responses—something the international community has been crying out for. A further, and quite radical, change that we propose in this area is the creation of an operational element that would extract and combine into a new body, working directly to the Deputy, the present relief and basic rehabilitation functions of UNHCR, UNICEF and WFP: those three organisations, with their residual protection and development functions, would then find a home in the Economic and Social Affairs area. We also see the Deputy Secretary-General for Humanitarian Affairs as having a particular responsibility to develop peace building strategies: poised between Political and Security Affairs and Economic and Social Affairs, as this functional area is, Humanitarian Affairs might be the logical location for the establishment of a small peace building planning and coordination unit.

Administration and Management

This is a grouping whose functions speak for themselves. The Deputy Secretary-General's primary objectives would be reform of UN financing, the comprehensive upgrading of systems for budgetary transparency, personnel evaluation, establishment review and efficiency audit and inspection. This is perhaps the place to make what should be the self-evident point that the growing demands on the UN, and the high expectations of it, require the very best people in the Secretariat. The selection of senior UN officials should be a transparent process with published job descriptions, and should pay particular regard to the injunction in Article 101.3 that the 'paramount consideration' in the employment of staff and in the determination of conditions of service should be the 'necessity of securing the highest standards of efficiency, competence and integrity'. Staff should be selected by open competition for publicly notified vacancies.

Priority 2: Solving the funding problem

The UN has long had serious problems with funding shortfalls and arrears both to its regular budget and to the budgets of peace keeping operations. Funding shortfalls have on occasion brought it close to insolvency. In August 1993 the Secretary-General advised member states of the 'enormity of the crisis': total cash reserves amounted to $380 million while the total monthly expenses of the UN amounted to $310 million. This situation cannot continue. The international community expects the UN to play a more effective role in maintaining international peace and security and the UN must be adequately resourced to do so. The ultimate obligation falls on member states to meet their assessed contributions, to the regular budget and for peace keeping, in full and on time.

As of August 1993, the outstanding assessed contributions of member states had reached $1,193 million for peace keeping and $848 million for the regular budget. This extraordinary level of arrears has accumulated over many years and reflects past political opposition to some peace keeping activities as well as a lack of seriousness on the part of some member states in meeting their financial obligations. If the bulk of these arrears were paid, the UN's finances would be in a very healthy state, both immediately and for the longer term. The Working Capital Fund, the Peace Keeping Reserve Fund and the Special Account could then all be replenished and could even be increased. The UN would also be in a position to meet all outstanding troop contributor costs.

In the light of these alarming statistics, no member state can be permitted to shirk its responsibility to pay its assessed contributions in full and on time. Failure by a member state to meet its financial obligations to the UN should be a matter of concern to all member states generally and not be left solely to the Secretariat and the Secretary-General to pursue. Member states should explore means of strengthening Article 19 of the Charter, for example by depriving a member state of voting rights if it is more than one year in arrears rather than two years at present.

It has to be acknowledged that the failure of the United States in the past to pay its assessed contributions in full is the major reason for the continuing financial weakness of the UN: as at August 1993 it was in arrears on its peace keeping budget obligations to the extent of $318 million, and on its pre-1993 regular budget obligations to the extent of $208 million. The new Clinton Administration took the welcome step of reaffirming the Bush administration's commitment to pay (with some exceptions) the arrears of the United States to the UN by the end of 1995. This step, together with the expectation that the United States would not in future fall back into arrears, gave some confidence for the future financial health of the UN.

The US Congress, however, is working against this commitment of the Administration by holding up the undertaking to pay arrears, blocking supplementary funding for current peace keeping commitments and signalling the possibility of reduced funding in future years. Many of the attitudes behind the position of the US Congress are outdated and take no account of the potential the UN offers for effective preventive diplomacy, conflict resolution and social and economic advancement provided member states are prepared to invest in this potential. There needs to be a recognition on the part of the US Congress—directly encouraged by the international community—of the current realities and promise of the UN, and a shift to support for the position of the Clinton Administration.

Some at least of the proposals that have been floated for raising additional revenue for the UN's peace and security functions warrant more consideration than they have so far received. As mentioned in the Volcker–Ogata report and by the Secretary-General in *An Agenda for Peace,* those proposals include commercial borrowing by the Secretary-General; a levy on arms sales listed in the UN Arms Transfer Register; a levy on international air tickets; tax exemptions for private contributions to the UN; and changes to the scale of assessment of contributions of member states.

Of these ideas, that of a levy on international airline travel seems to us to merit particularly close examination, not least because of the nexus between international peace and the availability of that travel. International Civil Aviation Organization's (ICAO) figures indicate that there were 300 million international passenger sectors travelled world-wide in 1992: a flat charge of just $5 applied to each such sector (hardly enough to be a disincentive to travel by that mode), collected on behalf of the UN by the airline at the time of ticket issue for what would presumably be a reasonably small administrative charge, could thus raise up to $1.5 billion annually. Of course, to be effective, such a proposal would require the cooperation of the airlines' organisation, the International Air Transport Association (IATA), and some persuasion of ICAO would no doubt be required in the light of its 1992 resolution that no tax be imposed on airlines or passengers not directly related to aviation activity. But this would be no ordinary tax, and there would be no harm in asking.

There are several administrative steps which the UN could usefully take to improve the financing of peace keeping operations, as we have already mentioned in Chapter 8. A unified UN peace keeping budget should be established, with separate line items for each operation and an annual assessment for all member states. This would allow the Secretary-General much more flexibility in financing the rapid deployment, as well as on-going funding, of peace keeping operations. It would improve considerably the administration of numerous and diverse peace keeping operation budgets, and allow the Secretariat to replace the current multi-billing process with an annual billing system for member states' assessed contributions. The Peace Keeping Reserve Fund should be dedicated solely to the start-up costs of new peace keeping operations, as originally intended, and the Secretary-General should have discretion to spend a greater amount of the estimated cost for each operation than he is permitted at present before the General Assembly's approval of the peace keeping budget is finalised.

It is important to keep in perspective the financial and other demands made on member states as a result of increased UN peace and security activities. Peace keeping costs may have risen steeply, but—as we pointed out in Chapter 8—they remain very small relative to expenditure by both developed and developing countries on arms procurement. Moreover, the cost of a modest investment now in strengthening and widening preventive diplomacy efforts should yield a considerable benefit. The establishment of adequately equipped preventive diplomacy units in six regional centres, with a total staff of 100 and funds for necessary travel, would require in the order of $21 million per annum: compare this with the expected UN peace keeping budget for 1993 of $3.7 billion, or the estimated cost of well over $70 billion for the Gulf War coalition, a single enforcement operation.

As part of the reform process, the UN needs to give consideration to ensuring that staff numbers allocated to key functions are consistent with relative priorities. At present, of the almost 14 000 people who work in the UN Secretariat, 850 staff work in the area which would become the responsibility of the suggested Deputy Secretary-General for Peace and Security Affairs; 5200 for the suggested Deputy Secretary-General for Economic and Social Affairs; only 100 for the Deputy Secretary-General for Humanitarian Affairs (although, of the relief organisations embraced by that area, the UNHCR alone has another 2300 personnel); 4300 for the Deputy Secretary-General for Administration and Management; and nearly 1000 in the Public Information and Legal Affairs areas that would remain attached directly to the Secretary-General. A comprehensive management review would be invaluable in determining where staff resources could be saved for reallocation to the areas which do clearly require strengthening—in particular peace operations, preventive diplomacy and peace making, and humanitarian operations.

Priority 3: Improving the management of peace operations

We have already discussed at length in Chapters 8 and 10 the further changes we believe are necessary, both at UN Headquarters and in the field, to make peace keeping and peace enforcement operations more administratively effective, and there is no need to repeat that here. The most overwhelming and urgent need is for a significant expansion in capacity of the small planning group established within the Department of Peace Operations, so that it includes sufficient military and civilian personnel to be able to meet simultaneous demands promptly, and plan effectively for the multi-dimensional operations now so characteristic of peace keeping. In the medium term, it would be helpful to convert that into a properly constituted General Staff, not necessarily very large in number but with a 'surge' capacity at times of greater demand, which would be responsible for both the planning and management of peace operations.

Priority 4: Giving priority to prevention

Giving priority to dispute resolution and conflict prevention goes to the heart of equipping the UN for taking its rightful place as the pre-eminent cooperative security institution in the post-Cold War era. As we argued at length in Chapter 5, and again need not repeat, the most promising approach to upgrading UN preventive diplomacy would be one which gave the organisation the capacity to offer a dispute resolution service to its members, providing skilled third party assistance through good offices and mediation. We have suggested in this respect the creation of a number of regionally located 'Peace and Security Resource Centres' to help carry out both preventive diplomacy and peace making functions closer to the area where problems arise. We have also argued for a substantial upgrading of the information and analytical capability available to the Department of Political Affairs for these and related purposes.

While all this will require additional resources, such outlays will lessen the later calls for the more expensive options of peace keeping or peace enforcement. The current distribution of resources is heavily skewed towards the more expensive later stages of conflict resolution (with around 40 staff in the Department of Political Affairs assigned to preventive diplomacy and peace making, compared to some 82 000 peace keepers in the field). We have already made the point earlier in this chapter about the comparative costs of keeping 100 preventive diplomacy practitioners in the field for a year ($21 million), as compared with the current annual peace keeping budget ($3.7 billion) and the six-week Gulf War peace enforcement coalition (more than $70 billion).

Priority 5: Rethinking humanitarian coordination

Identifying improvements in the functioning of the UN security system would be incomplete unless problems of UN humanitarian relief coordination were also addressed. The UN's recent resort to enforcement action in support of humanitarian objectives has provoked unease among some in the international community and has, in practice, run into considerable difficulties in Somalia. Improvements in the UN's ability to provide and coordinate humanitarian relief in response to catastrophic humanitarian situations should lessen the need for the international community to consider resorting to the radical step of intervention in the internal affairs of a member state.

As we argued in detail in Chapter 10, structural reasons would appear to lie at the heart of the inadequacies of the UN's present system of international humanitarian relief, and structural changes are necessary to make the system more effective. Our preference, as we have made clear, is for the creation of a new disaster response agency—combining the relief and basic rehabilitation functions of UNHCR, UNICEF and WFP—working directly to our proposed new Deputy Secretary-General for Humanitarian Affairs.

Priority 6: Raising the profile of peace building

Peace building is one of *the* fundamental tasks of the UN, if not previously much recognised as such. Peace building aims to meet basic human needs and to create the frameworks for orderly relations among states. If the foundations are properly laid to create fair systems of international conduct, and fair ways of distributing scarce resources, then the chances are that many potential problems, whether international or internal, will be contained or never emerge. Peace building is certainly essential in post-conflict situations, but it has an even wider and underlying pre-conflict role.

Peace building is in fact carried on in many parts of the UN system, reflecting the great diversity of peace building activities. It ranges from international law making to disarmament, economic and social advancement, sustainable development, democratisation and institution building. All too often these activities can be pursued in isolation from each other, without any overriding sense of common purpose. Linkages need to be created across the whole UN system so that those working, for example, in preventive diplomacy have in mind the importance of economic and social strategies and democratisation in their work, and can draw easily on the resources of the UN to supplement their own particular work.

There is a need for much more integration of peace building activities across the whole UN system. The pursuit of peace and security has to be seen to include the satisfaction of basic human needs as well as the prevention, containment and settlement of violent conflict. And the peace keeping function has to take account of the total needs of the communities with which peace keepers work, so that their development needs for post-conflict rehabilitation and long-term reconstruction are fully integrated into the UN's peace keeping role.

The creation of four Deputy Secretaries-General would provide the basic means of ensuring the creation of these linkages from the very top of the organisation, and down through it to all elements responsible to the Deputies. To achieve this necessary integration from the top down, the four Deputies should, as we have suggested earlier in this chapter, be located in New York, with their offices co-located on the same floor as the Secretary-General's office. They should meet on a regular basis, at least once a week and more often as issues arise on which their coordination and direction are required. Through the close coordination of the four Deputies under the Secretary-General, the offices and departments which work for them can in turn be aligned and encouraged to work with each other, and create the cross-organisational linkages which will make for effective peace building.

To assist this process, consideration could be given to the establishment of a new unit under the Deputy Secretary-General for Humanitarian Affairs, to advise the Secretary-General and his Deputies on structural and procedural changes which would facilitate integration for peace building across the whole UN system. The greatest encouragement for this essential coordination, however, would come from the development of a top structure which works to create permanent linkages from the very top down, throughout the whole organisation.

Priority 7: Regenerating the Security Council

The Security Council will continue to be the UN body with the primary responsibility for the maintenance of international peace and security, with all the power and responsibility this entails. To be effective, the Security Council must maintain broad international support for the decisions it makes. The composition of the Security Council no longer represents the make-up of the international community, as it was designed to do in 1945. Economic power, in particular, has spread to a number of new points on the globe, just as the realities of political power have changed dramatically over the past half century. As we have already discussed in Chapter 8, there is increasing concern about the extent to which this lack of representativeness is beginning to impact on the Council's legitimacy. The principle of limited expansion of the Security Council—from its present fifteen to twenty, or a maximum of twenty-five—is now generally accepted, but questions of 'who and how many' are the subject of intensive negotiation.

There is a close relationship between the composition of the Security Council and its ability to perform more effectively a number of the most pressing items on its agenda, especially in the field of arms control and disarmament. During the Cold War, the two most powerful and interrelated symbols of a powerful nation were the possession of nuclear weapons and permanent membership of the Security Council. Expansion of permanent membership in the way we and others have suggested should break that nexus once and for all.

If there is an expansion, then we support what appears to be a clearly emerging majority view that there be no extension of the veto power beyond the present permanent members of the Security Council. In practical terms, it is difficult to see how an increase in the number of members with the veto, irrespective of the way in which that veto might be exercised, would improve the efficiency of the Council's decision making: indeed it would probably make it unmanageable. Extension of the veto power would in any case be inconsistent with the diminishing use of the veto in the more collegial atmosphere for collective security decision-making that currently prevails.

To deal with the challenges of international security in the future, decision-making in the Security Council needs to operate more effectively. While recognising the strains upon Security Council members from their much-increased workload in recent years, the Council could improve the effectiveness of its decision-making through broader consultation by permanent members with non-permanent members, and with member states outside the Council whose interests are affected by a particular issue before it. Certainly troop contributing countries should be consulted as part of the Security Council's decision-making on the establishment or renewal of a peace operation.

The Security Council should also be better able to respond to emerging threats and disputes before their escalation into armed conflict. The Council should draw upon existing early warning systems in the humanitarian area, and on an augmented information system for more effective preventive diplomacy. ECOSOC should not hesitate to exercise its Article 65 mandate and advise the Security Council of potential emergencies arising out of economic and social conditions. With improved coordination of UN organisations and agencies devoted to economic and social progress, ECOSOC could better assist the Security Council's capacity for peace building and preventive strategies.

12

Cooperative Security for the 1990s and Beyond

Getting the culture right: the cooperative security instinct

The post-Cold War world has been tumultuous and chaotic, and shows no particular sign of becoming less so. The peace and security problems we feared most in the Cold War years have become less alarming, but others have taken their place, and there is no reason yet to believe that in terms of the capacity of states to do insult and injury to each other, or the capacity of peoples to inflict violence upon each other, the habits of millennia have yet changed. The purpose of this study, prompted by Secretary-General Boutros-Ghali's path-breaking *An Agenda for Peace*, has been to examine just what the international community might be able to do about this state of affairs.

One kind of answer is to say 'not very much'. This can be proclaimed not as a response of despair, but of hard-headed realism. There will always be those who will say that events just have to take their course; that real-politik will always prevail; that only when national interests are directly threatened, or domestic pressures are sufficiently strong, will reaction to international misbehaviour be possible; and that there is little that the international community can or should do, in an organised and systematic way, to advance the cause of peace and security, other than tinker at the margins.

This is *not* our answer. We believe that even if the world can never be made absolutely safe for all its peoples, we are beginning to learn how to make it very much safer than it has been. Technology, trade and telecommunications are bringing us closer together. There are more and more significant ways in which, across national borders, things are being done more alike, and in which institutions, practices, and outlooks are becoming more alike—as a result of which countries, cultures and peoples are becoming less alien to each other than has been the case in the past. This phenomenon of economic and cultural convergence is being overtaken by emergent new notions of community: nations are finding it progressively easier to talk together, build processes and institutions together, advance common interests and resolve common problems. They are beginning to learn that their best interests are advanced not by a culture of conflict, but by a culture of cooperation.

All this means that the concept of 'cooperative security', as we defined it in Chapter 1, is a meaningful way of approaching the peace and security problems with which this study is concerned. Cooperative security, as we saw, embraces the ideas both of common security (that nations' best protective option is to seek to achieve security with others, not against them) and collective security (the notion of members of a group renouncing force among themselves, and agreeing to come to the aid of any member attacked by a defector). More than that, cooperative security describes an approach which, among other things, is multi-dimensional, gradualist, about reassurance more than deterrence, and which stresses the value of creating habits of dialogue between potential antagonists.

So an important first objective of this study has been to encourage the international community to adopt what we might describe as the 'cooperative security instinct': in other words, to have confidence in the possibility of being able to achieve genuinely cooperative solutions to the peace and security problems with which we are bound to go on being confronted from time to time.

Getting the concepts right: asking the right questions

Having the right instinct, of course, does not take one very far. One has to have a sense of how to translate that instinct into an effective response. When a problem arises, how do we answer questions like: who should be doing what, when, how, and with who paying? So, coming a little closer to earth, a more specific objective of this study has been to try to offer some guidance as to how to answer these kinds of questions. That is not a simple enterprise, as should be apparent to anyone who has read the preceding chapters. There is no computer that one could program with so complete a set of criteria that it would only be a matter of keying in the data to get an unequivocal, correct answer. Every individual problem that forces itself upon the international community's attention does have its own distinctive characteristics, and the relevant considerations that bear upon its resolution can be almost infinitely variable.

But, as we said in Chapter 1, this reality should not be cause for despair. It should be possible to achieve, through argument and analysis, a strong measure of intellectual consensus about the nature of the problems which it is appropriate for the international community to tackle; about the broad scope of appropriate responses; and about the kind of detailed criteria it is appropriate to weigh and balance in coming to a conclusion about which, if any, response to apply to a particular problem. So we have tried, in this study, to develop that argument and analysis—stimulated by *An Agenda for Peace,* but taking the argument into rather more detailed terrain than was sketched in that document.

One of the things we have tried hardest to do in this study—and we hope it will be seen as a useful and distinctive contribution to the debate—is to map, at the outset, the *whole* terrain. There have been innumerable published studies of particular international peace and security problems, or sets of problems, and of particular kinds of responses to them by the international community. The literature, of which we give a sample in the Bibliography, is already enormous and growing monthly more so. But there have been very few attempts to bring all the different problem and response elements together into a single coherent picture: on a map-scale, as it were, that does not obliterate the necessary detail, but at the same time is large enough to be readily grasped. To attempt to do so, as we have—and Chart 1 on page 14 is the pictorial summary—is to embark on more than a merely intellectual exercise. It is to recognise that, in the real world of hard political decision-making—whether in the Security Council, or regional organisations, in national Cabinet rooms or anywhere else—decision-makers desperately need, before they set out, some sense of the total landscape and some compass bearings if they are to reduce the risk of losing their way.

While every situation *is* different, and has to be handled on its own merits and in its own international political context, it is always helpful for an individual decision-maker to be able to see at the outset where that situation might fit into the total picture, and a larger pattern of precedent. But, much more importantly for present purposes, where we are dealing with international problems and how the international community might respond cooperatively to them, it is

184

crucially important that there be enough intellectual consensus to enable those many different individual international actors to approach the issues with common objectives, common terminologyand, so far as possible, common criteria of evaluation.

Having such a measure of consensus does not mean that the responses will always prove right: the world is too complex and uncertain ever to be sure of that. But it should mean that decisions can be reached more quickly, and have a better *chance* of being right. And, extremely importantly as well, in a real world where we must assume that resources are always going to be limited and the demands for responses always greater than the capacity to satisfy them, having a strong measure of consensus about objectives, terminology and criteria should make it significantly easier to reach consensus about *prioritising* those demands and the allocation of resources to meet them.

It is not very easy, nor should it be necessary, to now try to distil the entire analysis of this study into some more succinctly formulated check lists: the preceding chapters will have to speak for themselves. But it may be useful, nonetheless, to spell out some basic questions which it could be helpful for decision makers to work through when wrestling with these problems in the future.

Question 1:   What can we do to prevent this possible problem becoming a real problem?

This is not a question asked as often as it should be.   In the international peace and security business, prevention—in all its various manifestations—is dramatically cheaper than cure.   Peace building—embracing international regimes (Chapter 3) and in-country development strategies both before and after conflict (Chapter 4)—should be at the heart of the global security agenda for the 1990s and beyond: not least because it is fertile common ground for those whose preoccupations are with economic and social, as well as political and security, issues. And many fewer emerging threats and disputes would escalate into armed conflicts or other major security crises if the international community were prepared to devote to preventive diplomacy (Chapter 5) just a fraction of the focus, time and resources it now spends on trying to restore or enforce the peace in situations that have blown out of control.

Question 2:   Is this problem one that demands a response by the international community?

There are, at any given time, a great many situations around the world that satisfy the descriptions of 'international security problems' that we gave in Chapter 1, being definable as 'emerging threats', 'disputes', 'armed conflicts' or 'major security crises'. Sometimes these problems, left to themselves, will resolve themselves: 'don't just do something, sit there' can often be good advice in international affairs, as elsewhere. But for many others a choice will be required, as to whether to place the issue on the international agenda—in particular of the UN, or a regional organisation—or rather leave it to be resolved by bilateral or other means. There may be not much room for choice with unequivocal cross-border aggression by one state against another, but for most other situations there will be. The important point for present purposes is that it be recognised that there *is* usually a choice, and that it should be made on consistent and articulate grounds—having regard to the principles of timeliness, graduation, effectiveness, affordability and, especially, consistency that we spelt out in Chapter 1. It is not very satisfactory that the main determinant be, for example, the views or interests of permanent members of the Security Council, or other militarily significant states. A cooperative security system able to attract the fullest measure of support by the world community would be one marked, in its agenda-setting, by a far greater degree of objectivity and consistency of evaluation and judgement than has been the case in the past.

Question 3: What is the best available category of response?

If the choice is made to address a problem, then this should be done intelligently or systematically, again having regard to the basic principles of timeliness, graduation, effectiveness, affordability and consistency. 'Being seen to be doing something' may sometimes be a domestic political imperative for national governments, but it is hardly a satisfactory foundation for international cooperative security effort. Whether the proper response strategy comes under the category of 'peace building' (Chapters 3 and 4), 'peace maintenance' (Chapters 5 and 6), 'peace restoration' (Chapters 7 and 8) or 'peace enforcement' (Chapters 9 and 10) depends entirely on its particular circumstances.

Question 4: Who is best placed to respond?

Although most attention in this study has inevitably been devoted to the UN, there are many other actors in the international community who have played, or are capable of playing a significant international security role: we listed the cast in Chapter 2, and have referred to them many times since. If a problem is being effectively addressed by a regional organisation, for example, or by non-government organisation-initiated dialogue process, then there is no point in the UN seeking to duplicate the effort. Equally, it should be recognised that it does not always need to be the case that actions decided upon by the UN be carried out by the UN. Resource constraints and efficiency considerations may well make it sensible on occasion for the UN to 'contract out' various tasks, whether they be of a humanitarian or military character, provided that the organisations, states or agencies which are carrying out the work do so in accordance with the decisions of the UN and report to it regularly on their conduct of it.

Question 5: How, in detail, should the preferred response be implemented?

In practice, the question of whether and by whom a particular response should be made will often be connected inextricably with how, in detail, it will have to be implemented. If the resource or other perceived cost of a particular strategy preferred in principle is seen to be too great, then the choice will have to be squarely confronted at the outset whether to opt for a less-preferred response, or not to respond at all. Sometimes in the past this dilemma has not been confronted as squarely as it should have been, and lower cost options never likely in practice to meet preferred objectives have been embarked upon with unhappier or less productive consequences than if no action at all had been taken. Successful cooperative security responses—in particular those involving significant field operations in peace keeping (Chapter 8) and peace enforcement (Chapter 10)—require, above all else, clear identification of objectives, sufficient resources to meet those objectives, and very sound management structures. Experience suggests that rather more attention should be paid to these matters by political decision-makers than has tended to be the case in the past: they are not mere matters of administrative implementation.

Question 6: What will be the cost of this response strategy, and are we prepared to see it through to its defined objectives?

The state of UN and most national budgets, combined with the wealth of recent experience in the conduct of various peace maintaining, restoring and enforcing strategies, has injected a stronger note of realism into the consideration of security responses than perhaps was previously the case. The crucial consideration here is that unless there is a clear commitment to see a preferred strategy through to its logical conclusion, it may well be preferable, on balance, not to embark upon that strategy, or indeed any other, at all. One cannot be unequivocal about these matters: sometimes a situation may be so uncertain, but at the same time so grave, that there is simply no alternative to proceeding one step at a time, in the knowledge that escalation of response—and new demands upon resources to match, which it may be difficult to meet—may be unavoidable. But it is important for decision makers to at least confront the question posed at the outset:

clear thinking, even with imperfect data, usually has an edge over muddled incrementalism.

Question 7 : What will we do if our preferred strategy fails, and some escalated response is called for?

The possibility of failure in a preferred strategy should always be acknowledged privately, if not publicly or to the parties or governments causing the problem in question. The issue arises quite sharply in the context of preventive deployment (Chapter 6) and higher-risk peace keeping operations (Chapter 8), where contingency planning for escalation ought logically to be part of the whole initial decision making process, but all too often has not been. It is a matter of calculating, first, the probability of failure of the preferred strategy against, secondly, the degree of difficulty (for resource or other reasons) in upgrading the response against, thirdly, the relative impact of trying and failing versus not trying at all. These are all obviously matters of fine judgement, about which it is very difficult to be prescriptive in advance, but the credibility of the cooperative security system is threatened whenever some risk eventuates that could reasonably have been foreseen, and the reaction is disarray or worse.

Getting the delivery right: cooperative security in action

All the clear thinking in the world about appropriate responses to different kinds of problems will not count for much if the strategies thus devised are flawed in their execution. We have already made clear in the previous chapter our view that the UN itself has, in all the circumstances, performed quite remarkably in adapting to the surge in new demands made upon it for cooperative security action in the post-Cold War period. And throughout the text, we have given many instances where regional organisations have played their own part, particularly in preventive diplomacy, or show a clear capacity—with more resources, and more encouragement—to do more. Similarly, individual states and combinations of states, as well as a variety of non-government actors, have all played useful niche roles from time to time in contributing to the resolution of particular problems.

Overwhelmingly, however, one is left with a sense that the international community could be doing much better in tackling these issues, particularly in the preventive and peace-building stage. And while there will continue to be a major, and growing, role for regional organisations—both the long established formal ones and the emergent new dialogue forums—overwhelmingly the major responsibility for doing better is going to have to be borne by the UN, the only fully empowered cooperative security body with global membership that we have. We have set out in detail in Chapter 11, and have no need here to repeat, the priority issues of structure, process and resources that we believe need to be tackled if the UN is to at last fully realise its potential.

The ideal of nations and communities living and working together in peace and security, enjoying—in the words of the UN Charter—'better standards of life in larger freedom'—should be closer now to realisation than at any previous time in modern world history. For all the reasons outlined at the outset of this chapter, there are signs of a culture of cooperation emerging to replace the culture of conflict that has prevailed so long.

What has to happen now is for that mood to be systematically tapped and translated into effective institutional structures and processes. As we said in Chapter 1, that kind of adjustment is never easy to achieve. It depends partly on achieving a measure of intellectual consensus among decision makers as to the applicable principles, and partly on there being a clearly defined set of widely-supported practical proposals for change: this study has been written essentially to help achieve those two objectives.

But what major change *also* needs is commitment, and stamina, from the governments and individuals who, at the end of the day, have to make it happen. Member states of the UN, when they accede to its Charter, commit themselves to cooperating both with other states and the organisation itself to achieve both international peace and security, and—through economic and social cooperation—the conditions of stability and well-being necessary for peaceful and friendly relations among nations.

There could be no better time than now for a renewal of that commitment, and a renewed pledge of determination to make the world a better and safer place for all its peoples. And there could be no better target date for making it all happen than the 50th Anniversary—on 24 October 1995—of the coming into force of the United Nations Charter.

Bibliography

Abi-Saab, Georges, *The United Nations Operations in the Congo 1960–1964*, Oxford University Press, Oxford, 1978.

Alagappa, Muthiah, 'Regionalism and the Quest for Security: ASEAN and the Cambodia Conflict', *Journal of International Affairs*, Vol. 46, No. 2, Winter 1993, pp. 439–467.

Assefa, H., 'Mediation in internal wars: the Ethiopia/Eritrea conflict', *Security Dialogue*, Vol. 23, No. 3, 1992, pp. 101–106.

Australia, Department of Foreign Affairs and Trade, *Cambodia: An Australian Peace Proposal*, AGPS, Canberra, 1990.

Australia, Senate, Standing Committee on Foreign Affairs, Defence and Trade, *United Nations Peacekeeping and Australia,* AGPS, Canberra, 1991.

Australia, Senate, Standing Committee on Foreign Affairs, Defence and Trade, Subcommittee on Security and National Defence, Issue No. 7, *Sixth Proceedings on: The Study of Peacekeeping*, 16 June 1992.

Axelrod, R., *The Evolution of Cooperation*, Basic Books, New York, 1984.

Azar, E.E. and J.W. Burton (eds), *International Conflict Resolution: Theory and Practice*, Wheatsheaf Books, Sussex, 1986.

Baev, Pavel K., 'Peace-keeping as a Challenge to European Borders', *Security Dialogue*, Vol. 24, No. 2, 1993, pp. 137–150.

Bailey, S.D., *The United Nations*, Pall Mall Press, London, 1963.

Bailey, Sydney, *How Wars End: The United Nations and the Termination of Armed Conflicts 1946–1964*, 2 vols, Clarendon Press, Oxford, 1982.

Ballaloud, Jacques, *L'ONU et les opérations de maintien de la paix*, Éditions Pédone, Paris, 1971.

Bibliography

Baranyi, S. and L. North, *Stretching the Limits of the Possible: United Nations Peacekeeping in Central America*, Aurora Papers 15, Canadian Centre for Global Security, Ottawa, 1992.

Baratta, J.P. *International peacekeeping: history and strengthening*, Monograph No. 6, The Center for UN Reform Education, Washington, D.C., 1989.

Barnaby, F. (ed.), *Building a More Democratic United Nations: Proceedings of CAMDUN-1*, Frank Cass, London, 1991.

Bell, Coral, 'The Fall and Rise of the UN', *Quadrant,* July–August 1993, pp. 50–56.

Belonogov, A.M., 'Soviet peace-keeping proposals', *Survival*, Vol. 32, No. 3, 1990, pp. 206–211.

Berridge, G.R., *Return to the UN: UN Diplomacy in Regional Conflicts*, Macmillan, London, 1991.

Blodgett, J.Q., 'The future of UN peacekeeping', *The Washington Quarterly*, Vol. 14, No. 1, Winter 1991, pp. 207–220.

Boulden, Jane, *Building on the past: future directions for peacekeeping*, Behind the headlines series, Vol. 48, No. 4, Canadian Institute of International Affairs, Toronto, Summer 1991.

Boutros-Ghali, Boutros, 'An Agenda for Peace: One Year Later', *Orbis*, Vol. 37, No. 3, Summer 1993, pp. 323–332.

Boyd, James M., *United Nations Peacekeeping Operations: A Military and Political Appraisal*, Praeger, New York, 1971.

Bremner, J.S. (Col), and Snell, J. M. (LtCol), 'The Changing Face of Peacekeeping', *Canadian Defense Quarterly*, Vol. 22, No. 1, special No. 2, August 1992.

Browne, M., *United Nations Reform: Issues for Congress*, Congressional Research Service, Washington, D.C., 1988.

Bull, Hedley, *Intervention in World Politics*, Clarendon Press, Oxford, 1984.

Burton, J.W. , *Global Conflict*, Wheatsheaf Books, Brighton, 1984.

Bustelo, M.R., and P. Alston, *Whose New World Order?, What Role for the United Nations?,* The Federation Press, Annandale, NSW, 1991.

Buzan, Barry, 'New Patterns of International Security in the 21st Century', *International Affairs*, Vol. 67, No. 3, 1991.

Canada, Standing Committee of Foreign Affairs, *Report on Peacekeeping*, February 1993.

Caradon, H., 'The Security Council as an instrument for peace', in Lall, A.S. (ed.) *Multilateral Negotiation and Mediation*, Pergamon Press, New York, 1985.

Carlsson, I., 'A new international order through the UN', *Security Dialogue*, Vol. 23, No. 4, December 1992, pp. 7–11.

Carter, Ashton B., William J. Perry and John D. Steinbruner, *A New Concept of Cooperative Security*, Brookings Occasional Papers, The Brookings Institution, Washington, D.C., 1992.

Cassese, A. (ed.), *United Nations Peacekeeping: Legal Essays*, Sijthoof & Noordhoff, Alphan Aan Den Rijn, 1978.

Childers, E.B., 'The future of the United Nations: The challenges of the 1990s', *Bulletin of Peace Proposals*, Vol. 21, No. 2, 1990, pp. 143–152.

Childers, E.B. and B. Urquhart, *Strengthening international response to humanitarian emergencies*, study done for the Dag Hammarskjöld Foundation and the Ford Foundation, October 1991.

Chopra, J. and T.G. Weiss, 'Sovereignty is no longer sacrosanct: codifying humanitarian intervention', *Ethics and International Affairs*, Vol. 6, 1992, pp. 95–117.

Claude, Inis, *Swords into Plowshares: The Problems and Progress of International Organization*, 3rd ed. (rev.), University of London Press, London, 1964.

Claude, Inis, *States and the Global System: Politics, Law and Organization*, St. Martin's Press, New York, 1988.

Coate, R.A. and D.J. Puchala, 'Global policies and the United Nations system: a current assessment', *Journal of Peace Research*, Vol. 27, No. 2, 1990, pp. 127–140.

Coleman, C.C. and I.J. Rikhye (eds), *Negotiators' Handbook*, International Peace Academy, New York, January 1990 (draft).

Connaughton, Richard Michael, *Military intervention in the 1990s: a new logic of war*, Routledge, New York, 1992.

Cox, D. (ed.), *The use of force by the Security Council for enforcement and deterrent purposes: a conference report*, The Canadian Centre for Arms Control and Disarmament, Ottawa, 1990.

Cox, David, *The reduction of the risk of war through multilateral means: a summary of conference proceedings*, Working Paper No. 18, Canadian Institute for International Peace And Security, Ottawa, 1989.

Danarosch, L.F. and D. Scheffer (eds), *Law and Force in the New International Order*, Westview Press, Boulder, Co., 1991.

Bibliography

Dawson, Pauline, *The Peacekeepers of Kashmir: The UN Military Observer Group in India and Pakistan*, St. Martin's Press, New York, 1992.

Day, Arthur D., and Michael W. Doyle, (eds), *Escalation and Intervention –Multilateral Security and its Alternatives*, Westview Press, Boulder, Co., 1986.

Dewitt, David B., 'Concepts of Security for the Asia-Pacific Region in the Post-Cold War Era: Common Security, Cooperative Security, Comprehensive Security', Paper presented at the Seventh Asia-Pacific Roundtable, 'Confidence building and conflict reduction in the Pacific', Kuala Lumpur, 6–9 June 1993.

Diehl, P.F., 'When peacekeeping does not lead to peace: some notes on conflict resolution', *Bulletin of Peace Proposals*, Vol. 18, No. 1, 1987, pp. 47–53.

Diehl, Paul F., 'Peacekeeping Operations and the Quest for Peace', *Political Science Quarterly*, Vol. 103, No. 3, 1988, pp. 485–507.

Diehl, Paul F., 'A Permanent U.N. Peacekeeping Force: An Evaluation', *Bulletin of Peace Proposals*, Vol. 20, No. 1, 1989, pp. 27–36.

Diehl, P.F., 'What are they fighting for? the importance of issues in international conflict research', *Journal of Peace Research*, Vol. 29, No. 3, 1990, pp. 333–344.

Diehl, Paul F., 'Institutional Alternatives to Traditional U.N. Peacekeeping: An Assessment of Regional and Multinational Options', *Armed Forces and Society*, Vol. 19, No. 2, Winter 1993, pp. 209–230.

Diehl, P.F. and S.R. Jurado, *United Nations Election Supervision in South Africa? Lessons from the Namibian Peacekeeping Experience*, ACDIS Occasional Paper, Program in Arms Control, Disarmament and International Security, University of Illinois at Urbana–Champaign, Urbana, Il ., 1992.

Diehl, Paul F. and Chetan Kumar, 'Mutual Benefits from International Intervention: New Roles for United Nations Peace-Keeping Forces', *Bulletin of Peace Proposals*, Vol. 22, No. 4, 1991, pp. 369–375.

Diehl, P.F. and C. Kumar, *United Nations Peacekeeping Operations: Some Win–Win Applications*, ACDIS Occasional Paper, Program in Arms Control, Disarmament and International Security, University of Illinois at Urbana–Champaign, Urbana, Il., 1992.

Djonovich, D.S., *United Nations Resolutions*, Oceana, New York, 1992.

Dorn, W., 'Keeping Watch for Peace: Fact-finding by the UN Secretary-General', unpublished paper, Parliamentarians for Global Action, New York, 1992.

Durch, W.J., 'Building on sand: UN peacekeeping in Western Sahara', *International Security*, Vol. 17, No. 4, Spring 1993, pp. 151–171.

Durch, William J. (ed.), *The Evolution of U.N. Peacekeeping: Case Studies and Comparative Analysis*, St. Martin's Press, New York, 1993.

Durch, Wiliam J. and Barry Blechman, *Keeping the Peace: the United Nations in the Emerging World Order*, Henry L. Stimson Center, Washington, D.C., March 1992.

Encyclopaedia of Public International Law, Vol. II, North–Holland, Amsterdam, 1989.

Evans, Senator Gareth D., *The Asia Pacific and Global Change*, Address by the Minister for Foreign Affairs and Trade of Australia to the Trilateral Commission, Tokyo, 20 April 1991.

Fabian, Larry, *Soldiers without Enemies: Preparing the United Nations for Peacekeeping*, The Brookings Institution, Washington, D.C., 1971.

Falk, R.A. *et al* (eds), *The United Nations and a Just World Order*, Westview Press, Boulder, Co., 1991.

Ferencz, Benjamin B., *Enforcing International Law – A Way to World Peace: a Documentary History and Analysis*, Oceana Publications, London/New York, 1983.

Fermann, Gunnar, *Bibliography on International Peacekeeping*, Martinus Nijhoff, Dordrecht, 1992.

Ferris, E.G. (ed.), *The Challenge to Intervene: A New Role for the United Nations?*, Conference Report 2, Life and Peace Institute, Uppsala, Sweden, 1992.

Fetherston, A.B., 'Towards a Theory of United Nations Peacekeeping', *Peace Research Report No. 31*, Department of Peace Studies, University of Bradford, Bradford, UK, 1993.

Findlay, T., *Conflict Resolution and Peacekeeping in the Post-Cold War Era: Implications for Regional Security*, Working Paper No. 118, Peace Research Centre, Australian National University, Canberra, 1992.

Finkelstein, L. (ed.), *Politics and the United Nations System*, Duke University Press, Durham, 1988.

Fisher, R.J., 'Prenegotiation problem-solving discussions: enhancing the potential for successful negotiation', *International Journal*, Vol. 44, No. 2, Spring 1989.

Fisher, R.J. and L. Keashly, 'The potential complementarity of mediation and consultation within a contingency model of third party intervention', *Journal of Peace Research,* Vol. 28, No. 1, 1991, pp. 29–42.

Fleitz, Frederick H., *United Nations peacekeeping operations, 1992: a reference aid*, Central Intelligence Agency, Directorate of Intelligence—Office of European Analysis, Washington, D.C., 1992.

Florini, Ann, *On the front lines: the United Nations' role in preventing and containing conflict*, United Nations Association of the U.S., New York, 1984.

Fortna, Virginia Page, *Regional Organizations and Peacekeeping*, Occasional Paper No. 11, Henry L. Stimson Center, Washington, D.C., June 1993.

Fromuth, Peter, 'The making of a security community: the United Nations after the Cold War', *Journal of International Affairs*, Vol. 46, No. 2, 1993, pp. 341–366.

Galtung, J., *The United Nations Today: Problems and Some Proposals*, Center for International Studies, Princeton University, Princeton, N.J., 1986.

Galtung, J. and H. Hveem, 'Participants in peacekeeping forces', in Galtung, J., *Peace, War and Defence: Essays in Peace Research*, Vol. III, Christian Ejlers, Copenhagen, 1976.

Gardner, R.N. and J.P. Lorenz, *Post-Gulf war challenges to the UN collective security system: two views on the issue of collective security*, Special Middle East Program in Peacemaking and Conflict Resolution, United States Institute of Peace, Washington, D.C., 1992.

Gati, T.T., *The 'New' UN: Through Soviet and American Eyes*, United Nations Association of the U.S., New York, 1989.

Gati, T.T. (ed.), *The US, the UN and the Management of Global Change*, New York University Press, New York, 1983.

Gerlach, Jeffrey R., 'A U.N. Army for the New World Order?', *Orbis*, Vol. 37, No. 2, Spring 1993, pp. 223–236.

Ghali, Mona, *The Multinational Forces: Non-UN Peacekeeping in the Middle East*, Occasional Paper No. 12, Henry L. Stimson Center, Washington, D.C., 1992.

Glasl, F., 'The Process of Conflict Escalation and Roles of Third Parties', in Blomers, G.B.J. and R.B. Peterson (eds) *Conflict Management and Industrial Relations*, Kluwer Nijhoff, Boston, Ma., 1982.

Goldman, Ralph Morris, *Is it time to revive the UN Military Staff Committee?*, Center for the Study of Armament and Disarmament, Occasional Paper No. 19, California State University, Los Angeles, Ca., 1990.

Goot, Murray and Tiffen, Rodney (eds), *Australia's Gulf War,* Melbourne University Press, Carlton, Victoria, 1992.

Goodrich, Leland M. and Simond, Anne P., *The United Nations and the Maintenance of International Peace and Security*, The Brookings Institution, Washington, D.C., 1966.

Goodrich, L. *et al, Charter of the United Nations: Commentary and Documents,* 3rd ed., Columbia University Press, New York, 1969.

Gordenker, Leon, *The UN Secretary-General and the Maintenance of Peace*, Columbia University Press, New York, 1967.

Gordenker, Leon, *The United Nations in the 1990s*, St. Martin's Press, New York, 1992.

Gordenker, Leon and Thomas G. Weiss (eds), *Soldiers, Peacekeepers and Disasters*, St. Martin's Press, New York, 1991.

Gordon, Nancy and Bernard Wood, 'Canada and the Reshaping of the United Nations', *International Journal*, Vol. 47, Summer 1992.

Goulding, Marrack, 'The evolution of United Nations peacekeeping', *International Affairs*, Vol. 69, No. 3, July 1993.

Greenwood, Christopher, "Is There a Right to Humanitarian Intervention?", *The World Today*, Vol. 49, No. 2, February 1992.

Gregory, Francis E. C., *The multinational force, aid or obstacle to conflict resolution?*, Conflict Studies No. 170, Institute for the Study of Conflict, London, 1984.

Grove, Eric, 'UN Armed Forces and the Military Staff Committee—A Look Back', *International Security*, Vol. 17, No. 4, Spring 1993.

Gurr, T.R., with B. Harff, 'The feasibility of an early warning system for ethnic conflicts in Europe', paper prepared for the PIOOM Symposium on Ethnic Conflicts and Human Rights Violations in Europe, Leiden, 25 June 1993.

Haas, E.B., *Why We Still Need the United Nations: Collective Management of International Conflict, 1945–1984*, Institute of International Studies, Berkeley, Ca., 1986.

Haas, Ernst B., *The United Nations and collective management of international conflict*, United Nations Institute for Training and Research, New York, 1986.

Hägglund, G., 'Peacekeeping in a modern war zone', *Survival*, Vol. 32, No. 3, 1990, pp. 233–240.

Harbottle, Michael, *The Blue Berets*, Leo Cooper, London, 1971.

Harbottle, M., *The United Nations and its capacity for keeping the peace*, Fellowship Briefing No. 4, The Fellowship of Reconciliation, UK, 1984.

Harbottle, M., *What is proper soldiering?: a study on new perspectives for the future uses of the armed forces in the 1990s*, The Centre for International Peacebuilding, Oxen, UK, 1991.

Harleman, C., 'Regional conflicts: peacekeeping and disarmament', *United Nations Disarmament Quarterly Review*, Vol. 3, 1992, pp. 171–190.

Harleman, C., 'Requirements for peacekeeping training within the United Nations', *UNITAR Newsletter*, Vol. 4, No. 1, 1992, pp. 4–6.

Hay, Robin, *Civilian Aspects of Peacekeeping. A Summary of Workshop Proceedings. Ottawa, 9–10 July 1991*, Working Paper No. 36, Canadian Institute for International Peace and Security, Ottawa, October 1991.

Hay, Robin, *Humanitarian Ceasefires: an Examination of their Potential Contribution to the Resolution of Conflict*, Working Paper No. 28, Canadian Institute for International Peace and Security, Ottawa, 17 July 1990.

Helman, Gerald B. and Steven R. Ratner, 'Saving Failed States', *Foreign Policy*, No. 89, Winter 1992–93, pp. 3–20.

Higgins, Rosalyn, *United Nations Peacekeeping 1947–1967: Documents and Commentary. Vol. I: The Middle East*, Oxford University Press, London, 1969.

Higgins, Rosalyn and Michael Harbottle, *United Nations peacekeeping: past lessons and future prospects; annual memorial lecture*, 25th November 1971, David Davies Memorial Institute of International Studies, London, 1972.

Hoffmann, W., (ed.) *Rethinking Basic Assumptions about the United Nations*, Conference Report, World Federalist Association, Washington, D.C., 1993.

Holiday, David, and Stanley William, 'Building the Peace: Preliminary lessons from El Salvador', *Journal of International Affairs*, Vol. 46, No. 2, Winter 1993, pp. 341–366.

Holmes, Kim R., 'New World Disorder: A critique of the United Nations', *Journal of International Affairs*, Vol. 46, No. 2, Winter 1993, pp. 323–346.

Hong Tat Soon, Mark, 'Role of Regional Groupings and Bodies in Cooperation with the UN', Paper presented at the Second Workshop on ASEAN–UN Cooperation for Peace and Preventive Diplomacy, Singapore, 6–7 July 1993.

Hume, Cameron R., *Negotiations Before Peacekeeping*, Occasional Paper No. 5, International Peace Academy, New York, 1991.

Independent Advisory Group on U.N. Financing, (Co-Chairs Shijuro Ogata and Paul Volcker), *Financing an Effective United Nations*, Ford Foundation, New York, 1993.

International Conference on Peacebuilding, 'Summary of Conference Proceedings', Shannon International Airport, Ireland, 28 April–3 May 1986.

James, A., 'Options for peacekeeping', in Howe, J.O. (ed.) *Armed Peace: The Search for World Security*, Macmillan, London, 1984.

James, A., 'The UN force in Cyprus', *International Affairs*, Vol. 65, No. 3, 1989, pp. 481–500.

James, A., 'International peacekeeping: the disputants' view', *Political Studies*, Vol. 18, No. 2, 1990, pp. 215–230.

James, A., *Peacekeeping and International Politics*, St. Martin's Press, New York, 1990.

Johansen, R.C., *Toward a Dependable Peace: A Proposal for an Appropriate Security System*, World Policy Paper No. 8, World Policy Institute, New York, 1983.

Johansen, R.C., 'UN peacekeeping: the changing utility of military force', *Third World Quarterly*, Vol. 12, No. 2, 1990.

Johansen, R.C., 'The United Nations after the Gulf War: Lessons for Collective Security', *World Policy Journal*, Vol. 8, No. 3, Summer 1991, pp. 561–574.

Johnson, E.J., The British government attitudes to United Nations peacekeeping in the post-war international system, Ph.D. diss., London University College, 1985.

Jones, Peter, *Peacekeeping: An Annotated Bibliography*, Ronald P. Frye, Toronto, 1990.

Kazimi, M. R., *Financing the U.N. Peace-keeping Operations*, Capital Pub. House, Delhi, 1988.

Kerr, Pauline and Andrew Mack, 'The Evolving Security Discourse in Asia-Pacific', Paper presented to the conference on 'Economic and Security Cooperation in the Asia-Pacific: Agendas for the 1990s', Canberra, 28–30 July 1993.

Kirgiz, Frederic L., Jr, *International Organizations in their Legal Setting*, 2nd ed., West Publishing, St Paul, Minn., 1993.

Kostakos, G., A.J.R. Groom, S. Manphet and P. Taylor, 'Britain and the New UN Agenda: Towards Global Riot Control?', *Review of International Studies*, January 1991.

Bibliography

Kozyrev, A. and G. Gatilov, 'The UN peacemaking system: problems and prospects', *International Affairs* (Moscow), No. 12, December 1990, pp. 79–88.

Krepon, M. and J.P. Tracey, 'Open Skies' and UN peace-keeping', *Survival.*, Vol. 32, No. 3, 1990, pp. 251–263.

Kriesberg, L. and S.L. Thorson (eds), *Timing the De-escalation of International Conflicts*, Syracuse University Press, Syracuse, New York, 1991.

Kriesberg, L., T.A. Northrup, and S.L. Thorson (eds), *Intractable Conflicts and their Transformation*, Syracuse University Press, Syracuse, New York, 1989.

Langille, P. and E.V. Simpson, 'A Training Centre for Peacekeepers', *Ploughshares Monitor*, December 1991.

Lawson, Stephanie, *The Politics of Authenticity: Ethnonationalist Conflict and the State*, Working Paper No. 125, Peace Research Centre, Australian National University, Canberra, November 1992.

Lee, John M., Robert von Pagenhardt, and Timothy W. Stanley, *To Unite Our Strength: Enhancing the United Nations Peace and Security System*, University Press of America/International Economic Studies Institute, Lanham, Md./Washington, D.C., 1992.

Lefever, Ernest W., 'Reining in the U.N.', *Foreign Affairs*, Vol. 72, No. 3, Summer 1993, pp. 17–20.

Legault, Albert, *Peace-keeping operations. Bibliography*, International Information Center on Peace-Keeping Operations, Paris, 1967.

Lewer, N. and O. Ramsbotham, 'Something must be done: towards an ethical framework for humanitarian intervention in international-social conflict', *Peace Research Report*, Department of Peace Studies, University of Bradford, Bradford, 1993 (draft copy).

Lillich, R.B. (ed.), *Humanitarian Intervention and the United Nations*, University Press of Virginia, Charlottesville, 1973.

Liu, F.T., *United Nations Peacekeeping: Management and Operations*, Occasional Paper No. 4, International Peace Academy, New York, 1990.

Liu, F.T., *United Nations Peacekeeping and the Non Use of Force*, Lynne Rienner, Boulder, Co., 1992.

Liu, F.T. and H. Wiseman (rapporteurs), *The Tokyo Symposium on the Evolution of UN Peacekeeping Operations: Recent Experiences and Future Prospects, 3–4 September 1991, Tokyo: Report*, United Nations University/International Peace Academy, Tokyo, 1991.

Lorenz, Joseph P., 'Collective Security After the Cold War', in *Resolving Third World Conflict—Challenges for a New Era*, United States Institute of Peace, Washington, D.C., 1992, pp. 213–238.

Luard, Evan, *The international regulation of civil wars*, New York University Press, New York, 1972.

Luard, Evan, *The United Nations: How It Works and What It Does*, Macmillan Press, London, 1975.

Lukacs, John, 'The End of the Twentieth Century: Historical Reflections on a misunderstood epoch', *Harper's Magazine*, January 1993, pp. 39–58

Luck, E.C. and T.T. Gati, 'Whose Collective Security?', *The Washington Quarterly*, Spring 1992.

Lyons, G.M., *The State of the United Nations: 1992*, The Academic Council on the United Nations System, Brown University, 1992.

Lyons, G.M. and M. Mastanduno, *Beyond Westphalia: International Intervention, State Sovereignty and the Future of International Society*, Dartmouth College, The Rockefeller Center, 1992.

Mackenzie, L., 'Military realities of UN peacekeeping operations', *RUSI Journal*, Vol. 138, No. 1, 1993, pp. 21–24.

Mackinlay, John, *The Peacekeepers—An Assesment of Peacekeeping Operations at the Arab Israeli Interface*, Unwin Hyman, London, 1989.

Mackinlay, John, 'Powerful peace-keepers', *Survival*, Vol. 32, No. 3, 1993, pp. 241–250.

Mackinlay, John and Jarat Chopra, 'Second Generation Multinational Operations', *The Washington Quarterly*, Vol. 15, No. 3, Summer 1992, pp. 113–134.

Mackinlay, John and Jarat Chopra, *A Draft Concept of Second Generation Multinational Operations 1993*, Thomas J. Watson Jr. Institute for International Studies, Brown University, Providence, RI, 1993.

MacQueen, Norman, *United Nations peacekeeping in a transforming system*, Working Paper No. 215, Strategic and Defence Studies Centre, Research School of Pacific Studies, Australian National University, Canberra, 1990.

Magnarella, Paul J., 'Expanding the Role of the International Court of Justice to Resolve Interethnic Conflict and Protect Minority Rights', *Journal of Transnational Law and Policy*, Vol. 2, No. 1, Spring 1993.

Mahmood, R. and R.A. Sani, *Confidence building and conflict reduction in the Pacific*, Proceedings of the Sixth Asia-Pacific Roundtable, Kuala

Lumpur, June 21–25, 1992, Institute of Strategic and International Studies (ISIS) Malaysia, Kuala Lumpur, 1993.

Martin, Lawrence, 'Peacekeeping as a Growth Industry', *The National Interest,* No. 32, Summer 1993, pp. 3–11.

Mayall, J., 'Non-intervention, self-determination and the New World Order', *International Affairs,* Vol. 67, No. 3, 1991, pp. 421–429.

Mazarr, Michael J., 'The Military Dilemmas of Humanitarian Intervention', *Security Dialogue,* Vol. 24, No. 2, June 1993, pp. 151–162.

McCoubrey, Hilaire and Nigel J. White, *International Law and Armed Conflict,* Dartmouth, Aldershot, 1992.

McDermott, A. and Skelsbaek, Kjell, *The Multinational Force in Beirut 1982–1984,* Florida International University Press, Miami, 1991.

McDermott, A. and Skelsbaek, Kjell (eds), *A Thankless Task: The Role of UNIFIL in Southern Lebanon,* Norwegian Institute of International Affairs, Oslo, 1988.

Miall, H., *The Peacemakers: Peaceful Settlement of Disputes Since 1945,* Macmillan, London, 1992.

Mills, Susan R., *The Financing of United Nations Peacekeeping Operations: the Need for a Sound Financial Basis,* Occasional Paper No. 3, International Peace Academy, New York, 1989.

Mitchell, Christopher R., *Conflict Resolution and Civil War: Reflections on the Sudanese Settlement of 1972,* Working Paper 3, Center for Conflict Analysis and Resolution, George Mason University, Virginia, 1989

Mitchell, C.R. and K. Webb (eds), *New Approaches to International Mediation,* Greenwood Press, Westport, 1988.

Mitchell, C.R., *The Structure of International Conflict,* Macmillan Press, London, 1981.

Mitchell, R., *Peacekeeping and peacemaking in Cyprus,* Background Paper No. 23, Canadian Institute for International Peace and Security, Ottawa, 1988.

Muller, J.W., *The Reform of the United Nations,* Oceana, New York, 1992.

Nerfin, M., 'The Future of the United Nations System: Some Questions on the Occasion of an Anniversary', *Development Dialogue,* 1, 1985.

Norton, A.R. and T.G. Weiss, 'Superpowers and peacekeepers', *Survival,* Vol. 32, No. 3, 1990, pp. 212–220.

Norton, A.R. and T.G. Weiss, 'UN peacekeepers: soldiers with a difference', *Headline Series,* No. 292, Foreign Policy Association, New York, 1990.

Ogunbanwo, S., 'The United Nations disarmament training for diplomats: hopes for the future', *Bulletin of Peace Proposals*, Vol. 22, No. 1, 1991, pp. 49–53.

Osgood, C.E., *An Alternative to War and Surrender*, University of Illinois Press, Urbana, Il., 1962.

Parliamentarians for Global Action, 'Towards a Global Security System for the 21st Century: A Submission to the Secretary-General of the United Nations', *PGA Newsletter*, June 1993, pp. 6–7.

Parsons, A., 'The United Nations and International Security', *Millenium*, Vol. 12, No. 2, 1983, pp. 101–109.

Parsons, Anthony, 'The United Nations in the Post-Cold War Era', *International Relations*, Vol. 11, No. 3, December 1992.

Patchen, Martin, *Resolving Disputes between Nations: Coercion or Conciliation?*, Duke University Press, Durham, 1988.

Paxman, John M. and Georges T. Boggs (eds), *The United Nations: A Reassessment; Sanctions, Peacekeeping and Humanitarian Assistance*, University Press of Virginia, Charlottesville, 1973.

Peacekeepers' Handbook, International Peace Academy, Pergamon, New York, 1984.

Petrovsky, V., 'The UN and World Politics', *International Affairs* (Moscow), July 1990, pp. 10–20.

Pillar, Paul R., *Negotiating Peace: War Termination as a Bargaining Process*, Princeton University Press, Princeton, N.J., 1983.

Plunkett, Mark, Submission to the Human Rights Sub-Committee of the Joint Parliamentary Committee on Foreign Affairs, Defence and Trade in its inquiry into 'Australia's Efforts to Promote and Protect Human Rights', 9 August 1993.

Powell, Colin L., 'US Forces: Challenges Ahead', *Foreign Affairs*, Vol. 71, No. 5, Winter 1992/93.

Prins, Gwyn, 'The United Nations and Peace-Keeping in the Post-Cold War World: the Case of Naval Power', *Bulletin of Peace Proposals*, Vol. 22, No. 2, 1991, pp. 135–155.

Puchala, D.J. and R.A. Coate, *The Challenge of Relevance: the United Nations in a Changing World Environment*, The Academic Council on the UN System, New York, 1989.

Pugh, M.C., *Multinational maritime forces: a breakout from traditional peacekeeping?*, Southampton Papers in International Policy, No. 1, Mountbatten Centre for International Studies, Southampton, UK, 1992.

Ramcharan, B.G., *The International Law and Practice of Early-Warning and Preventive Diplomacy: The Emerging Global Watch*, Martinus Nijhoff, Dordrecht, 1991.

Ramphal, S., 'Globalism and meaningful peace: a new world order rooted in international community', *Security Dialogue*, Vol. 23, No. 3, September 1992, pp. 81–87.

Renner Michael, *Critical Juncture: The Future of Peacekeeping*, WorldWatch Paper 114, Worldwatch Institute, Washington, D.C., 1993.

Richardson, James E., 'The end of geopolitics', in Richard Leaver and James E. Richardson (eds), *The Post-Cold War Order: Diagnoses and Prognoses*, Studies in World Affairs 2, Allen & Unwin/Department of International Relations, Research School of Pacific Studies, Australian National University, Canberra, 1993.

Rikhye, Indar Jit, *Preparation and training of United Nations peace-keeping forces*, Adelphi Papers No. 9, International Institute for Strategic Studies, London, 1964.

Rikhye, Indar Jit, *The Theory and Practice of Peacekeeping*, Hurst, London, 1984.

Rikhye, Indar Jit, *The Future of Peacekeeping*, Occasional Paper No. 2, International Peace Academy, New York, 1989.

Rikhye, Indar Jit, *Military Adviser to the Secretary-General: UN Peacekeeping and the Congo Crisis*, St. Martin's Press, New York, 1992.

Rikhye, Indar Jit, *Strengthening UN Peacekeeping—New Challenges and Proposals*, United States Institute of Peace, Washington, D.C., 1992.

Rikhye, Indar Jit, *The United Nations of the 1990s and International Peacekeeping Operations*, Southampton Papers in International Policy No. 3, Mounbatten Centre for International Studies, Southampton, UK, 1992.

Rikhye, Indar Jit, *The United Nations and the Aftermath of the Gulf Crisis*, Editions du Gref, Toronto, 1992.

Rikhye, Indar Jit, Michael Harbottle and Bjorn Egge *The Thin Blue Line - International Peacekeeping and its Future*, Yale University Press, New Haven, 1974.

Rikhye, Indar Jit and Skjelsbaek, Kjell (eds), *The United Nations and Peacekeeping—Results, Limitations and Prospects: The Lessons of 40 Years of Experience*, Macmillan Press, London, 1990.

Rittberger, V. 'International regimes and peaceful conflict resolution', in Wallensteen, P. (ed.)., *Peace Research: Achievements and Challenges*, Westview Press, London, 1988, pp. 144–165.

Roberts, A. and B. Kingsbury (eds), *United Nations, Divided World: The UN's Role in International Relations*, Clarendon Press, Oxford, 1988.

Roberts, Adam, 'The United Nations and International Security', *Survival*, Vol. 35, No. 2, Summer 1993.

Roberts, Adam, 'Humanitarian war: military intervention and human rights', *International Affairs*, Vol. 69, No. 3, July 1993.

Rosenau, J.N., *The United Nations in a Turbulent World*, International Peace Academy Occasional Paper, Lynne Rienner, Boulder, Co., 1992.

Russett, B. and J.S. Sutterlin, 'The UN in a new world order', *Foreign Affairs*, Vol. 70, No. 2, 1991, pp. 69–83.

Schachter, O., 'United Nations Law in the Gulf Conflict', *American Journal of International Law*, Vol. 85, No. 3, 1991, pp. 452–473.

Scheffer, David J., 'Toward a modern doctrine of Humanitarian Intervention', *The University of Toledo Law Review*, Vol. 23, No. 2, Winter 1992, pp. 253–293.

Seyersted, Finn., *United Nations Forces in the Law of Peace and War*, Sijthoff, Leyden, 1966.

Sherry, George L., *The United Nations reborn: conflict control in the post-Cold War world,* Council on Foreign Relations, New York, 1990.

Siekmann, Robert C.R., *Basic Documents on UN and Related Peacekeeping Forces*, 2nd enl. ed., Martinus Nijhoff, Dordrecht/Boston, 1989.

Siekmann, Robert C.R., *National contingents in United Nations peace-keeping forces,* Martinus Nijhoff, Dordrecht/Boston, 1991.

Singapore Symposium, 'The changing role of the United Nations in conflict resolution and peacekeeping', United Nations, New York, 1991.

Sivard, Ruth Leger, *World Military and Social Expenditures 1991,* 14th ed., World Priorities, Washington, D.C., 1991.

Skjelsbaek, K., 'Peaceful settlement of disputes by the United Nations and other intergovernmental bodies', *Cooperation and Conflict*, Vol. 21, No. 3, 1986, pp. 139–154.

Skjelsbaek, K., 'United Nations peacekeeping and the facilitation of withdrawals', *Bulletin of Peace Proposals*, Vol. 20, No. 3, 1989, pp. 253–264.

Skjelsbaek, K., 'The UN Secretary-General and the mediation of international disputes', *Journal of Peace Research*, Vol. 28, No. 1, 1991, pp. 99–115.

Skogmo, B., *UNIFIL: International Peacekeeping in Lebanon, 1978–1988.* Lynne Rienner, Boulder, Co., 1989.

Smith, H., 'Humanitarian Intervention: Morally right, Legally wrong?', *Current Affairs Bulletin*, Vol. 68, No. 4, 1991, pp. 4–11.

Smith, Hugh (ed.), *Australia and Peacekeeping*, Australian Defence Studies Centre, Canberra, 1990.

Snow, Donald M, *Peacekeeping, Peacemaking and Peace-enforcement: the U.S. Role in the New International Order*, U.S. Army War College, Carlisle Barracks, Penn., February 1993.

Solarz, S.J., 'Cambodia and the International Community', *Foreign Affairs*, Vol. 69, No. 2, 1990, pp. 99–115.

Soldiers with a Difference: The Rediscovery of Peacekeeping, Foreign Policy Association, New York, 1990.

Staley, Robert Stephens, *The Wave of the Future: the United Nations and Naval Peacekeeping*, Lynne Rienner, Boulder, Co., 1992.

Stedman, John, 'The New Interventionists', *Foreign Affairs*, Vol. 71, No. 1, Winter 1993.

Stegenga, James A., *The United Nations Force in Cyprus*, Ohio State University Press, Ohio, 1968.

Stein, Eric, 'The United Nations and the Enforcement Of Peace', *Michigan Journal of International Law*, Vol. 10, No. 1, Winter 1989, p. 304.

Stein, J.M. 'Getting to the table: processes of international prenegotiation', *International Journal.*, Vol. 44, 1989, pp. 231–236.

Stockholm International Peace Research Institute, *SIPRI Yearbook 1992: World Armaments and Disarmament*, SIPRI/Oxford University Press, 1992.

Strategic Survey 1992–1993, Brassey's/International Institute for Strategic Studies, London, 1993.

Sutterlin, J.S., *Military Force in the Service of Peace*, Aurora Papers 18, Canadian Centre for Global Security, Ottawa, 1993.

Swift, Richard N., *The United Nations Special Committee on Peace-keeping Operations: status and prospects*, Center for International Studies, New York University Press, New York, 1970.

Taboury, Mala, *The Multinational Forces and Observers in the Sinai: Organisation, Structures and Function*, Westview Press, Boulder, Co.,1986.

Thakur, Ramesh, *International Peacekeeping in Lebanon: United Nations Authority and Multinational Force*, Westview Studies on Peace, Conflict and Conflict Resolution, Westview Press, Boulder, Co., 1988.

Thakur, Ramesh, 'The United Nations in a Changing World', *Security Dialogue*, Vol. 24, No. 1, March 1993, pp. 7–20.

Thakur, Ramesh (ed.), *International Conflict Resolution*, Westview Press, Boulder, Co., 1988.

Tinbergen, Jan, *Supranational Decision-Making: A More Effective United Nations*, Waging Peace Series, Booklet 29, Nuclear Age Peace Foundation, Santa Barbara, Ca., 1991.

Touval, S., 'Multilateral negotiation: an analytic approach', *Negotiation Journal*, Vol. 5, No. 2, 1989, pp. 159–174.

Umbricht, V. *Multilateral Mediation: Practical Experiences and Lessons*, Martinus Nijhoff, Boston, 1988.

UNITAR, *The United Nations and the Maintenance of International Peace and Security*, Martinus Nijhoff, Dordrecht, 1987.

United Kingdom, House of Commons, Foreign Affairs Committee, *The Expanding Role of the United Nations and its Implications for United Kingdom Policy*, Volume 1, HMSO, London, 23 June 1993.

United Nations Handbook, 1992 , Ministry of External Relations and Trade, Wellington, New Zealand, 1992.

United Nations, *Status of Multilateral Arms Regulations and Disarmament Agreements*, United Nations, New York, 1988.

United Nations, *The Blue Helmets: A Review of United Nations Peacekeeping*, 2nd ed., United Nations, New York, 1991.

United Nations, 'United Nations Peace-keeping Operations: Information Notes', United Nations, New York, 1993.

United Nations, Department for Disarmament Affairs, *Challenges to multilateral disarmament in the post-Cold War and post-Gulf War period*, Disarmament Topical Papers No. 8, United Nations, New York, 1992.

United Nations, General Assembly, Special Committee on Peace-Keeping Operations, *Comprehensive review of the whole question of peace-keeping operations in all their aspects: rapporteur, Shaffie Abdel-Hamid*, United Nations, New York, 1967.

United Nations, Office of Legal Affairs, Codification Division, *Handbook on the Peaceful Settlement of Disputes between States*, United Nations, New York, 1992.

United Nations, Secretary-General, *An Agenda for Peace—Preventive Diplomacy, Peacemaking and Peace-Keeping*, United Nations, New York, June 1992.

Bibliography

United Nations, Secretary-General, *Comprehensive review of the whole question of peace-keeping operations in all their aspects*, United Nations, New York, 1965.

United Nations, Secretary-General, *New Dimensions of Arms Regulation and Disarmament in the Post-Cold War Era*, Report of the Secretary-General, United Nations, New York, 27 October 1992.

United Nations, Secretary-General, *Implementation of the Recommendations Contained in 'An Agenda for Peace'*, Report of the Secretary-General, A/47/965 S/25944, United Nations, New York, 15 June 1993.

United States Congress, House, *The costs of world peacekeeping: report / by Barratt O'Hara, Peter H.B. Frelinghuysen, members of the United States Delegation to the 20th session of the United Nations General Assembly, September 21 to December 21, 1965, pursuant to H. Res. 84*, House Report No. 1404, Washington, D.C., 89th Cong., 2nd sess., 1966.

United States Congress, House, Committee on Foreign Affairs, *The Future of U.N. Peacekeeping Operations: Joint hearing before the Committee on Foreign Affairs*, Washington, D.C., 102nd Cong., 2nd sess., 25 March 1992.

United States Congress, House, Committee on Foreign Affairs. *Consideration of authorizations for fiscal years 1992–93 for the former Soviet Republics; peacekeeping activities; implementation of the Salvadoran Peace Accords; and the Nonproliferation and Disarmament Fund*, Washington, D.C., 102nd Cong., 2nd sess., 25 February, 11 March, and 10 June 1992.

United States Congress, Senate, Committee on Foreign Relations. *United Nations Peacekeeping Efforts*, Washington, D.C., 102nd Cong., 2nd sess., 9 June 1992.

United States Congress, Senate, Committee on Foreign Relations, *Arming the United Nations Security Council—the Collective Security Participation Resolution, S.J. Res. 325*, Washington, D.C., 102nd Cong., 2nd sess., 24 September 1992.

United States Congress, Senate, Committee on Foreign Relations, *Situation in Bosnia and Appropriate U.S. and Western Response*, Washington, D.C., 102nd Cong., 2nd sess., 11 August 1992.

United States, Department of Defense, *Conduct of the Persian Gulf War, Final Report to Congress*, Washington, D.C., April 1992.

Urquhart, B., 'International peace and security: thoughts on the twentieth anniversary of Dag Hammarskjöld's death', *Foreign Affairs*, 1981.

Urquhart, B., 'The future of peacekeeping', *Negotiation Journal*, Vol. 5, No. 1, January 1989, pp. 25–32.

Urquhart, B., 'The United Nations system and the future', *International Affairs*, Vol. 65, No. 2, 1989, pp. 225–231.

Urquhart, B., 'Beyond the Sheriff's Posse', *Survival*, Vol. 32, No. 3, May/June 1990, pp. 196–205.

Urquhart, B., *The United Nations: from peacekeeping to a collective system?* Adelphi Papers, No. 265, International Institute for Strategic Studies, London, Winter 1991–92.

Urquhart, B., 'For a UN Volunteer Military Force', *The New York Review of Books*, 10 June 1993, pp. 3–4. See also 'A UN Volunteer Military Force—Four Views', *The New York Review of Books*, 24 June 1993, pp. 58–60.

Urquhart, B. and E. Childers, 'A world in need of leadership: tomorrow's United Nations', *Development Dialogue*, 1–2, 1990.

Urquhart, B. and E. Childers, *Reorganization of the United Nations Secretariat: a suggested outline for needed reforms*, Ford Foundation, New York, 1991.

Urquhart, B. and E. Childers, *Towards a More Effective United Nations*, Dag Hammarskjöld Foundation, Uppsala, 1992.

Ury, W.L., 'Strengthening international mediation', *Negotiation Journal*, Vol. 3, No. 3, 1987, pp. 225–229.

Väyrynen, R., 'Is there a role for the United Nations in conflict resolution', *Journal of Peace Research*, Vol. 22, No. 3, 1985, pp. 189–196.

Väyrynen, R., 'The United Nations and the Resolution of International Conflicts', *Cooperation and Conflict,* Vol. 20, No. 3, September 1985, pp. 141–171.

Väyrynen, R., (ed.), *New Directions in Conflict Theory: Conflict Resolution and Conflict Transformation*, Sage, London, 1991.

Verrier, Anthony, *International Peacekeeping*, Harmondsworth, Penguin, 1981.

Wainhouse, David W., *International Peacekeeping at the Crossroads: National Support, Experience and Prospects*, John Hopkins University Press, Baltimore, 1984.

Waldman, Robert Joseph, 'International Peacekeeping: Conditions for Conflict Control', PhD diss., University of Maryland, 1991.

Walker, Jenonne, 'International mediation of ethnic conflicts', *Survival*, Vol. 35, No. 1, 1993, pp. 102–117.

Wallensteen, P. and K. Axell, 'Armed conflict at the end of the Cold War, 1989–92', *Journal of Peace Research*. Vol. 30, No. 3, 1993, pp. 331–46.

Washington Centre of Foreign Policy Research, *National Support of International Peacekeeping and Peace Observation Operations*, Washington Center of Foreign Policy Research, John Hopkins University, Washington D.C., 1970, (Vols 1–5).

Weber, T., 'The problems of peacekeeping', *Interdisciplinary Peace Research*, Vol. 1, No. 2, 1989, pp. 3–26.

Weiss, Thomas G., 'New Challenges for U.N. Operations: Implementing an Agenda for Peace', *The Washington Quarterly*, Vol. 16. No. 1, Winter 1993.

Weiss, Thomas G. (ed.), *UN Conflict Management—American, Soviet and Third World Views*, International Peace Academy, New York, 1990.

Weiss, T.G. (ed.), *Collective Security in a Changing World*, Lynne Rienner, Boulder, Co., 1993.

Weiss, Thomas G. and Kurt M. Campbell, 'Military Humanitarianism', *Survival*, Vol. 33, No. 5, September/October 1991, pp. 451–465.

Weiss, Thomas G. and Jarat Chopra (eds), *United Nations Peacekeeping; an ACUNS teaching text*, Academic Council on the United Nations System, Hanover, N.H., 1992.

Weston, B.H., *Toward Post-Cold War Global Security: A Legal Perspective*, Waging Peace Series, Booklet 32, Nuclear Age Peace Foundation, Santa Barbara, Ca., 1992.

White, Nigel D., *The United Nations and the Maintenance of International Peace and Security*, St. Martin's Press, New York, 1990.

Wilson, J.B. (Brig.), 'Experiences in and Lessons from UN Operations in Yugoslavia', Paper presented at Chief of the General Staff Exercise, Land Warfare Centre, Canungra, Queensland, 21–25 June 1993.

Wiseman, H., *Peacekeeping and Peacemaking*, Pergamon Press, New York, 1983.

Wiseman, H., *Peacekeeping, Appraisals and Proposals*, International Peace Academy/Pergamon Press, New York, 1983.

Wiseman, H., *Peacekeeping and the Management of International Conflict*, Background Paper No. 15, Canadian Institute for International Peace and Security, Ottawa, 1987.

Wiseman, H., 'Civilian participation in UN peacekeeping operations', Paper presented to the International Peace Academy, Vienna Seminar, 7–18 July 1991.

Index

Index

Index

Index